PEACE AND CONFLICT 2008

J. Joseph Hewitt

Jonathan Wilkenfeld

Ted Robert Gurr

Center for International Development and Conflict Management
University of Maryland

Paradigm Publishers
Boulder • London

All rights reserved. No part of this publication may be transmitted or reproduced in any media or form, including electronic, mechanical, photocopy, recording, or informational storage and retrieval systems, without the express written consent of the copyright holder.

Copyright © 2008 University of Maryland

Published in the United States by Paradigm Publishers, 3360 Mitchell Lane, Suite E, Boulder, CO 80301 USA.

Paradigm Publishers is the trade name of Birkenkamp & Company, LLC, Dean Birkenkamp, President and Publisher.

ISBN 978-1-59451-400-5 (hardcover)
ISBN 978-1-59451-401-2 (paperback)

Library of Congress Cataloging-in-Publication Data

Hewitt, J. Joseph.
    Peace and conflict 2008 / J. Joseph Hewitt, Jonathan Wilkenfeld, Ted Robert Gurr.
        p. cm.
    Includes bibliographical references.
    ISBN 978-1-59451-400-5 (hardcover : alk. paper) — ISBN 978-1-59451-401-2
(pbk. : alk. paper) 1. War. 2. Peace-building. 3. Conflict management.
4. Democratization. 5. Self-determination, National. I. Wilkenfeld, Jonathan.
II. Gurr, Ted Robert, 1936– III. University of Maryland (College Park, Md.).
Center for International Development and Conflict Management. IV. Title.
    JZ6385.H49 2008
    303.6—dc22
                                                                      2007020919

Printed and bound in the United States of America on acid-free paper that meets the standards of the American National Standard for Permanence of Paper for Printed Library Materials.

CONTENTS

A Note on the 2008 Publication

Peace and Conflict is the flagship publication of the Center for International Development and Conflict Management at the University of Maryland. Readers of this fourth volume in the series will note changes in authorship, approach, data resources, substantive scope, and mission. The first three volumes (2001, 2003, and 2005) were prepared and written by Monty G. Marshall and Ted Robert Gurr. Monty Marshall is now Director of Research, Center for Global Policy, School of Public Policy, George Mason University. Joseph Hewitt and Jonathan Wilkenfeld have joined Ted Robert Gurr in the preparation of the 2008 volume.

Beginning with this volume, all analyses will use sources that have been released to the public and are available for further analysis and replication. This publication continues coverage of several topics that appeared in earlier ones: the Peace and Conflict Instability Ledger, trends in global conflict, the spread of democracy, and self-determination movements and their outcomes. It also includes five chapters on a special theme: "Challenges to the Stability of States."

The partnership between CIDCM and Paradigm Publishers will facilitate wider dissemination of *Peace and Conflict* to the academic and policy communities and provide the opportunity for students to understand, replicate, and extend our analyses. CIDCM will continue to make its findings available to the policy community; an executive summary can be found on the CIDCM Web site (**www.cidcm.umd.edu**) and is available from the Center upon request (cidcm@cidcm.umd.edu).

This volume also introduces two new outlets for resources and research related to the contents of the book. The *Peace and Conflict* companion Web site features a suite of data analysis tools (**www.cidcm.umd.edu/pc**). Users will be able to explore data used for analyses reported in this issue by manipulating the data and making modifications to produce their own customized analyses. We are also launching the Web-based Peace and Conflict Working Paper Series which will feature article-length papers that expand on issues related to the contents of *Peace and Conflict*.

During the transition to this new format and approach, we have been guided by the advice of our newly appointed Editorial Board, chaired by Ted Robert Gurr, the founding author of the *Peace and Conflict* publications. These specialists provided careful reviews of each of the substantive chapters in this volume. In the future they will participate in biennial consultations and advise on the content and shape of future volumes. We are very grateful for their valuable contributions to this book. The members are identified at the end of this volume.

1. INTRODUCTION TO PEACE AND CONFLICT 2008

The modern age demands that we think in terms of human security...a concept that acknowledges the inherent linkages between economic and social development, respect for human rights, and peace....Until we understand and act accordingly, we will not have either national or international security.

Mohamed ElBaradei, October 24, 2006
Sadat Lecture for Peace, University of Maryland

Previous editions of *Peace and Conflict* reported evidence of a sustained post-Cold War decline in armed conflicts within states and a growing capacity of states, acting singly and multilaterally, to avoid and end internal wars. This volume has no such clear story line. New evidence, and a closer look at old evidence, suggests that if there was a global movement toward peace in the 1990s and early years of the 21st century, it has stalled. Some positive trends are still evident but they are offset by new challenges. These challenges point to a *conflict syndrome*—a collection of factors that often operate concurrently to undermine the stability of states and erode the foundations of human security. Taken together, the essays in this volume explore aspects of these factors.

- Has the magnitude of armed conflict declined? The answer is yes when judged by falling numbers of internal wars and their average death-tolls across the last 20 years. But when we tabulate the number of states engaged in armed conflicts, either their own or multilateral wars as in Iraq and Afghanistan, the long-run trend is up. A larger portion of the global community of states is involved now than in any other time in the past six decades (see chapter 11). And the historic low of 19 ongoing armed conflicts in 2004 was followed by an increase to 25 in 2005.

- Are deadly conflicts more avoidable now than in the past? International crises, which in the past often led to armed conflict within and among states, have declined in number since the mid-1980s (see chapters 3 and 8). Many separatist conflicts have been contained, especially long-lasting ones like those in Northern Ireland and Indonesia's Aceh province (see chapter 5). But overall new armed conflicts have been erupting at roughly the same pace for the past 60 years. Moreover, an unusually large number of "new" conflicts began in 2005–06, and some were born from the failure of past peace processes, as in Sri Lanka and Azerbaijan.

- Has the "third wave" of democratization continued to rise? Full democracies have numbered about 80 since the mid-1990s (77 in 2006) compared with less than 40 autocratic regimes (34 in 2006). Democratic governance is the norm in the early 21st century but in recent years more regimes have edged into anocracy—a middling category of regimes with an incoherent mix of authoritarian and democratic features (chapter 4). The existence of 49 anocratic polities in 2005 is of particular concern because, as a group, they are much more susceptible than either full democracies or autocracies to political instability and armed conflict (chapter 2), to terrorist attacks (chapter 6), and to international crises (chapter 8).

- Is state failure merely a local concern? While the global community is increasingly aware of the dreadful conditions facing the populations of unstable and failing states, *Peace and Conflict* carefully traces the dangerous propensity for these states to host domestic and international terrorist organizations (see chapter 6). Equally alarming is the likelihood that these states will become participants in crises either on the regional or global stage. A staggering 77 percent of all international crises in the post-Cold War era have involved at least one unstable or failing state (see chapter 8). As Mohamed ElBaradei (2006) has recently observed, we must acknowledge the inherent linkages between economic and social development, respect for human rights, and peace.

- How is the international community responding to old and new conflict challenges? Since 2000, the number of active peacekeeping operations has been more than double the number at any point during the Cold War. They are about equally divided between UN operations and those by regional organizations. In one-fifth of all 126 missions undertaken since 1948 there was no "peace" to keep, and instead peacekeepers had to use force proactively. Success rates have been about equally good for UN and regional missions, and substantially higher than alleged by skeptics (chapter 10).

- Are civilians more secure from armed conflict? The average lethality of war has declined for those caught up in combat, but not for civilians in guerrilla wars. Of 81 states that fought large-scale insurgencies from 1945 to 2000, one in three resorted to mass killing of civilians thought to support the rebels. The greater the civilian support for guerrillas and the greater the guerrilla's threat to the government, the more likely governments are to choose a deliberate policy of mass killing (chapter 9). Such a policy of genocidal violence and ethnic cleansing has caused at least a quarter-million deaths in Sudan's Darfur region in the last three years. A weak African Union peacekeeping force with a limited mandate can do little more than observe the suffering. Darfur is the worst failure of the international responsibility to protect civilians since the Rwandan genocide of 1994.

Local and regional threats to peace are of greater concern to most people than global patterns. From 1980 to 2005 there were no significant trends, up or down, in fatalities from warfare in either Asia (if the Afghan civil war of 1976–2003 is excluded) or the Middle East (excluding the Iran-Iraq war of 1980–88). Africa experienced an irregular decline, more pronounced if the Congo-centered wars of the late 1990s are excluded. In Europe the wars accompanying the breakup of Yugoslavia sent the trend sharply upward until 2001. Only the Americas show a steady and significant declining trend over the 25-year span (chapter 11).

Regional trends are of little help in anticipating specific future challenges to security. The *Peace and Conflict* Instability Ledger in chapter 2 assesses each country's risks of future political instability based on five factors as measured in 2004. They are regime anocracy, high infant mortality, lack of integration in the global economy, high levels of militarization, and warfare in neighboring states. Of the 25 countries with the highest risks for political instability and internal war—ten or more times greater than the average risks in the OECD democracies—19 are in Africa, two in the Middle East (Iraq and Lebanon), three in Asia (Afghanistan, India, and Bangladesh, with Cambodia just below the threshold), and only one in the Americas (Haiti, though Brazil and Bolivia are not far behind). Some of these countries, including India and Ethiopia as well as Iraq and Afghanistan, confront ongoing insurgencies. The risk factors used are background conditions, not predicated on armed conflict per se, so prospects for peace in these countries are not good irrespective of current events or conflict outcomes.

Country risks of instability do shift over time: Mozambique, Iran, and Peru were among the ten highest-risk countries as of 2000 but now have moved down to middle levels of risk—principally because of domestic political changes in Iran from anocracy toward autocracy, and in Peru from anocracy toward restoration of full democracy. Congo and Rwanda, both devastated by civil war and mass killings in the 1990s, also are now at middle levels of risk, appreciably lower than most of their neighbors (see chapter 2).

Terrorism, especially by Islamists, is an existential threat to security in all world regions. This issue of *Peace and Conflict* reports on two new data collection projects that have already yielded several important generalizations about global and regional patterns of terror. One analysis, in chapter 7, is specific to ethnic and religious minorities in the Middle East and reports two particularly striking findings. First, most of the 112 organizations representing minorities in this region did not use terrorism between 1980 and 2004—the period covered by the study. Those that do typically have alternated among electoral politics, protest, and violence—often pursuing several strategies simultaneously. Terrorism is used, avoided, or abandoned depending on political circumstances. Second, democratization in the Middle East has led to increases in *both* conventional politics and terrorism. It remains to be seen whether these patterns also will be observed in other world regions.

Chapter 6 reports a first-ever global study that includes all international and domestic terrorist events. Currently it covers 1970 to 1997 and is being extended to the present. One distinctive pattern can be seen—the principal locales of terrorism are shifting over time. In the 1970s terrorism was mainly a European problem, in the 1980s a serious threat in Latin America, in the 1990s an Asian and African challenge (chapter 6). When data collection is current it will no doubt confirm the perception that terrorism is now most common in, and likely to originate from, the Islamic world.

Let us revisit an issue raised by Monty Marshall and Ted Robert Gurr in their conclusions to the 2003 and 2005 editions of *Peace and Conflict*. What has been the impact of changing US policy on trends in global and regional security? This volume provides suggestive evidence. The US invasions of Afghanistan and Iraq created or exacerbated international crises and pulled many allied states into combat operations in both countries. The lethality of conflict in Iraq has reached horrendous proportions for civilians. These wars also provide provocations and targets for terrorist attacks on the US and its allies. How far these attacks will spread and persist is beyond the current reach of our data and vision. Moreover the US promotion of democracy in these two countries provides space for partisan electoral politics by ethnic and religious groups but also, paradoxically, increases risks of terrorism. International efforts at peacekeeping continue apace, at the highest level of the past half-century, so it cannot be said that US invasions and unilateralism have dented the post-Cold War commitment of most international actors to contain and resolve local and regional conflicts. US policies may have exacerbated the problem but have not stopped the international community, or even US policymakers, from attempting to manage local wars and regional crises.

Peace and security are shifting targets. Armed conflicts declined to a historic low of 19 in 2004 only to increase in the following years. New conflicts begin, "settled" conflicts can reemerge or manifest themselves in new ways. Democratic regimes are generally more effective in containing conflicts and more likely to join international projects of conflict management, but new and partial democracies are potentially unstable. Their leaders may prove to be autocrats who, when tempted or challenged, will put aside democratic pretenses.

By itself, terrorism is not likely to be the most serious future challenge to international security. Rather, the most important threat to human security and state stability is the impact of a set of associated hazards, a *conflict syndrome*, that poses the gravest danger. The evidence presented in this volume leads us to conclude that high-risk states are simultaneously politically unstable, challenged by rebels and terrorists, tempted to resort to mass killings of civilians, and enmeshed in international crises. There are predictable pathways into these syndromes but no clearly marked exits.

Ted Robert Gurr
Joseph Hewitt
Jonathan Wilkenfeld

A conflict syndrome…poses the gravest danger.…High-risk states are simultaneously politically unstable, challenged by rebels and terrorists, tempted to resort to mass killings of civilians, and enmeshed in international crises. There are predictable pathways into these syndromes but no clearly marked exits.

2. THE PEACE AND CONFLICT INSTABILITY LEDGER: RANKING STATES ON FUTURE RISKS

J. Joseph Hewitt

Which countries are at greatest risk of future civil conflict and instability? A definitive answer to that question would have great value to policy-makers. With reliable early warning about the states at greatest risk, scarce resources could be directed accordingly. Investment of preventive resources in high-risk states is preferable to managing the consequences of state failure. Those consequences are often enormous and catastrophic. In the wake of state failure, humanitarian crises and increased military violence can leave a gruesome human death toll. Failed states are more likely to provide havens for terrorist organizations. They may trigger international crises. Spillovers can destabilize nearby states and entire regions. The international costs to rebuild failed states are large, which can divert resources from other states at risk and contribute to conditions that may lead to a cascade of state collapses elsewhere. Effective early warning makes it more likely that these scenarios can be avoided or their harsh consequences mitigated.

This chapter presents the new *Peace and Conflict* Instability Ledger—a ranking of 160 countries in terms of their *risk of future state instability*. The full listing of all states appears at the end of this chapter (see pp. 15–18). As we present details about the new ledger, we encourage readers to periodically consult it. The risk estimate for each country was obtained using a statistical model based on several variables known to be strongly related to the onset of instability events (or armed civil conflict). These include the incoherence of the governing regime, high infant mortality rates, lack of integration with the global economy, the militarization of society, and the presence of armed conflict in neighboring states. For each country, the ledger presents a single score that captures the overall risk of future instability. In addition, the ledger gives information about the level of statistical confidence corresponding to the risk estimate. This information can be just as important as the reporting of the estimate itself. A high level of confidence about an estimate for a state at risk can provide part of the basis for prioritizing resources for that state.

In previous issues of *Peace and Conflict*, the ledger presented the results of Ted Gurr and Monty Marhall's pioneering research on measuring the *peace-building capacity of states* (Gurr, Marshall, and Khosla 2001; Marshall and Gurr 2003, 2005). They constructed a composite index based on seven components thought to be related to a state's ability to manage the sources of domestic disputes in order to avoid the outbreak of armed conflict. In this issue of *Peace and Conflict*, we depart from Gurr and Marshall's approach and offer something different, albeit related. Our ranking of states based on the estimated risk for the onset of future political instability or state fragility differs from the previous approach in two important ways.

First, the former ledgers ranked states based on a measurement of a particular attribute of a state—the capacity to manage disputes and avert outbreaks of violence.

The current ledger offers a forecast of the future risk of instability. The concepts are certainly related. All things being equal, states with low peace-building capacity are more at risk for future instability than states with high peace-building capacity. As Marshall explains about the former ledger, "These rankings do not necessarily indicate impending risks of armed conflict or instability [in the states with lowest peace-building scores], rather that these states are vulnerable to such challenges." (Marshall 2005: 3). The new ledger now offers an explicit measurement of that risk and ranks states accordingly.

Second, the former and current ledgers are based on different methodologies. Current risk estimates are derived explicitly and systematically from a statistical model that explains the onset of various types of instability events by accounting for patterns in the evidence for 160 countries over the last six decades. This approach allows us to verify that each factor included in our model is indeed statistically related to future instability with a high degree of confidence. The weights of each causal factor in determining overall risk are estimated directly from the contours in the evidence from the historical experiences of all countries in the last half-century.

Index construction—the former approach—is a different methodological approach. Gurr and Marshall obtained their index by combining composite scores on individual items through summing and averaging. This approach is well-suited for measuring a state's peace-building capacity because the richness and complexity of the concept defy easy measurement through a single quantitative indicator. A difficult challenge to effective index construction relates to the researcher's decisions about the weights to assign each component in the ultimate combination of scores. The past ledgers assign equal causal weight to all seven of the factors they considered. An advantage of the current modeling approach is that these decisions, which can sometimes be arbitrary, are averted in favor of letting the data drive the estimates of causal weight.

Presenting a New Ledger

Figure 2.1 presents a global map that summarizes the results of our analyses. Countries in the highest risk category are depicted in red, while countries with moderate risk are shown in gold. The low-risk countries are shaded in light blue. A cursory scan of the map reveals some well-known patterns about the regions most likely to be affected by political instability (and those that are not). For example, most African countries qualify for moderate or high risk. Not surprisingly, many countries with well-documented difficulties with past instability (e.g., Somalia, Haiti, and Afghanistan) have been found to have high-risk scores for future instability. And, of course, the analyses found that Western democracies with advanced, post-industrial economies tend to have a very low risk of instability. Clearly, it is worthwhile to note that the analysis confirms some of the broadest intuitions about political instability worldwide, but the findings from this research extend well beyond confirming what is already well-known. To explore some of the

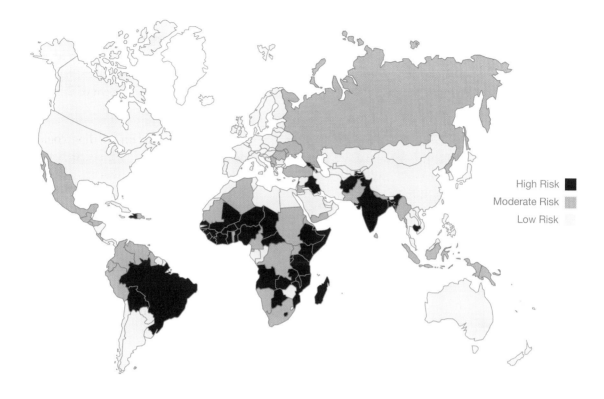

High Risk ■
Moderate Risk ▥
Low Risk ▫

more nuanced findings reported below, we turn first to a description of how the analysis was constructed.

This analysis is based on a conceptualization of political instability developed through the work of the Political Instability Task Force (PITF).[1] For more than a decade, the PITF has refined a broad definition of political instability that encompasses a wide variety of events that create significant challenges to the stability of states. These include revolutionary wars, ethnic wars, adverse regime changes, and genocides or politicides. The onset of any of these types of episodes for a state marks the beginning of an instability period. The task force has collected data on all instability events that satisfy the definitional requirements for these categories in the period 1950–2005.[2] The defining events selected by the PITF are quite diverse. However, the unifying connection is that the onset of any of these events signals the arrival of a period in which serious disruption to stable governance has occurred.

---

1 For overviews of some of the PITF's work, see Esty et al. (1995), Goldstone et al. (2000), Goldstone et al. (2005).

2 The initial compilation of state failure events for the Task Force was done at CIDCM in 1994–95 under the direction of Ted Robert Gurr. The roster of genocides and politicides was provided by Barbara Harff. Subsequent research by Monty G. Marshall and others has refined and updated the dataset. The PITF presents full definitions for revolutionary wars, ethnic wars, adverse regime changes, genocide, and politicide in Esty et al. (1998). A summary can be found in chapter 8 of this volume, which examines the relationship between instability and international crises.

The ledger represents a synthesis of some of the leading research on explaining and forecasting state instability.[3] It is noteworthy that the definition of instability used here covers a more heterogeneous set of events than an alternative definition that focuses exclusively on either the onset of armed civil conflict or political instability. By attempting to estimate the risks of future instability more broadly defined, the results may differ from other efforts that focus only on forecasting conflict or state collapse (absent conflict).

This chapter focuses on a small set of factors representing four broad categories of state features and functions: the political domain, the economic domain, the security domain, and the social domain. Instability can emerge from factors in each of these domains, or—most likely—from combinations of them. Interested readers will find a detailed explanation of the quantitative indicators used to measure these five factors immediately following the full ledger at the end of the chapter.

Institutional Consistency: From the political domain, the ledger accounts for the impact of *institutional consistency*. This refers to the extent to which the institutions comprising a country's political system are uniformly and consistently autocratic or democratic. Political institutions with a mix of democratic and autocratic features are inconsistent, a common attribute of polities in the midst of a democratic transition. Based on a series of findings reported in the academic literature, we expect regimes with inconsistent institutions to be more likely to experience political instability (Gurr 1974; Gates et al. 2006; Hegre et al. 2001)

Economic Openness: The ledger accounts for the impact of the economic domain with two factors. The first is *economic openness*, which is the extent to which a country's economy is integrated with the global economy. Countries that are more tightly connected to global markets have been found to experience less instability (Hegre et al. 2003; Goldstone et al. 2000).

Infant Mortality Rate: The ledger examines the impact of *infant mortality rates*, an indicator that serves as a proxy for a country's overall economic development and the level of advancement in social welfare policy. In this respect, this indicator taps into both the economic and social domains of a country. Research findings reported by the PITF have been especially notable for the strong relationship found between high infant mortality rates and the likelihood of future instability (Esty et al. 1999; Goldstone et al. 2005).

Militarization: To account for the security domain, the ledger focuses on a country's *level of militarization*. Instability is most likely in countries where the opportunities for armed conflict are greatest. In societies where the infrastructure and capital for organized armed conflict are more plentiful and accessible, the likelihood for civil conflict increases (Collier and Hoeffler 2004). Extensive militarization in a country typically implies that a large portion of the society's population has military skill

---

3 A sampling of some of the more significant recent contributions includes Collier and Hoeffler (2004), Esty et al. (1999), Fearon and Laitin (2003), Goldstone et al. (2005), Hegre and Sambanis (2006), Hegre et al. (2001), King and Zeng (2001), Sambanis (2002, 2004), and the United States Agency for International Development (2005).

and training, weapons stocks are more widely available, and other pieces of military equipment are more diffused throughout the country. The likelihood of instability is greater in this setting because increased access to and availability of these resources multiplies the opportunities for organizing and mobilizing.[4]

Neighborhood Security: The likelihood of political instability in a state increases substantially when a neighboring state is currently experiencing armed conflict. This risk is especially acute when ethnic or other communal groups span across borders. A number of studies have shown that neighborhood conflict is a significant predictor of political instability (Sambanis 2001; Hegre and Sambanis 2006; Goldstone et al. 2005).

The ledger is based on a model that estimates the statistical relationship between the future likelihood of instability and each of the five factors discussed above. The analysis accounts for the experiences of 160 countries over the past six decades.[5] Each case in our data collection is an annual observation for each country that records the values for the five factors that predict instability. We organize the data to enable a forecast of the likelihood of a new instability event occuring three years after any given year. Each observation in the data collection, therefore, records whether the country experienced an onset of a new instability event three years after the present year. We estimated our model based on data for the period 1950–2003 and found that each of our five factors was strongly related to the future risk of instability. Using the model estimates for the causal weight assigned to each factor, we used data from 2004, the last year for which complete data are available for all five of our factors, to produce a three-year forecast indicating the risk of instability in 2007.[6]

The ledger presents the likelihood of future instability in a country as a *risk ratio*. The risk ratio gives the relative risk of instability in a country compared to the average estimated likelihood of instability for 28 member countries of the Organization for Economic Cooperation and Development (OECD).[7] The member states of the OECD were selected as a baseline because the organization's membership is widely

---

4 We note, however, that high levels of militarization might also strengthen the government's capacity to tamp down the sources of instability. Hegre and Sambanis (2006) found that high levels of militarization reduced the likelihood of armed civil conflict. However, that study used a different measure of militarization than the one utilized here, and it focused only on the onset of armed conflict. These differences may account for why we found the oppposite relationship here.

5 The *Peace and Conflict* companion Web site (*http://www.cidcm.umd.edu/pc*) contains a full description of model specification details, along with a discussion of all data used in the analysis.

6 We recognize that forecasts reaching further into the future would have great value. The 2005 data necessary to compute those forecasts are unavailable at the time of this writing. We note, however, that risk estimates computed from structural models such as this one change only incrementally from year to year, which suggests that the estimates in the ledger will maintain their relevance for nearly all countries beyond the end of 2007.

7 Those members are Australia, Austria, Belgium, Canada, Czech Republic, Denmark, Finland, France, Germany, Greece, Hungary, Ireland, Italy, Japan, South Korea, Mexico, Netherlands, New Zealand, Norway, Poland, Portugal, Slovak Republic, Spain, Sweden, Switzerland, Turkey, United Kingdom, and the United States. (Two members of the OECD have been excluded from the average: Iceland and Luxembourg. Neither country is included in the overall analysis because its population does not meet the minimum threshold of 500,000.)

viewed as representing the most politically stable countries in the world. Indeed, the average estimated probability for future instability for these 28 countries is quite small: 0.003. The risk ratio for any country is computed by dividing that country's estimated probability for future instability by the baseline OECD probability of 0.003. For example, the model estimates a 0.012 probability that Jordan will experience future instability. Accordingly, Jordan's risk ratio is 4.00, indicating that it is about four times as likely as an average OECD country to experience instability. Ethiopia, one of the highest-rated countries in terms of risk for future instability (estimated 0.077 probability for future instability), has a risk ratio of 25.7.[8]

The ledger categorizes states into three groupings: low risk, moderate risk, and high risk. Any state with a risk ratio in the top 25th percentile of all states qualifies for high risk (denoted with a red circle in the ledger). Accordingly, a risk ratio greater than 7.3 places a state in the top 25th percentile. Any state with a risk ratio less than the global median (3.56, the threshold for the lower 50th percentile) qualifies for the low-risk category (denoted with a green circle). Any state with a ratio between 3.56 and 7.3 qualifies for moderate risk (denoted with a gold circle).

The risk ratios appearing in the ledger are statistical estimates and, accordingly, are accompanied by varying levels of confidence depending on the particular attributes of a given country. This point warrants some elaboration. Statistical models make inferences about the direction (positive or negative) and the strength of the relationship between variables. These inferences are based on samples of evidence collected from the real world. The tools from inferential statistics provide guidance about whether we can safely conclude that the relationships we observe in our sample are likely to be the "true" relationship in the real world. An under-appreciated characteristic of statistical inferences is that they are *always* associated with some level of uncertainty. For instance, in the model used to create the ledger, infant mortality rates were found to be positively related to the onset of instability. The level of uncertainty for that estimate was sufficiently small to rule out the possibility that the model was pointing erroneously to a positive relationship when the "true" relationship was actually negative (or nonexistent). However, uncertainty around the estimate remains. The uncertainty exists because many countries with high infant mortality rates have not experienced instability (e.g., Malawi, Saudi Arabia, or Bolivia) and some with a low rate do (e.g., Israel). These outlier states create "noise" in the estimated relationship between instability and infant mortality rates. Each of the variables in the model is accompanied by this kind of uncertainty or noise.

For each country, the ledger reports a single best estimate of the overall risk of instability.

Information extracted from the statistical model for instability can be used to compute the total amount of uncertainty surrounding an individual country's estimate for instability risk. The ledger reports this level of uncertainty. For each

---

8 Some of the states in the ledger are currently in the midst of an ongoing instability event. We report the risk of future instability in these states with a caveat to the reader to interpret these risk ratios cautiously.

country, the ledger reports a single best estimate of the overall risk of instability. Additionally, the ledger reports a range of values within which the best estimate lies. Statistically speaking, the "true" risk of instability lies within this range with a 95 percent probability. A narrow confidence range indicates a high degree of certainty about the estimate. In contrast, wide confidence ranges can sometimes render an estimate nearly meaningless because uncertainty is so great.

Discussion of Key Findings

Let us begin to present some of the findings from the analyses that produced the ledger by referring back to Figure 2.1. It can be seen that no region rivals Africa in terms of the number of states at the highest level of risk for future instability. Of the 51 African states in the analysis, 28 are in this category. Even more staggering, many of these states are among the most at-risk states in the world. Many others qualify for moderate risk, leaving just 7 states on the entire continent qualifying at the lowest level of risk.

Looking through the ledger's listing of African states, it can be seen that the primary factors driving the high-risk estimates are regime inconsistency, lack of economic openness, and high infant mortality.[9] Progress in each of these three areas will produce a tripod upon which future stability in Africa can be advanced. Although that diagnosis is well-known and widely accepted, steady progress has proven elusive. Certainly, future democratic consolidation is expected to bolster state stability, but, in the interim, mixed regimes lack the capacity to reinforce stability, as competing elites often have the authority to undermine newly rooted democratic institutions. At the same time, enduring inability to make great strides in improving social welfare through effective delivery of services (captured in part by measurements of infant mortality) is a problem common to most of the African high-risk states. Further, many African states continue to struggle in their attempts to shephard economic growth through greater integration with the global economy. It is notable, and perhaps surprising, that problems related to extreme militarization and regional security threats are somewhat less applicable in Africa. While this had not been true until relatively recently (especially with the end of the civil war in the Democratic Republic of Congo), these factors are now relatively less pronounced in most of the highest-risk states in the African region.

Many Latin American states qualify for the moderate or high-risk categories. Notably, Brazil qualifies at the high-risk level, barely satisfying the threshold for this category. Brazil's low level of economic openness is the primary factor driving this estimate. Of all South American states, Brazil's ratio of total trade to GDP is the lowest. An increase in trade to the median ratio for the region would reduce Brazil's estimate for instability substantially, placing it solidly in the moderate risk category.

---

9 We remind the reader that the color codes used to present a country's standing on each of the five predictors of instability reflect the 2004 values used to produce a three-year forecast.

Table 2.1: Top 25 Highest Risk for Instability		
Rank	Country	Risk Ratio
1	Afghanistan	39.3
2	Iraq	29.9
3	Niger	29.7
4	Ethiopia	25.7
5	Liberia	21.1
6	Sierra Leone	20.9
7	Mali	20.7
8	Tanzania	18.9
9	Central African Republic	18.4
10	Djibouti	17.1
11	Ivory Coast	17.0
12	Zambia	14.8
13	Somalia	13.7
14	Nigeria	13.4
15	Bangladesh	13.1
16	Malawi	13.1
17	Benin	13.0
18	Kenya	12.9
19	Mozambique	12.7
20	Lebanon	12.1
21	Haiti	11.7
22	Chad	11.2
23	Burundi	11.1
24	India	10.7
25	Angola	10.5

Table 2.1 lists the 25 states with the highest estimated risk levels. Approximately three-fourths (19 of 25) of these states are African, another indication of the acute nature of the problems found in that region.

The methodology used to generate the rankings in the ledger can also be used to make assessments about progress over time. To illustrate, we produce risk ratios using data from 2000, creating an estimate for the likelihood of instability in 2003. Table 2.2 presents the 10 countries with the highest risk in 2003 alongside the 10 highest-risk countries from our current analysis. Since 2000, four countries (Peru, Iran, Mozambique, and Guinea-Bissau) have seen sufficient improvement in their circumstances to drop from the current top 10.

The sharp drop in Peru's risk of instability is due in large measure to significant steps toward democratic consolidation, improvements in social welfare policy, and increased integration with the global economy. In late 2000, amidst allegations of corruption and serious human rights abuses, President Alberto Fujimori fled his country and resigned his office. At the time of Fujimori's election to office in 1990, Peru had enjoyed a decade of relatively stable democratic rule. His election, however, was soon followed by a series of reversals to democratic governance as Fujimori relied on increasingly authoritarian measures to deal with guerrilla insurgency in the country. By 2000, mounting dissatisfaction contributed to pressures that led to his resignation. From 1990 to 2000, Peru's scores for regime consistency plummeted as it transitioned from a fairly stable, consolidated democracy to a regime with a combination of democratic and autocratic features, culminating in a risk ratio in 2000 of 14.9. Since Fujimori's departure and the elections of President Alejandro Toledo in 2001 and Alan Garcia in 2006, democratic attributes have strengthened considerably in Peru, leading to a restoration of high scores on regime consistency. Since 2000, Peru has also seen a 25 percent decline in its infant mortality rate, a reflection of greater governmental effectiveness in improving social welfare standards in the country. Also, Peru's total trade as a percentage of GDP increased modestly from 2000 to 2004, a reflection of growing integration with global markets and strong overall economic performance during this period. In all, positive developments in each of these three areas (regime consistency, infant mortality, and economic openness) lead to a dramatically lower estimated risk of instability for Peru (5.5). Peru ranked ninth in the world for risk of instability in 2000. Today, its ranking places it squarely in the middle of the pack among all Latin American countries.

Table 2.2: Change Over Time: Top 10 Highest Risk Countries in 2003 and 2007				
	2003 Forecast		2007 Forecast	
Rank	Country	Risk Ratio	Country	Risk Ratio
1	Ethiopia	26.6	Afghanistan**	39.3
2	Niger	23.0	Iraq**	29.9
3	Tanzania	18.8	Niger	29.7
4	Central African Rep.	17.6	Ethiopia	25.7
5	Sierra Leone	16.4	Liberia**	21.1
6	Iran*	16.3	Sierra Leone	20.9
7	Djibouti	15.8	Mali**	20.7
8	Mozambique*	15.3	Tanzania	18.9
9	Peru*	14.9	Central African Rep.	18.4
10	Guinea-Bissau*	14.8	Djibouti	17.1
* Falls out of top 10 in 2007, ** New to top 10 in 2007				

Iran's experience is much like Peru's—an unusual, yet fitting comparison. As in Peru, dramatic changes in regime consistency in Iran explain the shift in its estimated risk for instability. While Peru moved from inconsistency toward greater democratic consolidation, Iran shifted toward a more coherent autocracy. Efforts at democratic reform in the latter half of the 1990s have been reversed recently, leading to a strengthening of autocracy in Iran and a lower estimated risk for instability. Also, the ratio of Iran's total trade to GDP has increased since 2000, partly a reflection of higher oil prices in recent years, which has also contributed to the marked decrease in Iran's estimated risk.

Mozambique's reduction in risk is not as dramatic as that for Peru or Iran (a decline in its risk score from 15.3 to 12.7), but its experience illustrates the sensitivity of our estimates to changes in the neighborhood security context. Of the five factors we track, only one changed significantly for Mozambique in the period 2000–2004. The termination of the devastating civil war in the Democratic Republic of the Congo (DRC) in 2001 meant that neighboring Zimbabwe, which had sent troops to fight directly on behalf of DRC's government, was no longer at war. While we do not claim that the civil war in DRC posed a direct and tangible threat to state stability in Mozambique, global evidence over the last 50 years indicates that the presence of a neighborhood war is a powerful predictor of instability. Wars have far-reaching consequences, carrying powerful contagion effects that can seriously disrupt the interactions between and within neighboring states. The same logic underlies Guinea-Bissau's significant decline in risk (from 14.8 in 2000, to 9.3 in 2004). In this case, the cessation of internal violence in neighboring Senegal in 2003 reduces the estimated risk.

Table 2.2 shows four newcomers to the top 10 list in 2004 that were not included in 2000. Two of these had very high risk estimates in 2000 and their appearance in the list does not reflect a significant change in risk (Liberia and Mali). However, the estimates for Afghanistan (4.3 in 2000) and Iraq (2.1 in 2000) have increased sharply, which warrants some explanation. The higher estimates for these two countries are reflections of the effort to democratize both states. In 2000, both states were consolidated autocracies with a high degree of regime coherence. Today, both states are transitional regimes with little coherence. The increased risk of instability today stems from this particular change. Indeed, with the exception of infant mortality in Iraq, none of the other four factors changed significantly from their 2000 values. Some readers may be tempted to conclude that the higher risk estimates for these two states is evidence that military action by US-led coalitions in both contexts has backfired. We caution our readers against such a conclusion. Rather, the increase in their estimated risks is due to changes in regime characteristics. While the US-led coalition's military actions precipitated these changes in both Afghanistan and Iraq, the estimated risks would have been the same if these regime transitions had occurred without military intervention. The model limits its focus to the changes in regime characteristics, not to other contextual details in the respective countries that may also bode poorly for future state stability. For instance, many other factors that observers point to as harbingers of future problems in Iraq (e.g., increased sectarian violence, weakened domestic security forces, diminished state capacity to provide essential services) are not accounted for explicitly in our framework. Increased infant mortality rates in Iraq do capture some of the government's inability to deliver services to society, but this change contributes only modestly to the upward shift in Iraq's risk.

To conclude, we note that the estimates listed in the following pages are based on measurements of large, structural forces that govern the possibilities for instability in any given country. This analysis should be complemented by other early-warning analyses that focus on more detailed information about high-risk countries that can be updated in weekly or monthly intervals. The ledger does more than simply highlight high-risk states. It provides information about the level of confidence attached to country assessments, which can serve as a basis for making distinctions among states with roughly equal risk levels. More important, the approach allows us to assess the progress of states as they move through periods of transition. This has great potential value because, for any given country, shifts in the constellation of key structural factors can alter future risks considerably. In the future, we will continue to monitor how changes in these structural factors affect assessments for high-risk states, as well as for states with borderline estimates. We will also be attentive to advances in identifying other indicators that are found to be effective predictors of future instability. This will serve to improve our underlying model by further reducing uncertainty about our predictions and strengthening the quality of forecasts.

The Peace and Conflict Instability Ledger ranks states according to the forecasted risk of future instability. See notes on pp. 19–20 for a description of the color codes for each indicator and also a detailed explanation of the confidence range (note 10).

Recent Instability	Country	Regime Consistency	Infant Mortality	Economic Openness	Militarization	Neighborhood War	Risk Category	Risk Score	Confidence Range
Africa									
	Niger	●	●	●	●	●	●	29.7	17.7 – 44.4
	Ethiopia	●	●	●	●	●	●	25.7	16.1 – 39.5
	Liberia	●	●	●	●	●	●	21.1	11.4 – 36.9
	Sierra Leone	●	●	●	●	●	●	20.9	11.5 – 35.2
	Mali	●	●	●	●	●	●	20.7	11.8 – 32.5
	Tanzania	●	●	●	●	●	●	18.9	12.3 – 27.9
	Central African Rep.	●	●	●	●	●	●	18.4	10.4 – 29.1
	Djibouti	●	●	●	●	●	●	17.1	8.4 – 31.3
■	Ivory Coast	●	●	●	●	●	●	17.0	9.7 – 27.7
	Zambia	●	●	●	●	●	●	14.8	9.1 – 23.1
■	Somalia	●	●	●	●	●	●	13.7	8.6 – 21.6
	Nigeria	●	●	●	●	●	●	13.4	7.6 – 21.5
	Malawi	●	●	●	●	●	●	13.1	7.3 – 21.8
	Benin	●	●	●	●	●	●	13.0	8.4 – 19.3
	Kenya	●	●	●	●	●	●	12.9	7.4 – 20.7
	Mozambique	●	●	●	●	●	●	12.7	7.3 – 20.9
	Chad	●	●	●	●	●	●	11.2	5.4 – 20.7
	Burundi	●	●	●	●	●	●	11.1	6.5 – 18.0
	Angola	●	●	●	●	●	●	10.5	4.7 – 20.6
	Guinea-Bissau	●	●	●	●	●	●	9.3	4.8 – 16.6
	Botswana	●	●	●	●	●	●	9.1	4.7 – 15.1
	Madagascar	●	●	●	●	●	●	9.1	5.3 – 14.6
	Senegal	●	●	●	●	●	●	8.8	5.0 – 14.1
	Burkina Faso	●	●	●	●	●	●	8.3	5.0 – 12.9
	Guinea	●	●	●	●	●	●	8.1	4.6 – 12.8
	Lesotho	●	●	●	●	●	●	7.7	3.7 – 14.2
	Ghana	●	●	●	●	●	●	7.5	4.1 – 12.1
	Rwanda	●	●	●	●	●	●	7.5	4.5 – 11.6
	Namibia	●	●	●	●	●	●	7.3	4.4 – 11.3
■	Dem. Rep. of Congo	●	●	●	●	●	●	6.9	3.7 – 11.8
	Cameroon	●	●	●	●	●	●	6.8	4.2 – 10.5
	South Africa	●	●	●	●	●	●	6.5	3.8 – 10.3
	Togo	●	●	●	●	●	●	5.9	3.3 – 9.9
	Eritrea	●	●	●	●	●	●	5.2	2.3 – 9.9
	Mauritania	●	●	●	●	●	●	5.1	3.1 – 7.5
■	Uganda	●	●	●	●	●	●	4.9	2.8 – 8.1
	Equatorial Guinea	●	●	●	●	●	●	4.5	3.0 – 6.6
	Comoros	●	●	●	●	●	●	4.0	2.5 – 5.8
■	Sudan	●	●	●	●	●	●	3.7	2.2 – 5.6
	Gambia	●	●	●	●	●	●	2.8	1.6 – 4.5
	Congo	●	●	●	●	●	●	2.7	1.5 – 4.5
	Zimbabwe	●	●	●	●	●	●	2.5	1.6 – 3.9
	Gabon	●	●	●	●	●	●	2.3	1.3 – 3.8
	Swaziland	●	●	●	●	●	●	2.2	1.0 – 4.3
	Cape Verde	●	●	●	●	●	●	1.4	0.7 – 2.5
	Mauritius	●	●	●	●	●	●	0.8	0.4 – 1.5

Recent Instability	Country	Regime Consistency	Infant Mortality	Economic Openness	Militarization	Neighborhood War	Risk Category	Risk Score	Confidence Range
Asia									
■	Afghanistan	●	●	●	○	○	●	39.3	26.5 — 56.3
	Bangladesh	○	○	●	○	○	●	13.1	9.1 — 18.7
■	India	○	○	●	○	●	●	10.7	6.5 — 16.5
	Cambodia	○	●	○	●	○	●	7.9	3.8 — 14.0
	Tajikistan	○	○	○	○	○	●	7.3	3.6 — 13.4
	North Korea	○	○	●	●	●	○	7.2	2.6 — 16.0
■	Nepal	○	○	●	○	○	○	6.4	3.8 — 10.0
■	Myanmar (Burma)	○	○	●	●	○	○	6.2	3.9 — 9.3
■	Pakistan	○	●	●	○	○	○	5.2	3.3 — 7.9
	Papua New Guinea	○	○	●	○	○	○	5.1	2.5 — 9.3
	Indonesia	○	○	○	○	○	○	4.4	2.7 — 6.8
	Sri Lanka	●	○	○	●	○	○	4.4	2.3 — 7.8
	Fiji	○	○	●	○	○	○	3.6	1.9 — 6.0
■	Philippines	○	○	○	○	○	○	3.5	2.0 — 5.7
	Kyrgyzstan	○	○	○	○	○	○	3.5	1.7 — 6.2
	Kazakhstan	○	○	○	○	○	○	3.2	1.8 — 5.3
	Laos	○	○	○	●	○	○	3.2	1.9 — 4.8
	Malaysia	●	○	○	○	●	○	3.1	1.3 — 6.2
	Turkmenistan	○	●	○	○	●	○	2.8	1.5 — 4.9
	Bhutan	○	○	○	○	○	○	2.8	1.6 — 4.6
	Mongolia	○	○	○	○	○	○	2.7	1.2 — 5.2
■	Thailand	○	○	○	○	○	○	2.4	1.2 — 4.0
	Vietnam	○	○	○	●	○	○	2.3	0.6 — 5.8
	Uzbekistan	○	○	○	○	●	○	2.2	1.3 — 3.8
	China	○	○	○	○	●	○	1.5	0.8 — 2.8
	South Korea	○	○	○	●	○	○	1.3	0.5 — 2.5
	Singapore	○	○	○	●	○	○	0.9	0.3 — 2.6
	Taiwan	○	○	○	●	○	○	0.6	0.3 — 1.2
	Japan	○	○	●	○	○	○	0.5	0.2 — 1.1
	New Zealand	○	○	●	○	○	○	0.5	0.2 — 1.0
	Australia	○	○	●	○	○	○	0.5	0.2 — 1.0
Eastern Europe									
	Armenia	●	○	○	●	●	●	9.4	5.7 — 15.3
	Georgia	○	○	○	○	●	●	8.2	4.7 — 12.9
■	Russia	○	○	○	●	●	○	5.0	2.8 — 8.1
	Yugoslavia	○	○	○	●	●	○	4.5	2.4 — 8.0
	Albania	○	○	○	●	○	○	4.5	2.6 — 7.3
	Moldova	○	○	●	○	○	○	4.3	2.3 — 7.5
	Romania	○	○	○	●	●	○	3.8	2.2 — 6.1
	Ukraine	○	○	○	○	●	○	3.7	1.8 — 6.5
	Bosnia	●	○	○	○	○	○	3.6	1.6 — 6.9
	Azerbaijan	○	○	○	●	●	○	3.4	1.9 — 5.7
	Bulgaria	○	○	○	●	●	○	2.8	1.5 — 4.8
	Latvia	○	○	○	○	●	○	2.3	1.1 — 4.2
	Croatia	○	○	○	○	○	○	1.9	0.8 — 3.7
	Estonia	○	○	○	○	●	○	1.8	0.7 — 3.6
	Slovakia	○	○	○	○	●	○	1.4	0.6 — 2.8
	Lithuania	○	○	○	●	●	○	0.8	0.4 — 1.6
	Poland	○	○	○	○	●	○	0.7	0.4 — 1.4
	Belarus	○	○	○	●	●	○	0.7	0.3 — 1.6

Recent Instability	Country	Regime Consistency	Infant Mortality	Economic Openness	Militarization	Neighborhood War	Risk Category	Risk Score	Confidence Range
Eastern Europe (continued)									
	Hungary	○	○	○	○	●	○	0.7	0.3 — 1.4
	Slovenia	○	○	○	○	○	○	0.5	0.2 — 1.0
	Czech Republic	○	○	○	○	●	○	0.4	0.2 — 0.9
Latin America and the Caribbean									
	Haiti	○	○	●	○	○	●	11.7	6.7 — 18.3
	Bolivia	○	○	○	○	○	●	7.6	4.5 — 12.1
	Brazil	○	○	●	○	○	●	7.5	5.1 — 10.9
	Guatemala	○	○	●	○	●	○	7.3	4.8 — 11.0
	Honduras	○	○	○	○	●	○	6.6	3.9 — 10.1
	Ecuador	○	○	○	○	○	○	6.3	3.8 — 10.0
	Guyana	○	○	○	○	○	○	6.0	2.9 — 10.4
	Nicaragua	○	○	○	○	●	○	5.9	3.4 — 9.5
	El Salvador	○	○	○	○	●	○	5.5	3.2 — 8.8
	Peru	○	○	●	○	○	○	5.5	3.4 — 8.4
	Mexico	○	○	○	○	○	○	4.9	3.0 — 7.9
	Venezuela	○	○	○	○	○	○	4.6	2.6 — 7.8
	Dominican Republic	○	○	○	○	○	○	3.8	2.3 — 6.2
■	Colombia	○	○	●	○	○	○	3.6	2.2 — 5.8
	Paraguay	○	○	○	○	○	○	3.2	1.9 — 5.1
	Argentina	○	○	●	○	○	○	2.9	1.6 — 4.9
	Jamaica	○	○	○	○	○	○	2.2	1.2 — 3.9
	Panama	○	○	○	○	○	○	1.6	0.8 — 2.8
	Chile	○	○	○	○	○	○	1.4	0.7 — 2.7
	Uruguay	○	○	○	○	○	○	1.1	0.6 — 1.8
	Costa Rica	○	○	○	○	○	○	1.0	0.4 — 1.8
	Trinidad and Tobago	○	○	○	○	○	○	1.0	0.5 — 1.6
	Cuba	○	○	●	○	○	○	0.5	0.2 — 1.2
Middle East and North Africa									
■	Iraq	●	●	●	○	○	●	29.9	20.0 — 43.2
	Lebanon	●	○	○	●	○	●	12.1	6.4 — 21.4
■	Turkey	○	○	○	●	●	○	7.2	4.6 — 11.0
■	Yemen	○	●	○	○	○	○	7.2	4.2 — 11.5
	Jordan	○	○	○	●	●	○	4.0	1.9 — 7.2
	Algeria	○	○	○	●	○	○	3.7	2.2 — 6.1
	Tunisia	○	○	○	○	○	○	2.8	1.4 — 5.1
	Morocco	○	○	○	●	●	○	2.4	1.3 — 4.0
	Iran	○	○	○	○	●	○	2.1	1.1 — 3.5
	Egypt	○	○	○	●	●	○	2.0	1.0 — 3.4
	Syria	○	○	○	●	●	○	1.4	0.7 — 2.5
	Libya	○	○	○	●	●	○	1.4	0.7 — 2.5
	Saudi Arabia	○	○	○	●	●	○	1.0	0.5 — 1.8
	Kuwait	○	○	○	●	○	○	0.7	0.3 — 1.6
	Bahrain	○	○	○	●	○	○	0.7	0.3 — 1.4
	Qatar	○	○	○	●	○	○	0.7	0.4 — 1.1
	Oman	○	○	○	●	○	○	0.6	0.3 — 1.1
■	Israel	○	○	○	●	○	○	0.5	0.2 — 1.1
	UAE	○	○	○	●	○	○	0.3	0.1 — 0.7
North Atlantic									
	Macedonia	○	○	○	●	●	○	2.9	1.5 — 5.0
	United States	○	○	●	○	●	○	1.0	0.4 — 1.9

Recent Instability	Country	Regime Consistency	Infant Mortality	Economic Openness	Militarization	Neighborhood War	Risk Category	Risk Score	Confidence Range
	North Atlantic (continued)								
	Cyprus	●	●	●	●	●	●	0.7	0.3 ▌ 1.4
	Greece	●	●	●	●	●	●	0.7	0.3 ▌ 1.3
	United Kingdom	●	●	●	●	●	●	0.7	0.3 ▌ 1.3
	France	●	●	●	●	●	●	0.6	0.2 ▌ 1.4
	Canada	●	●	●	●	●	●	0.6	0.3 ▌ 1.2
	Italy	●	●	●	●	●	●	0.6	0.2 ▌ 1.2
	Portugal	●	●	●	●	●	●	0.6	0.2 ▌ 1.1
	Denmark	●	●	●	●	●	●	0.5	0.2 ▌ 1.1
	Germany	●	●	●	●	●	●	0.5	0.2 ▌ 1.1
	Netherlands	●	●	●	●	●	●	0.5	0.2 ▌ 1.1
	Austria	●	●	●	●	●	●	0.5	0.2 ▌ 1.0
	Ireland	●	●	●	●	●	●	0.5	0.2 ▌ 1.0
	Switzerland	●	●	●	●	●	●	0.5	0.2 ▌ 1.0
	Spain	●	●	●	●	●	●	0.5	0.2 ▌ 1.0
	Norway	●	●	●	●	●	●	0.5	0.2 ▌ 1.0
	Belgium	●	●	●	●	●	●	0.4	0.2 ▌ 0.9
	Sweden	●	●	●	●	●	●	0.4	0.1 ▌ 0.9
	Finland	●	●	●	●	●	●	0.4	0.1 ▌ 0.9

The ledger is based on a model that estimates the statistical relationship between the future likelihood of instability and each of the five factors in the chapter. We estimated the model based on data for the period 1950–2003 and found that each of the five factors were strongly related to the future risk of instability. Using the model estimates for the causal weight assigned to each factor, we used data from 2004, the last year for which complete data are available for all five of our factors, to produce a three-year forecast indicating the risk of instability in 2007. The color codes used in the ledger to present a country's standing on each of the five factors are based on the values in 2004. The notes below explain the various color codings.

(1) Recent Instability   This column indicates (with a red square) whether the country has been coded by the Political Instability Task Force (PITF) as being involved in an instability event as of the end of 2005. The country's risk score (see column 9) provides an assessment of the likelihood of the country's experiencing future instability. One might interpret the risk score for countries currently experiencing instability as the risk of continued instability, but we caution readers that the causal factors that drive the continuation of instability are likely not the same as the factors that drive the onset of instability.

(2) Country   The ledger examines only those countries with populations greater than 500,000 in 2004.

(3) Regime Consistency   The risk of future instability is strongly related to the extent to which the institutions comprising a country's political system are uniformly and consistently autocratic or democratic. Political institutions with a mix of democratic and autocratic features are deemed inconsistent, a common attribute of polities in the midst of a democratic transition (or a reversal from democratic rule to more autocratic governance). We expect regimes with inconsistent institutions to be more likely to experience political instability. In the ledger, highly consistent democracies (Polity score greater than or equal to 6) and autocracies (Polity score less than or equal to -6) receive a green marker. A red marker has been assigned to regimes with inconsistent characteristics that also qualify as partial democracies according to PITF. Regimes with these characteristics have been found to have the highest risk for instability. We assign a gold marker to partial autocracies because the propensity for instability in these regimes is somewhat less than in partial democracies.

(4) Infant Mortality   Infant mortality rates serve as a proxy for overall governmental effectiveness in executing policies and delivering services that improve social welfare in a country. High infant mortality rates are associated with an increased likelihood of future instability. The states with the best records are indicated with a green marker (scoring in the bottom 25th percentile of global infant mortality rates). States with the worst record (scoring in the highest 25th percentile) are indicated with a red marker. States in the middle 50th percentile are indicated with a gold marker.

(5) Economic Openness   Closer integration with global markets reduces the potential likelihood of armed civil conflict and political instability. Policies that integrate global and domestic markets can produce higher growth rates and sometimes reduce inequality. To that extent, economic openness can remove or weaken common drivers for civil unrest related to economic grievances. We focus on the proportion of a country's GDP accounted for by the value of all trade (exports plus imports) as a measure for economic openness. The countries with the lowest score for economic openness are considered to be at the highest risk for instability. We designate these states with a red marker. The highest 25th percentile of states receive a green marker in the ledger. The middle 50th percentile receives a gold marker.

(6) Militarization   Instability is most likely in countries where the opportunities for armed conflict are greatest. In societies where the infrastructure and capital for organized armed conflict are more plentiful and accessible, the likelihood for civil conflict increases. The ledger measures militarization as the number of individuals in a country's active armed forces as a percentage of the country's total population. Countries with militarization scores in the bottom 25th percentile are indicated with a green marker. Countries in the top 25th percentile are presented with a red marker. The middle 50th percentile is indicated with a gold marker.

(7) Neighborhood War   The presence of an armed conflict in a neighboring state (internal or interstate) increases the risk of state instability. The contagion effects of regional armed conflict can heighten the risk of state instability, especially when ethnic or other communal groups span across borders. We use conflict data from the Uppsala Conflict Data Project at the International Peace Research Institute (Gleditsch et al. 2002) to determine the conflict status of states in 2004. For a neighbor to be considered involved in armed conflict, we further require that the conflict produces 25 or more battle-related fatalities per year. A red marker indicates when two or more neighbors are involved in armed conflict. A gold marker indicates the presence of armed conflict in only one neighboring state. A green marker indicates the absence of armed conflict in all neighboring states.

(8) Risk Category States have been placed in one of three categories corresponding to their risk score. Any state with a risk ratio in the top 25th percentile of all states qualifies for high risk (denoted with a red marker). A risk ratio greater than 7.3 places a state in the top 25th percentile. Any state with a risk ratio less than the global median (3.56) qualifies for the low-risk category (denoted with a green marker). Any state with a ratio between 3.56 and 7.3 qualifies for moderate risk (denoted with a gold marker).

(9) Risk Score The risk score gives a three-year forecast of the relative risk (compared to an average member of the OECD) of experiencing instability. The score is computed based on the results of estimating a statistical model using global data from the period 1950-2003. Then, using the model estimates, data

from 2004 were used to obtain the three-year forecasts for each country for 2007.

(10) Confidence Range The confidence range provides information about the degree of uncertainty corresponding to a country's estimated risk score. Statistically speaking, the "true" risk of instability lies within this range with a 95 percent probability. The width of the confidence range is drawn to scale. The widest confidence range observed in the data has been set to the width of the full column with all other confidence ranges drawn accordingly. When the bar is one color, the confidence range is confined to a single risk category. In cases where the confidence range spans multiple risk categories, the different colors of the bar reflect the extent of the overlap with those categories. Using a sample country (Ghana), the key below illustrates how to read the information contained in the graphic for each country's confidence range. The color green indicates the low-risk range, gold indicates the moderate-risk range, and red indicates the high-risk range.

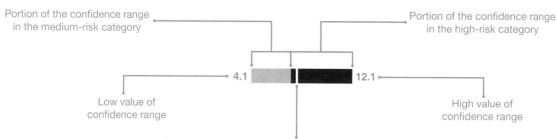

Portion of the confidence range in the medium-risk category

Portion of the confidence range in the high-risk category

4.1   12.1

Low value of confidence range

High value of confidence range

The location of the risk score estimate (from Column 9) within the confidence range is depicted with a vertical white line. In this example, the estimate is approximately 7.5. Note, the location of the risk score estimate does not necessarily fall in the midpoint of the confidence range.

3. TRENDS IN GLOBAL CONFLICT, 1946–2005

J. Joseph Hewitt

This chapter presents an overview of important trends in armed global conflict. The analyses offered here show a downward trend in the number of armed conflicts. That downward trend, which has been documented in previous volumes of *Peace and Conflict* as well as in other sources, begins as the Cold War fades away. However, the number of active armed conflicts in the last year of complete data (2005) rose sharply from the previous total in 2004, a sobering reminder of the resiliency of human temptation to use force to resolve disputes. The chapter presents some new analyses that indicate that the downward trend in conflict is not the result of effective prevention of new conflicts. Rather, the decline in active conflict worldwide is more the result of effective resolution of older conflicts that have been ongoing for several years. Still, there is indirect evidence suggesting that new conflicts may be erupting at a slower pace. International crises, the precursors of serious interstate war, have been steadily declining in number over the past two decades. The evidence presented in this brief overview raises questions about some explanations that have been advanced to explain the post-Cold War decline in armed conflict—a point that will be addressed in the conclusion.

Figure 3.1 presents the number of active armed conflicts in every year beginning with 1946. The detailed definitions for the different types of conflict can be found

Figure 3.1: Global Trends in Violent Conflict, 1946–2005

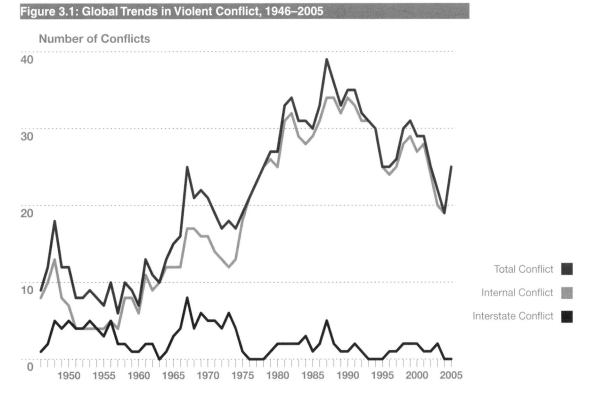

Number of Conflicts

Total Conflict
Internal Conflict
Interstate Conflict

Box 3.1: Definition of Armed Conflict	
The UCDP/PRIO Armed Conflict Dataset defines conflict as "a contested incompatibility that concerns government and/or territory where the use of armed force between two parties, of which at least one is the government of a state, results in at least 25 battle-related deaths" (from the UCDP/PRIO Armed Conflict Dataset Codebook, page 4). Although UCDP/PRIO tracks conflicts with low-level intensity, we limit our focus to conflicts that have exceeded 1,000 battle-related deaths. Specifically, to be counted as an active conflict in any given year, the battle-deaths in the conflict must have a cumulative total greater than 1,000 since the conflict's inception and must have recorded 25 or more battle-related deaths in that year. The UCDP/PRIO dataset identifies four types of armed conflict: extrasystemic armed conflict, interstate armed conflict, internal armed conflict, and internationalized internal armed conflict.	
Interstate Conflict	
Extrasystemic Armed Conflict	Extrasystemic armed conflict involves a state against a non-state actor outside the territory of the state. An example includes the armed conflict between France and the forces of the Viet Minh from 1946–1954. There have been no extrasystemic armed conflicts since the mid-1970s.
Interstate Armed Conflict	Interstate armed conflict involves two or more independent states (e.g., Iran and Iraq, 1980–1988)
Internal Conflict	
Internal Armed Conflict	Internal armed conflict involves the government of a state against one or more internal actors (e.g., domestic opposition groups, guerrilla forces, etc.) India's longstanding conflict with Kashmir insurgents is an example.
Internationalized Internal Armed Conflict	Internationalized internal armed conflict involves the government of a state against one or more internal actors with outside intervention by at least one other state in support of either the government or the internal opposition groups. The five-year civil war (1996–2001) in the Democratic Republic of the Congo is an example, as is the current civil war in Iraq.

in Box 3.1. Since the end of the Cold War (approximately 1990), the number of active armed conflicts around the world has gradually declined. The number of active conflicts reached its highest point since the end of World War II in 1987 with 39 total conflicts (5 interstate conflicts and 34 internal or civil conflicts). By 1996, that number had dropped to 25 (1 interstate conflict and 24 internal conflicts). After a brief resurgence in global conflict from 1997–2001, the numbers declined further, reaching a new low in 2004 with just 19 conflicts, all of which were internal conflicts. The figure depicts these patterns, showing separate trend lines for all interstate conflict, internal conflict, and combined total conflict.

These patterns will be familiar to readers of past *Peace and Conflict* books. Marshall (2001, 2003, 2005) was among the first scholars to document these trends. Others, like Gleditsch et al. (2002) and Harbom and Wallensteen (2005) have offered careful descriptions of these trends for more academic audiences. These patterns caught many observers of international politics by surprise. Indeed, the substantial media attention given to *Peace and Conflict 2005* was focused almost exclusively on the findings about the downward trends in conflict (see, for example, the comments by *New York Times* columnist John Tierney (May, 28, 2005) and by Gregg Easterbrook in *The New Republic* in May 2005.)

This volume will continue to assess global trends in armed conflict, but with some changes in approach and emphasis. Our analyses, like that presented in Figure 3.1, will be based on a data set on armed conflict different from those offered in previous volumes. The UCDP/PRIO Armed Conflict Dataset (Gleditsch et al. 2002), a product of the Uppsala Conflict Data Program and the International Peace Research Institute, will now serve as the basis for our analyses. This collection is well-suited for the goals of this publication. Among a variety of advantages, the data collection is updated annually and is publicly available (and widely used) for research in both the academic and policy communities.

Trends

As noted above, Figure 3.1 shows trends in global armed conflict since the end of World War II. The graph combines the four types of conflict tracked by UCDP/PRIO into two categories. We combine extrasystemic armed conflict and interstate armed conflict into one category for interstate conflict. Our second category, internal conflict, comprises internal armed conflict and internationalized internal armed conflict. Since the early 1960s, the vast majority of active conflicts worldwide are internal affairs. Moreover, the steady rise in global conflict from the 1960s through the 1980s is due to a rise in internal conflict. In the same vein, the decline in armed conflict since the late 1980s is due to the decline in civil conflict. Since the end of the Vietnam War, interstate wars have had little impact on overall global conflict trends. After a period of heightened interstate warfare from the mid 1960s through the mid-1970s, there is no distinguishable trend, upward or downward, in the frequency of war between sovereign states.[1]

A substantial increase in the amount of internal warfare in 2005 brought the global total of active conflicts to 25, the highest total since 2001. Even more sobering, the increase from 2004's total of 19 represents the single biggest annual increase in global conflict since 1990. A closer look at what happened in 2005 reveals that much of the "new" conflict in that year came from renewed hostility in longstanding conflicts that had temporarily subsided. For instance, in late 2005 violence broke out in Sri Lanka, rupturing a 2002 cease-fire agreement between the government and the Liberation Tigers of Tamil Eelam (LTTE). In Azerbaijan, sporadic clashes broke out over the disputed region of Nagorno-Karabakh, intensifying hostilities that had been relatively quiet for a number of years. Similar renewals of violence occurred in Myanmar (Burma) and India.[2]

The reversal in 2005 of the downward trend in global conflict points to the importance of recognizing that old adversaries are the most significant source of today's active conflicts. Figure 3.2 is a stacked bar graph showing the total number of active armed conflicts in each year during the period 1980–2005. The brown portion at the bottom of each bar represents the number of new conflict onsets in any given year. The gold segment shows the number of conflicts that began in a previous calendar

---

1 The noticeable decline in the number of active interstate wars starting in the mid-1970s is the result of the termination of the remaining colonial wars that emerged with the independence of many states after World War II.

2 The Appendix contains a full listing of all active conflicts.

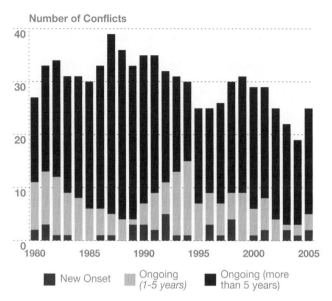

Figure 3.2: Ongoing Conflict, New Onsets (1980–2005)

Number of Conflicts

New Onset   Ongoing (1-5 years)   Ongoing (more than 5 years)

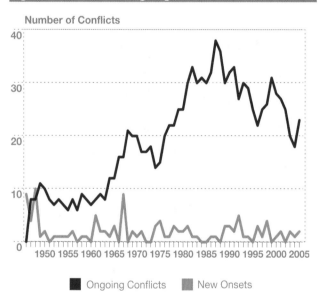

Figure 3.3: Trends In Ongoing and New Conflict

Number of Conflicts

Ongoing Conflicts   New Onsets

year and have been ongoing for up to five years. The red portion shows the number that have been ongoing for more than five years. The graph offers a clear presentation of an important, but often overlooked, feature of global conflict. Most of today's active armed conflicts began several years ago. For any given year, the majority of active conflicts were initiated more than five years previous. Only a small fraction began in that year.

The patterns evident in Figure 3.2 raise an important question. Is the downward overall trend in active conflict due to a reduction in the outbreak of new conflicts or to greater effectiveness at resolving old ones? To see this more easily, Figure 3.3 separates the annual trends in new conflict onsets from ongoing conflicts. It can be seen that the top red line depicting the number of active, ongoing conflicts declines noticeably during the post-Cold War period. The line depicting the number of new conflict onsets shows no trend. Accordingly, we conclude that the downward trend in active conflicts is attributable to the resolution of longstanding conflicts that have burned for several years. The downward trend is not due to a reduction in the outbreak of new conflicts. New conflicts have been erupting at roughly the same pace for the past 60 years. In that regard, the post-Cold War era has been no different than any other period since the end of World War II. Beginning in the 1960s the world witnessed a gradual buildup of stubborn conflicts that defied resolution. While new conflicts erupted at a fairly consistent pace, the pace of resolution dragged behind. The result was an accumulation of enduring conflicts that did not begin to diminish until the late 1980s. The evidence suggests that efforts at conflict resolution have become more effective, while nothing in the analyses presented so far shows any improvement in the prevention of new conflicts.

We turn our attention to another data source for insights about the origins of new conflict onsets, although with a scope limited to only interstate interactions. An examination of the circumstances that breed interstate wars reveals an interesting finding. Figure 3.4 depicts trends in international

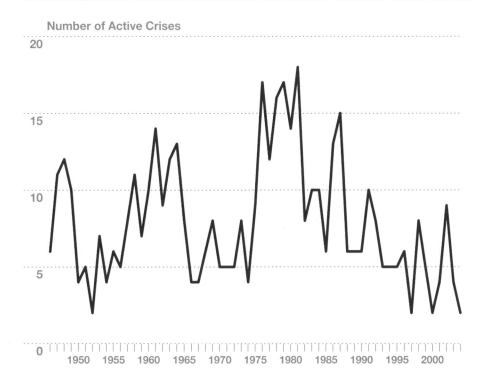

Figure 3.4: Global Trends in Active International Crises (1946–2004)

Number of Active Crises

crises, situations characterized by heightened interstate threats, significant time pressure, and a greater likelihood of military hostilities. The data come from the International Crisis Behavior (ICB) Project (Brecher and Wilkenfeld 2000), which tracks interstate involvement and behavior in international crises since the end of World War I. International crises can be the precursors to full-scale wars, but not all crises escalate to wars. According to the ICB data, for the entire 1918–2004 period, approximately one out of every five crises escalates to full-scale war.

Figure 3.4 depicts a downward trend in the number of crises beginning in the late 1980s, although with notable volatility. While the onset of interstate wars has remained roughly unchanged over the same period (referring back to the trend line for interstate war in Figure 3.1), the number of precipitating events has declined. Without more detailed research, it is difficult to interpret these trends conclusively because they offer mixed messages about overall risks of serious interstate warfare. The situations that give rise to war were more prevalent in the ten-year period spanning 1975–1985. Since 1985, international crises declined significantly and this would certainly appear to be good news. The downward trend in international crises does point to a significant decline in the number of lower-intensity armed confrontations worldwide. While the drop in crises does not seem to affect the number of full-scale interstate wars, the reduction in armed contests that fall short of war is still a notable positive development.

Conclusion

This short overview reports on a number of positive developments regarding trends in global conflict. Despite a substantial increase in the number of active conflicts in the last year of complete data (2005), the overall picture since the end of the Cold War continues to suggest a decline. Whether developments in 2005 represent a momentary blip before a return to the downward trend or the beginning of a complete reversal cannot be known. However, the decline in the number of international crises, another positive finding reported here, is a potential source of encouragement regarding the future.

A key finding of this brief presentation is that the downward trend in active global conflict is largely the result of the resolution of ongoing societal warfare that had simmered and burned for a number of years. Given the specifics of what we have presented here, it is not obvious what causal factors contributed to this trend. Certainly, the end of the Cold War is one potential contributing factor, as argued in the 2005 issue of the *Human Security Report* (Human Security Centre 2005). That argument asserts that the demise of superpower rivalry enabled a surge in activity by international organizations that facilitated the end of many societal conflicts that had once been fueled by Cold War politics and willing proxies. As Wallensteen and Heldt document in chapter 10, both global and regional institutions have been particularly active in helping to manage and resolve conflicts throughout the world.

Aspects of the evidence highlighted in this overview raise questions for this line of argument, though. Many terminated conflicts had endured for several years, proving resistant to ongoing and extensive involvement by international organizations, before finally settling. Accordingly, to be more confident about claims crediting the community of international institutions for the decline in conflict, future research should carefully assess the connections between terminated conflicts and the specific efforts that were thought to be critical for bringing about lasting settlements. This is especially true for conflicts that defied intermediaries for several years before finally settling. In the meantime, we close by reminding the reader that many dormant societal conflicts came back to life in the most recent year of available data (2005), producing the largest annual increase in the amount of active global conflict since 1990. Whatever the cause of the post–Cold War decline in conflict, its effect appears to be intermittent or waning.

A key finding…is that the downward trend in active global conflict is largely the result of the resolution of ongoing societal warfare that had simmered and burned for a number of years.

4. TRENDS IN DEMOCRATIZATION:
A FOCUS ON INSTABILITY IN ANOCRACIES

Amy Pate

In 1950, the world was almost equally divided among autocracies, anocracies (or hybrid regimes), and democracies. In the following two decades, the departure of colonial powers from Africa and Asia resulted in an explosion in the number of independent countries. While newly independent colonies were almost as likely to adopt democratic constitutions as authoritarian structures, the institutional vacuums left by rapidly departing colonial powers most often resulted in a reversion to autocratic, frequently one-party, rule. By 1977, the year in which the number of autocratic regimes peaked, there were 89 autocracies, 16 anocracies and 35 democracies. Then, beginning in the late 1970s and accelerating through the 1980s, a wave of democratization took place. In 1991, shortly after the Cold War ended, there were more democracies (66) than either anocracies (47) or autocracies (44). The spread of democracy continued throughout the 1990s, and by 2006, there were 77 democratic countries, 49 anocracies, and only 34 autocracies in the

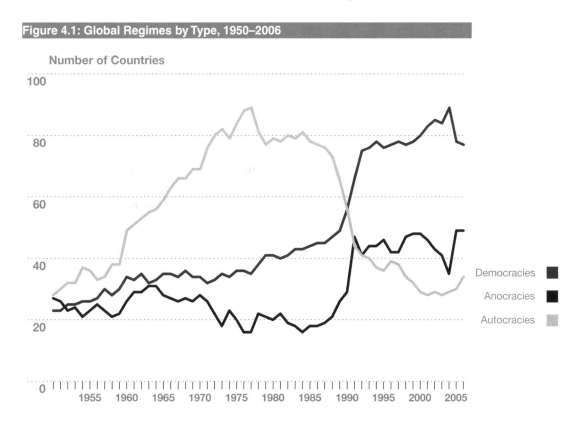

Figure 4.1: Global Regimes by Type, 1950–2006

Number of Countries

Democracies
Anocracies
Autocracies

world. Figure 4.1 summarizes these trends.[1] Box 4.1 presents definitions for the three regime types.

Democracy is clearly the norm in the twenty-first century. However, the majority of democracies today are relatively young, having had democratic institutions for less than a generation. Reflecting, perhaps, a lack of democratic consolidation in these younger democracies, the average Polity score for democracies in the post-Cold War era is significantly lower than the average during the Cold War era. So, while the continued spread of democracy is good news for the international community, the slow pace of democratic consolidation in younger democracies could be a concern. However, the larger proportion of young regimes in the democratic category does not seem to have increased their relative risk of falling into serious state instability, as will be shown below.

The larger proportion of young regimes in the democratic category does not seem to have increased their relative risk of falling into serious state instability.

Also a matter of concern is the relatively large number of anocracies in the international system. It is anocracies—a middling category of regimes having a mix of authoritarian and democratic institutional feature—that will be the focus of the remainder of this chapter. First, a large-N analysis comparing the occurrence of political instability in anocracies to that in democracies and autocracies is reported. Then, two countries in Francophone West Africa are examined in closer detail to illustrate some mechanisms that lead to regime instability in anocracies.

Regime Type and Political Instability

Multiple studies find a relationship between political instability and regime type, with instability operationalized in a variety of forms. In one of the earliest studies of regime type and stability (or the lack thereof), Gurr (1974) operationalizes stability as comprising both durability and flexibility. Muller and Weede (1990) explore the occurrence of political violence as a form of instability. A more recent treatment by Gates et al. (2006) also uses regime durability but with a different operationalization of regime change. The following analysis explores extreme political instability in the context of regime type.

---

1 Polity scores are publicly available only through 2004 (see the Polity Project Web site at *http://www.cidcm.umd.edu/polity/*). Estimated scores for 2005 and 2006 were generated using a conversion factor based on the Freedom House political liberties indicator. (Freedom House data are available through 2006 online at *http://www.freedomhouse.org/*). The Polity score from 2004 was carried through 2005–2006 for those countries that did not show a change in the Freedom House score. If a country's Freedom House rating changed for either year, the conversion factor was applied. For more information on the development of the conversion factor and how it was applied, please refer to the *Peace and Conflict* companion Web site (*http://www.cidcm.umd.edu/pc*).

Box 4.1: Defining Regime Type

The Polity Project scores all independent countries of the world with a population of at least 500,000 on autocratic and democratic features, resulting in a 21-point scale from -10 to 10 to measure regime type. Polity categorizes all regimes as autocracies, anocracies, or democracies, based on Polity scores.

Autocracies	Autocracies are those regimes scored between -10 and -6 on the Polity scale. Autocracies are characterized by closed political recruitment, lack of restraints on executive political power, and limitations on political competition. Autocracies in 2006 include hereditary monarchies, such as Saudi Arabia; one-party states, such as Zimbabwe; and countries ruled by military juntas, such as Myanmar (Burma).
Anocracies	Anocracies are hybrid regimes, with both authoritarian and democratic institutional features. Countries with Polity scores ranging from -5 to 5 are classified as anocracies. Some anocracies are competitive authoritarian regimes, in which elections are contested but not freely nor fairly, such as Chad and Kyrgyzstan. Other anocracies are weakly institutionalized electoral democracies, such as Niger and Cambodia.
Democracies	Democracies are characterized by open political recruitment, restraints on executive power, and political competition. Countries with Polity scores ranging from 6 to 10 are classified as democracies. Democracies include both parliamentary regimes, such as the United Kingdom and India; and presidential systems, such as the United States, South Africa, and Argentina.

Gates et al. (2006) postulate that autocracies and democracies are more stable because institutions in these regimes are self-reinforcing. In authoritarian regimes, institutions work together to concentrate power into the hands of the executive. In democratic regimes, institutions work together to diffuse power across political actors. Anocracies, on the other hand, are inconsistent polities. In short, they have dual tendencies—with some institutions working to concentrate power while others serve to diffuse it. This institutional tug-of-war is what leads to regime instability. In anocracies, power is neither concentrated enough nor diffuse enough to make challenges to authority too costly.

Data from the Political Instability Task Force (PITF),[2] updated through 2005, are used to explore the occurrence of instability events within different regime types. PITF defines four types of instability events: ethnic wars, revolutionary wars, adverse regime changes, and genocides/politicides.[3] As a category, anocracies are more likely throughout the time period (see Table 4.1, part A) to experience instability.

---

2 More information on the Political Instability Task Force—formerly called the State Failure Task Force—is available on its Web site, *http://globalpolicy.gmu.edu/pitf/index.htm*.

3 PITF defines ethnic wars as "episodes of sustained violent conflict in which national, ethnic, religious or other communal minorities challenge governments to seek major changes in their status"; revolutionary wars are "episodes of sustained, violent conflict between governments and politically organized challengers that seek to overthrow the central government, to replace its leaders, or to seize power in one region"; adverse regime changes include collapses of central state authority, contested dissolution of federated states, and shifts towards authoritarian rule of 6 points or greater on the Polity scale; genocides and politicides are "sustained policies by states or their agents…that result in the deaths of a substantial portion of a communal or political group." Wilkenfeld's chapter in this volume, "Unstable States and International Crises," contains a more detailed summary of the PITF definitions (chapter 8).

Between 1955 and 2005, anocracies experienced 93 instability onsets, almost twice the number as either democracies (52) or autocracies (56). Furthermore, their relative risk[4] of experiencing each type of instability was higher for the entire time period than for either autocracies or democracies. For example, anocracies were more than two times as likely to experience genocide/politicide and nearly two-and-a-half times as likely to experience an adverse regime change.

During the Cold War era, adverse regime changes were the primary source of political instability in anocratic regimes (see Table 4.1, part B). Anocracies were also more likely than either democracies or autocracies to experience other forms of instability.

Anocracies are also more stable in the post–Cold War era.... The improvement in anocratic stability, however, is not as dramatic as the improvement in democratic stability.

The post–Cold War era presents a different picture (see Table 4.1, part C). Anocracies are still more likely to experience political instability (31 onsets) than either autocracies (10) or democracies (14). Ethnic and revolutionary wars become more prominent sources of instability among anocracies in the post–Cold War era, likely owing to the relatively large number of post-Communist anocracies that experienced ethnic conflict during this time period. The break-up of the former Yugoslavia, which was an anocracy at that time, offers a prime example. Genocides and politicides, while more likely than either ethnic war or revolutionary war during the Cold War, are a small fraction of onsets in post–Cold War anocracies. However, the higher relative risk of instability for anocracies continues in the post–Cold War era, not because anocracies themselves are less stable now than they were twenty years ago. Rather, it is because democracies are significantly less likely to experience instability in the post–Cold War era than they did during the Cold War era—an encouraging sign, given the relatively higher number of young and unconsolidated democracies in the post–Cold War era. In a separate calculation based on numbers from these two periods, the relative risk that democracies will experience instability in the post–Cold War era as compared to the Cold War era is .43. Anocracies are also more stable in the post–Cold War era, with a relative risk of experiencing instability of .74. The improvement in anocratic stability, however, is not as dramatic as the improvement in democratic stability. There is no significant overall difference in regime stability for autocracies in the post–Cold War era as compared to the Cold War era. However, the distribution of risk across types of instability shifts toward higher likelihoods of genocide/politicide.

---

4 The risk ratios in Table 4.1 measure how likely each regime type is to experience a particular form of state failure as compared to the average risk of all regime types experiencing that form of state failure. A risk ratio greater than 1 indicates a higher-than-average risk. A relative risk less than 1 indicates a lower-than-average risk.

Table 4.1: Regime Type and Relative Risk of State Failure

	Ethnic War	Revolutionary War	Adverse Regime Change	Genocide or Politicide
(A) Complete Period, 1955–2005				
Autocracy	0.79	1.11	0.16	1.12
Anocracy	1.71	1.90	2.42	2.07
Democracy	0.82	0.33	1.13	0.21
(B) Cold War, 1955–1989				
Autocracy	0.69	1.11	0.18	0.90
Anocracy	1.49	1.37	2.98	2.36
Democracy	1.25	0.58	1.26	0.30
(C) Post-Cold War (1990–2005)				
Autocracy	1.21	0.87	0.00	2.17
Anocracy	2.02	2.91	1.82	1.82
Democracy	0.34	0.00	1.01	0.00

Note, figures are risk ratios. Risk ratios reflect the frequency of the type of state failure in that regime type relative to the frequency in all regime types.

Instability in Two West African Anocracies

Senegal and Côte d'Ivoire are both former French colonies in West Africa. They are highlighted here because they are located in the same region and share colonial backgrounds, thus controlling for important theoretical factors. Their post-colonial leaderships also share similarities, as does the manner in which authoritarianism declined, although that decline was a decade later in the case of Côte d'Ivoire. However, their paths diverge in important ways that are illustrative to an examination of regime instability.

Emerging from colonial rule, both countries were led by charismatic leaders of single parties—in Senegal, Leopold Sedar Senghor of the Union Progressiste Senegalaise (UPS, later renamed Parti Socialiste) and in Côte d'Ivoire, Felix Houphouet-Boigny of the Parti Democratique de la Côte d'Ivoire (PDCI). Though authoritarian, both countries were hailed at various times as African success stories—politically stable states with burgeoning economies. Both Senghor and Houphouet-Boigny began political liberalization shortly before leaving office. In Senegal, Senghor opened politics to two opposition parties in 1976 and ran for president under this managed pluralism in 1978. He resigned two years later, giving way to his hand-picked successor Abdou Diouf (Galvin 2001). In Côte d'Ivoire, the first multiparty elections were held in 1990, three years before Houphouet-Boigny's death. He was succeeded by Henri Konan Bédié, then president of the National Assembly (Toungara 2001). Both Diouf and Bédié—lacking the credentials of their predecessors—faced almost immediate challenges to their rule, with oppositions forcing decreases in executive powers. Furthermore, their accessions to power also coincided with downturns in their countries' economic condition (Galvin 2001, Toungara 2001). At this point, the stories diverge. While Senegal eventually underwent a successful democratic transition, Côte d'Ivoire became a failed state. Both experienced high levels of regime instability, but for only one did that instability lead to an adverse outcome.

Elite choices, perhaps more so than institutional factors, were a driving reason behind the disparate outcomes of Senegal and Côte d'Ivoire. In Senegal, Diouf further opened up the political process after facing challenges to his authority and accepted election results when he lost (Galvin 2001). In Côte d'Ivoire, Bédié attempted through repression and ethnic division to reconsolidate power before being ousted in a coup in December 1999 (Toungara 2001). Furthermore, junta leader General Robert Gueï excluded from elections the most popular opposition figure Alassane Ouattara and then suspended vote counting to announce victory (Toungara 2001). While a popular uprising forced Gueï to flee the country and installed Laurent Gbagdo as president, Gbagdo continued the exclusionary policies of his predecessors. A coup attempt in 2002—led by former associates of Gueï—resulted in the division of the country (International Crisis Group 2003). Owing to the unwillingness of political elites to diffuse power across political actors and their inability to reconcentrate power, political players in Côte d'Ivoire continue to jockey for position.

Conclusion

The outlook for political stability among different regime types is mixed. Democracies have seen radical improvement, in terms of resistance to instability. This is despite the fact that the number of young democracies is relatively high. This is good news. Anocracies—although still more susceptible to instability than either autocracies or democracies—have seen gains in resistance to instability in the post-Cold War era. This is also good news. However, entrenched authoritarian regimes have not seen the same improvement and seem resistant to whatever factors are leading to improvements in democracies and anocracies.

Elite choices help determine whether regime instability trends in more positive directions—such as increased democracy and respect for human rights—or in more negative directions—such as increased exclusion and violence.

It is important to note that not all regime instability has adverse outcomes, and state failure is still relatively rare. Elite choices help determine whether regime instability trends in more positive directions—such as increased democracy and respect for human rights—or in more negative directions—such as increased exclusion and violence. As such, elite decision-making—in addition to institutional structures—also deserves further analysis and theorizing if we are to identify states at greatest risk of failure.

5. SELF-DETERMINATION MOVEMENTS AND THEIR OUTCOMES

David Quinn[1]

The quest of national and indigenous peoples for self-governance has reshaped the political landscape in many countries and the international system as a whole during recent decades. Some states and many autonomous regions within states have been formed as a result of such movements. In addition, some of the worst humanitarian crises of the last 50 years have been associated with the struggles between ethnic groups and states over the legitimate sphere of state sovereignty, always a highly contentious issue. This chapter will highlight recent developments with regard to armed self-determination wars.

Since the 1950s, 79 territorially concentrated ethnic groups have waged armed conflicts for autonomy or independence, not counting the peoples of former European colonies. While no new conflicts have erupted since the 2005 volume, two previously contained self-determination movements experienced renewed hostilities in recent years: the Kurds in Iran and the South Ossetians in Georgia. A violent demonstration staged by Kurds in Iran in July 2005 to protest the death of a Kurdish man at the hands of Iranian police served as the trigger to a low-intensity self-determination conflict waged primarily by Pejak, a new Iran-based radical faction of the Kurdistan Workers' Party (PKK). In addition, a growing crisis between Georgia and its South Ossetian breakaway region—stoked by South Ossetia's push for independence—erupted into a steady stream of low-level violent incidents between the two sides that began in July 2006.

Self-Determination Trends

As of late 2006, 26 armed self-determination conflicts were ongoing, including the Assamese, Kashmiri Muslims, Khasis/Jaintas, Meteis, Tripuras, and Scheduled Tribes in India; the Chin/Zomis Karens, Karenni, and Shan in Myanmar; the Palestinians in Israel; the Oromos and Somalis in Ethiopia; the Corsicans in France, and the Chechens in Russia. Despite instances of continuing warfare, the last two years have witnessed a continuation of a previously documented pattern: beginning in the early 1990s a sustained decline in the total number of armed self-determination conflicts and a countervailing shift toward containment and settlement (see Table 5.1 and Figure 5.1). This decline has occurred despite a spike in the number of new armed conflicts (20) in the five-year period immediately following the end of the Cold War. Six violent self-determination conflicts were settled and 15 were contained from 2001 to 2006. Settlements were reached that ended the fighting of Afars in

---

1 Accompanying this chapter are two detailed appendices containing newly updated information on all armed self-determination conflicts and their outcomes for the period 1955–2006 and all non-violent self-determination movements since World War II. This appendix, along with a more extended version of this chapter, can be found at the *Peace and Conflict* companion Web site (*http://www.cidcm. umd.edu/pc*).

Table 5.1: Armed Conflicts for Self-Determination and Outcomes (1956–2006)				
Period	New Armed Conflicts	Ongoing at End of Period	Conflicts Contained	Conflicts Settled or Won
before 1956		4		
1956–1960	4	8	0	0
1961–1965	5	12	0	1
1966–1970	5	15	2	0
1971–1975	11	23	0	3
1976–1980	10	31	2	0
1981–1985	7	37	0	1
1986–1990	11	43	2	3
1991–1995	20	45	9	9
1996–2000	6	38	7	7
2001–2006*	8	26	15	6

Based on conflicts listed in the web-based appendix. Date used for listing conflicts "contained" or "settled or won" is the date when the period of armed conflict ended. "Settled" conflicts include five that ended with the establishment of a new, internationally recognized state. In cases where a settlement/containment of an earlier conflict lasted for five or more years before the outbreak of new fighting, the new outbreak of fighting is counted as a separate armed conflict and a subsequent settlement/containment may then be counted as a new event.

(*) This period covers six years; the others cover five. This applies in Figure 5.1, as well.

Djibouti; Albanians in Macedonia; and Easterners, Nuba, and non-Muslim Black Africans in southern Sudan.[2] In addition, four conflicts were contained in 2005–2006 alone. Papuans in Indonesia and Basques in Spain announced ceasefires in 2006 but have yet to engage in formal, meaningful peace negotiations. Acehnese in Indonesia and Cabindans in Angola agreed to more extensive peace plans as part of their cessations of hostilities. Ceasefires and interim agreements continue to provide some combination of political recognition, greater rights, and regional autonomy to most populations represented by these movements. For a more detailed discussion of the factors contributing to the decline in self-determination conflicts since the end of the Cold War, interested readers are encouraged to visit the companion Web site (*http://www.cidcm.umd.edu/pc*).

However, not all factions of those fighting for self-determination accept the conditions of peace accords. In fact, sometimes interim agreements with one or more rebel organizations have little to no containment effect on the conflict writ large. In the high-profile case of the Muslim Black Africans of Darfur, the Sudanese government signed a peace pact with the major faction of the Sudanese Liberation Movement/Army (SLM/A) in May 2006. However, Khartoum continued major counterinsurgency campaigns (aided by local Arab "janjaweed" militias) against a minor SLM/A faction and the other main rebel group, the Justice and Equality Movement (JEM), who together comprise a majority of Darfurian militants.

2 An additional group, the Casamancais in Senegal, reached a settlement in 2001, but recent developments have caused us to change the current classification of their conflict to "contained."

Figure 5.1: Trends in Armed Conflicts for Self-Determination (1956–2006)

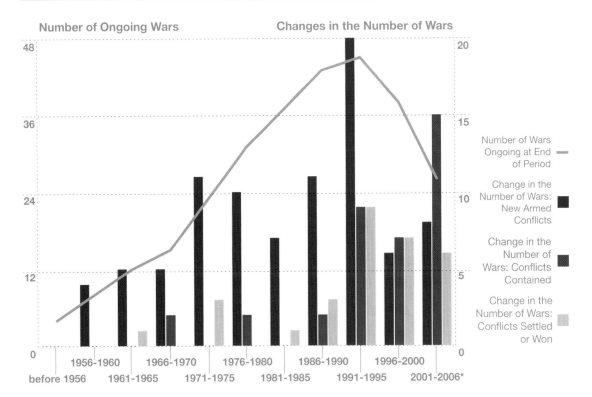

Number of Ongoing Wars

Changes in the Number of Wars

Number of Wars Ongoing at End of Period

Change in the Number of Wars: New Armed Conflicts

Change in the Number of Wars: Conflicts Contained

Change in the Number of Wars: Conflicts Settled or Won

Not all self-determination movements have relied on violent tactics; 55 of these groups currently support significant movements using conventional political means in pursuit of self-determination goals. Forty other groups employ a strategy mixing conventional means with militant tactics that include disruptive acts but fall short of anything but isolated incidents of armed attacks. Leaders of these groups rely mainly on building mass support, publicly representing group interests, and carrying out electoral and/or protest campaigns. Some, such as the Flemish and Walloons in Belgium, the Buryat and Yakut in Russia, and the Jurassians in Switzerland, act through local political institutions that were created to satisfy group demands for autonomy. One group included in the 2005 edition of *Peace and Conflict* has even achieved its own state—Montenegro (formerly part of Serbia-Montenegro, aka Yugoslavia) became the newest member of the international system in July 2006.

Phases of Self-Determination Conflicts

The political dynamics of self-determination movements in conflict with state authorities change over time in response to altered circumstances in the terms and expectations of their relationship. The general character of group tactics and strategies often moves through distinct phases. This movement may be a more or less linear progression from conventional politics to militancy, armed conflict, negotiation, settlement, and sometimes, independent statehood. More often, however, movements are neither linear nor necessarily progressive. Movements may be thwarted by repressive policies, de-radicalized by government concessions, or induced to alter their tactics by new leadership, resource surpluses or deficiencies, or external influences. Armed conflicts that had been contained, or even settled, may resume. The following section describes a diagnostic scheme with ten phases developed to simplify the tracking and comparison of conflicts.

1. Conventional politics (2 groups): Self-determination currently is pursued through conventional political strategies including advocacy, representation of group interests to officials, and electoral politics. Groups with self-administered regions and power-sharing arrangements in existing states are also included here. Protagonists who once fought armed conflicts but now rely on conventional politics include Serbs in Croatia and Gaguaz in Moldova. Another 55 that have not openly rebelled in the past also use these tactics now.

2. Militant politics (3 groups): Self-determination goals are pursued by organizing and inciting group members to use disruptive tactics such as mass protest, boycotts, and resistance to authorities; disruption strategies are often accompanied by, or give rise to, a few symbolic acts of violence. Former rebel groups using these strategies at present include Tibetans and Uighers in China and Ibos in Nigeria. Another 40 groups that have not engaged in large-scale violence in the last half-century currently use militant politics.

3. Low-level hostilities (16 groups): Self-determination is pursued through localized use of violent strategies such as riots, local rebellions, bombings, and armed attacks against authorities. Kurds in Iran began engaging authorities in low-intensity armed conflict in 2005 after primarily pursuing their goals via conventional means for nine years. However, most groups that moved into this phase in the last two years did so after a period of high-level hostile interactions with states, including highly repressed and weakening Russian Chechens, as well as Igorots in Philippines, and Scheduled Tribes and Tripuras in India.

4. High-level hostilities (10 groups): Self-determination is sought by widespread armed violence against authorities. Most groups have engaged in serious fighting for at least a few years, such as Palestinians in Israel; Oromos and Somalis in Ethiopia; and Assamese, Kashmiri Muslims, and Meteis in India (the three Indian groups have been engaged in such high-level hostilities for over 15 years).

5. Talk-fight (2 groups): Group representatives negotiate with authorities about settlement and implementation while substantial armed violence continues. Fighting may be done by the principals or by factions that reject efforts at settlement. Since mid-2001, negotiations between the Moros and the Philippine government have been punctuated by periods of significant violence. Karen rebels and Myanmarese authorities opened talks in 2006, even though high-level violence is ongoing.

6. Cessation of open hostilities (13 groups): Most fighting is over but one or more principals are ready to resume armed violence if efforts at settlement fail. Conflicts in which hostilities were checked by international peacekeeping forces, in the absence of agreements also are classified here. This kind of tenuous peace held at the end of 2006 for Armenians in Azerbaijan; Kurds in Iraq; and Dimasas, Garos, Karbis, and Nagas in India.

7. Contested agreement (20 groups): An interim or final agreement for group autonomy within an existing state has been negotiated between the principals but some parties, within the group or the government or both, reject and attempt to subvert the agreement. This is the current situation of the Serbs and Croats in Bosnia, the Chittagong Hill Tribals in Bangladesh, the Bougainvilleans in Papua New Guinea, and the Malaitans and Guadalcanalese in the Solomon Islands.

8. Uncontested agreement (7 groups): A final agreement for group autonomy is in place, is accepted in principle by all parties, and is being implemented. All seven of the groups currently in this phase are found in Africa. Sustained negotiations since 2002 between the southern Sudanese and the Khartoum government produced a final, comprehensive agreement signed in early 2005. The accord also includes provisions for the settlement of the conflict in the Nuba Mountains region of Sudan, although some Nuba spokespeople have expressed dissatisfaction with the final outcome. With help from Algerian mediators, Tuaregs and the Malian government updated their 1995 agreement in negotiations that followed an incident in which Tuaregs seized and attacked several military camps in May 2006.

9. Implemented agreement (1 group): A final settlement for group autonomy has been largely or fully implemented; the Mizos in India are the sole case.

10. Independence (5 groups): The group has achieved its own internationally recognized state. The former Indonesian province of East Timor is the newest member of this group that includes the Croats and Slovenes in the former Yugoslavia, the Eritreans in Ethiopia, and the Bengalis in Pakistan.

Self-determination conflicts do not move inevitably through all phases, and owing to their complex dynamics, there often is movement back and forth between phases. Former rebels that have used conventional politics for longer periods of time (e.g., Croatian Serbs) are very likely to continue to do so. However, groups that have signaled objectives through militant politics or low-level hostilities increase the risk of further escalation. Even among groups that have heretofore not used violence to pursue self-determination goals, movement from strictly conventional means to more militant tactics may be a prelude to more intense disruptive campaigns (or it may simply be a short-term tactical innovation). Nonviolent groups that incorporated more militant tactics into their repertoire in 2005–2006 include Indigenous Peoples in Canada, Puerto Ricans in the United States, Uzbeks in Kyrgyzstan, Indigenous Peoples in Colombia, Kashmiri Hindus in India, and Sarakis and Sindhis in Pakistan.

Sometimes the movement between phases is sudden rather than gradual. Iranian Kurds had pursued conventional politics for almost nine years before a mid-2005 series of violent demonstrations quickly moved from a set of isolated incidents to more frequent low-level clashes with the Iranian state. In the case of Tamils in Sri Lanka, a ceasefire between the Liberation Tigers of Tamil Eelam (LTTE) and the Sri Lankan government had held for almost four years. Within a few months beginning in late 2005, the conflict had shifted to a full-blown, high-level armed confrontation. The recent upsurge in this conflict is reaching civil-war like proportions accompanied by an increasingly severe humanitarian crisis, with casualty estimates in the several thousands, refugee estimates in the several hundreds of thousands, deteriorating health and living conditions, and reported difficulties created by both sides in allowing international humanitarian aid to get to those that need it the most.

While we are encouraged by the downward trend in the number of…armed self-determination conflicts since the end of the Cold War, we are simultaneously concerned that relatively few…can be confidently considered ended.

Conclusion

While we are encouraged by the downward trend in the number of new and ongoing armed self-determination conflicts since the end of the Cold War, we are simultaneously concerned that relatively few post-World War II self-determination conflicts can be confidently considered ended. The most critical phases in the settlement of self-determination conflicts are "talk-fight" and "cessation of open hostilities." In the absence of final agreements any of the 15 conflicts in these two phases may revert to open warfare. In these situations, preventive actions and efforts at mediation and peacekeeping from international actors should be redoubled to keep the conflicting parties moving toward agreement (or a quick ceasefire) and away from hostilities. Such efforts are especially advisable during the early years of self-determination wars, when they are easiest to settle. Although many observers are concerned that autonomy agreements will set the stage for all-out wars for independence and result in the redrawing of international boundaries, these fears are rarely realized. More commonly, conflicts end with governments and group representatives agreeing on a framework that acknowledges collective rights, provides institutional means for pursuing collective interests within states, and/or devolves some amount of central power to autonomous regional institutions.

It is clear that the greatest risk in autonomy agreements is not the eventual breakup of the state; rather it is that spoilers or the state may employ stall tactics and otherwise block full implementation in an attempt to force greater concessions, thereby dragging out the conflict and wasting resources that might otherwise be used to strengthen autonomous institutions. Only a small number of settlement agreements have been fully implemented, signaling a potential for renewed resistance by former rebels in most formerly violent self-determination conflicts. Contested agreements are particularly problematic because significant elements on one or both sides of a conflict reject them. Nonetheless, however challenging it is to reach an initial agreement, it may be still more difficult, and require greater international engagement, to move from formal agreement to the actual implementation of the terms of that agreement.

6. GLOBAL TERRORISM AND FAILED STATES

Gary LaFree, Laura Dugan, and Susan Fahey[1]

Researchers commonly date the beginning of modern terrorism in the late 1960s (Hoffman 1998). A pivotal event in this regard was the aerial hijacking of an Israeli El Al commercial flight en route from Rome to Tel Aviv in July 1968 by three armed Palestinian men, belonging to the Popular Front for the Liberation of Palestine. Although commercial aircraft had been hijacked many times before, this hijacking was unique in that it had a specific political purpose (trading the passengers held hostage for imprisoned Palestinians). The targeting of the main Israeli airline was symbolic, and perhaps most importantly, because of recent advances in television broadcasting, it instantly attracted worldwide media attention. It is no coincidence that major developments in open-source databases on terrorism—which rely heavily on unclassified media and newspaper accounts—got under way at about the same time.

Compared to most types of criminal violence, terrorism poses special data collection challenges, which have led to growing interest in open-source terrorist event databases (i.e., data collected and refined based on publicly available, nonclassified resources). One of the major problems with these databases in the past is that they have been limited to international events—those involving a national or group of nationals from one country attacking targets physically located in another country, or attacking foreign nationals within their own country. Past research shows that domestic incidents greatly outnumber international incidents (Schmid and Jongman 1988, LaFree and Dugan 2007). During the past few years, researchers at the National Consortium for the Study of Terrorism and Responses to Terrorism (START) have compiled the most comprehensive of these event databases—about seven times larger than any of the other existing open-source terrorism event databases (LaFree and Dugan 2007).

As international interest in terrorism has grown—and especially since the events of 9/11—researchers and policymakers have increasingly sought to understand terrorism by looking at the social, economic, and political characteristics of countries. This chapter will examine connections between a newly available measure of terrorist attacks and one such characteristic: whether a country was undergoing a period of state failure. For this purpose we rely on the most common definition of state failure as a country that is "utterly incapable of sustaining itself as a member of the international community" (Helman and Ratner 1993).

---

1 Support for this work was provided by the Department of Homeland Security (DHS) through the National Center for the Study of Terrorism and Responses to Terrorism (START), grant number N00140510629. The authors wish to thank Ted Gurr, Alex P. Schmid, and the editors for helpful comments on an earlier draft. Any opinions, findings, or recommendations in this document are those of the authors and do not necessarily reflect the views of DHS.

Domestic and International Terrorism Data

We began the Global Terrorism Database (GTD) by computerizing nearly 70,000 domestic and international terrorism events originally collected by the Pinkerton Global Intelligence Service (PGIS). From 1970 to 1997, PGIS trained researchers to identify and record terrorism incidents from wire services (including Reuters and the Foreign Broadcast Information Service), US State Department reports, other US and foreign government reporting, national and international newspapers, and information provided by PGIS offices around the world.

The main reason why the GTD database is so much larger than other secondary databases on terrorism is that it includes information on all terrorist events—both domestic and international. To underscore the importance of this difference, consider that two of the most noteworthy terrorist events of the 1990s—the March 1995 nerve gas attack on the Tokyo subway and the April 1995 bombing of the federal office building in Oklahoma City—both lack any known foreign involvement and hence were pure acts of domestic terrorism.

"Terrorism is as much about the threat of violence as the violent act itself."

A secondary reason for the larger number of cases is that the GTD is based on a broader definition of terrorism than the one used by most of the other major open-source databases: *the threatened or actual use of illegal force and violence to attain a political, economic, religious, or social goal through fear, coercion, or intimidation.* For example, neither the US State Department nor the FBI definition of terrorism includes threats of force. Yet as Hoffman (1998, 38) points out, "Terrorism is as much about the threat of violence as the violent act itself." In fact, many, perhaps most, aerial hijackings involve only the threatened use of force (e.g., "I have a bomb and I will use it unless you follow my demands"). Similarly, kidnappers almost always employ force to seize victims, but then threaten to kill or otherwise harm victims unless demands are satisfied. Also, the State Department definition is limited to "politically motivated violence." By contrast, the GTD also includes economic, religious, and social objectives.

We completed computerizing the original PGIS data in December 2005. Since then we have actively searched open sources to update, correct, and extend the data.[2] We now refer to the resulting database—constructed on the original PGIS platform—as the Global Terrorism Database. In April 2006 a START Center team led by Gary Ackerman began the process of systematically updating the GTD to extend it beyond 1997 (hereafter referred to as the GTD2). The new procedures capture more than 120 variables and, unlike the PGIS data, the new data collection

---

2 During the transfer of the PGIS data to the University of Maryland for computerization, we discovered that one year of the PGIS data—1993—had been lost in an earlier office move. These data were never recovered. We were able to reconstruct marginal totals for events and fatalities in 1993 by country from annual reports prepared by PGIS. However, the research in this chapter omits any data from 1993. We are currently in the process of collecting data to replace the missing 1993 cases (see LaFree and Dugan 2007 for more details).

also records the original open-source texts upon which each event is based. GTD2 data collection includes from 25 to 35 data collectors, fluent in six language groups (English, French, Spanish, Russian, Arabic, and Mandarin). Based on current procedures, we expect to complete the GTD2 data collection through 2005 by June 2007. Eventually, we plan to release new additions to the data on an annual basis. However, at the time this chapter was being prepared, the post-1997 data were not yet available.

Given that the GTD data have not been previously available to the research community and that they are considerably more inclusive than earlier open-source terrorism databases, we believe that it is important to introduce them to researchers and policy makers as quickly as possible. However, we also want to make it clear that the trends reported in this chapter are preliminary and may well change substantially when the data are extended to more recent years. To state the obvious, it is reasonable to expect that terrorism has evolved considerably since 1997.

State Failure Data

The data used to identify failed states in this analysis come from the Political Instability Task Force (PITF), a multidisciplinary group assembled in 1994 (Bates et al. 2006). The PITF has done substantial research on the occurrence and predictors of state failure.[3] For example, using these data, the PITF group found that the level of democracy is an important predictor of state failure. More specifically, governments that are either full democracies or full autocracies are less likely to fail when compared to partial democracies. The scope of the data collected by the PITF includes all countries with a population over 500,000 (162 countries) for the years between 1955 and 2005 (see Esty et al. 1995, 1999; and Goldstone et al. 2005 for full details).

The PITF defines state failure broadly as including "civil conflicts, political crises, and massive human rights violations that are typically associated with state breakdown" (Esty et al. 1995, 1). We refer readers to Box 8.1 in chapter 8 for an extensive summary of the PITF definition and, of course, to the PITF's own project reports.

Because the coverage of the GTD is from 1970 to 1997, only failures between these years were included in this analysis. Further, because one of the criteria for state failure is protracted episodes of terrorism, we were concerned that considering a country as failed because it experiences extensive terrorist attacks would confound our main predictor variable, state failure, with our main outcome variable, terrorist attacks. Accordingly, we excluded as indicators of state failure analysis of protracted terrorism campaigns that took place in Algeria, China, Egypt, Iran, Israel, Northern

---

3 We recognize that the PITF has recently discarded the terminology of "state failure" in favor of "political instability" because the events tracked by the task force often fell short of complete collapse of governmental institutions. Nonetheless, we retain the former term to draw attention to the fact that these states are certainly at heightened risk for such a collapse. It is the fact of state failure (or the heightened risk of it) that we believe provides an important connection to patterns of global terrorism.

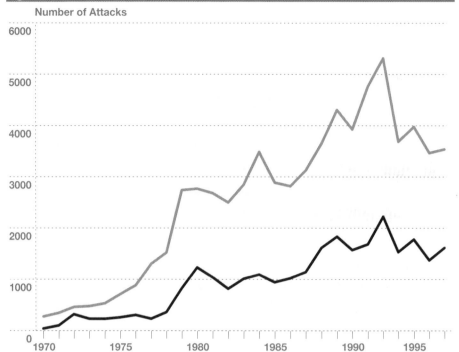

Number of Attacks

Lethal Attacks

Total Attacks

Ireland/UK, Peru, and the Philippines. In addition, we also excluded as indicators of state failure any direct governmental responses to such campaigns of terrorism.[4]

Because both the GTD and the PITF include attacks against the military (although by different types of perpetrators), some attacks reported in the GTD could have been used by the PITF to indicate state failure.[5] To reduce possible bias owing to this definitional overlap, we also excluded from all of our terrorism-state failure analyses any GTD attacks where the target was identified as military. By omitting these cases, we feel that we provide a conservative estimate of any resulting association found between state failure and terrorism.[6]

Global Terrorism Trends

In this section we consider global trends in terrorism since 1970 based on the GTD. In Figure 6.1 we present total incidents and fatalities over time. Figure 6.1 shows that terrorism events increased steadily from 1970 to a peak in 1992 with

---

4 It is also important to note that many of these countries had other failure problems co-occurring or occurring very closely in time to terrorism campaigns. If we determined that these other failures would have occurred independent of the terrorism episodes, we classified the country as having failed.

5 While the GTD excludes attacks on the military by uniformed military or by guerrilla organizations, it includes military targets that are attacked by sub-state groups where there is a political, economic or social motive.

6 We recognize that this is one of many decisions that could be made to try to guard against confounding the predictor, state failure, with the outcome, terrorism. A strength of the GTD is that it allows researchers to filter the data based on different definitions of terrorism.

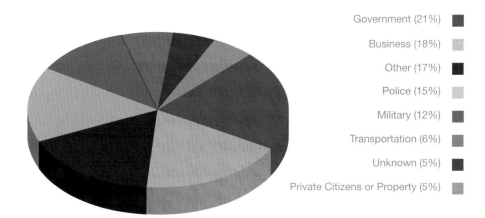

Government (21%) ■
Business (18%) ▨
Other (17%) ■
Police (15%) ▨
Military (12%) ■
Transportation (6%) ■
Unknown (5%) ■
Private Citizens or Property (5%) ■

5,318 events worldwide. Through 1976, terrorist attacks were relatively infrequent, with fewer than 1,000 incidents each year. But from 1978 to 1979 the frequency of events nearly doubled. The number of terrorist events continues to increase until 1992, with smaller peaks in 1984, at almost 3,500 incidents, and 1989, with more than 4,300 events. After the global peak in 1992, the number of terrorist incidents declined to just over 3,500 incidents at the end of the original data collection in 1997.

The number of lethal attacks clearly follows the pattern of total attacks (r = 0.97), but at a substantially lower magnitude (averaging 986 lethal attacks per year compared to 2,558 total attacks per year worldwide). Lethal attacks rise above 1,000 per year for the first time in 1980. After hovering close to 1,000 attacks annually for most of the 1980s, they more than double between 1985 and 1992. As with total incidents, fatal incidents declined somewhat from 1992 to the end of the series in 1997. We should point out that media-related information sources have also increased dramatically since the beginning of the GTD data collection, especially media penetration of the industrializing world, which might account for at least part of the rapid increase in attacks and fatalities since 1970.

In Figure 6.2 we examine the targets of global terrorist strikes for all attacks in the GTD. We can see that there is considerable variation in target types. The top three targets are government agents or facilities, businesses, and police (disregarding, for the moment, the 'Other' category). Together, these three targets account for just under 60 percent of the total. Following the top three in order are military, transportation, an 'Unknown' category, and private citizens and property. The 'Other' category here encompasses a diverse range of targets, including airports and airlines, diplomatic targets, utilities, journalists and media outlets, religious figures and institutions, nongovernmental organizations, educational institutions, and tourists. As noted above, for the remainder of this chapter we omit the 12 percent of the GTD attacks where the military is targeted. After omitting military targets, total attacks drop from 69,071 to 60,847.

Box 6.1: Incident Type Definitions	
Assassination	The objective of the act is to kill a specific person or persons. Normally the victim is a personage of note, a policeman, government official, etc. The key is—what was the objective of the act? For example, an attack on a police jeep usually is a facility attack, but an attack against a single police officer on a post is an assassination, i.e., the aim was to kill that specific man. Some incidents of this nature will be judgment calls and may be categorized either as assassinations or facility attacks. Generally, when the attack is against a jeep full of police, a police post, a military outpost, military vehicles, etc., it is coded as a facility attack. In an assassination, the thrust is concerning an identified person or persons rather than several unknowns, as would be the case in an attack on a police vehicle occupied by several persons or against a police/military post.
Bombing	The object of the act normally is destruction/or damage of a facility through the covert placement of bombs. The action is clandestine in contrast to a facility attack. Normally, the identity of the perpetrator(s) is not known at the time, although claims of responsibility often follow. The devices are usually placed at night or at least covertly and detonate after the bombers have departed. Bombings do not involve taking a facility or installation by attack and then placing bombs. In contrast to a facility attack, which often is aimed at physically taking over the installation, a bombing is designed simply to destroy or damage it. The clandestine nature of bombing separates it from facility attacks, as does the fact that there is no intention to take the installation or occupy it, or to take hostages. The target of a bombing often is unoccupied or its occupants asleep.
Facility Attack	The objective of the act is to rob, damage, or occupy a specific installation. The term installation includes towns, buildings, and in some cases, as mentioned previously, vehicles. Thus a bank robbery is a facility attack although all its guards may have been killed. The objective in such an action was robbery of a facility, not killing the guards. The occupation of a town, wherein persons may be killed or wounded, also is a facility attack since the objective was to take the town (installation), not to kill or wound persons. Again, it is the objective of the operation that is the determining factor. The idea or objective of the operation is important if, for example, bombs are left behind by the attackers. In such a case, the bombing of the building was not the aim—the aim was to take it over by assault. Bombs were left to do additional damage and/or cause disruption to facilitate the escape of the attackers. Facility attacks may be carried out using automatic weapons, explosives, incendiaries, etc. Normally, a multimember team is involved. The operation is carried out openly—in contrast to the covert placement of bombs at night. Hostages may be taken, but this is not the primary objective of the act.
Hijacking	The objective of the act is to assume control by force or threat of force of a conveyance such as an aircraft, boat, ship, bus, automobile, or other vehicle for the purpose of diverting it to an unprogrammed destination, obtain payment of a ransom, force the release of prisoners, or some other political objective.
Kidnapping	The objective of the act is to obtain payment of a ransom, force the release of political prisoner(s), or achieve some other political objective. If the person is killed in the course of the kidnapping process, this does not make it an assassination. It still remains a kidnapping. Kidnapping is aimed at a specific person(s). A facility attack against a bank, wherein hostages may be taken, is not a kidnapping because the hostage-taking is incidental to the primary objective.

The incidents in the GTD are divided into five main types: bombings, facility attacks, assassinations, kidnappings and aerial hijackings (LaFree and Dugan 2007). Box 6.1 presents detailed definitions for each of these types. Bombings are considered to be clandestine attacks, while facility attacks (which might include bombs) are carried out openly. The upper pie chart in Figure 6.3 shows the proportion of total attacks for four of the five main types. In terms of total attacks, bombings

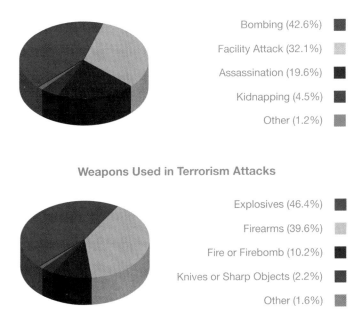

Type of Terrorist Attack

Bombing (42.6%)

Facility Attack (32.1%)

Assassination (19.6%)

Kidnapping (4.5%)

Other (1.2%)

Weapons Used in Terrorism Attacks

Explosives (46.4%)

Firearms (39.6%)

Fire or Firebomb (10.2%)

Knives or Sharp Objects (2.2%)

Other (1.6%)

are the largest single type in the GTD, accounting for over 40 percent of the total incidents. Facility attacks are next most common, accounting for over 30 percent of the incidents. Assassinations account for nearly one-fifth of the total incidents. Kidnappings account for more than four percent of the total. Aerial hijackings, the fifth of the five main types, account for less than one half of one percent and have been included in the "Other" category.

The lower pie chart in Figure 6.3 shows the primary weapons used in the commission of the terrorist incidents included in the database. Explosives and firearms are by far the most common, accounting for 86 percent of the total. Explosives include weapons such as dynamite, car bombs, grenades, and mortars. Some of the most common firearms used include automatic weapons, shot guns, and pistols. Fire or firebombs account for about ten percent of the incidents, knives and sharp objects for just over two percent. Chemical agents account for less than one-fifth of one percent of all incidents and have been included in the "Other" category.

To develop geographic comparisons for terrorist attacks and failed states, we next divided the countries of the world into six major regions.[7] The upper pie chart in Figure 6.4 shows that terrorism and terrorism-related fatalities occur in Latin

---

7 The composition of countries within each region was determined by PGIS. Note that for purposes of this analysis, we treat the country as the target. Thus, an attack on the US embassy in Nigeria would be treated here as a Nigerian attack. Similarly, an attack on a Nigerian ambassador living in the US would be counted as a US attack. Although it is the case that the vast majority of cases in the database involve attacks on a specific country's national interests, targeting nationals from that country within that country, the country attacked, the nationality of the target attacked, and whether the national target is outside the country being attacked are all important variables in their own right. We are

Attacks By Region

Asia (18.7%)
Europe (21.1%)
Latin America (39.1%)
Middle East/North Africa (13.2%)
North America (1.8%)
Sub-Saharan Africa (6.1%)

Fatalities By Region

Asia (28.4%)
Europe (5.8%)
Latin America (31.6%)
Middle East/North Africa (16.1%)
North America (0.6%)
Sub-Saharan Africa (17.4%)

America nearly twice as often as in any other region of the world; more than six times as often as Sub-Saharan Africa; and more than 20 times more often than North America.[8] Europe rates second in terms of total incidents with more than 21 percent of all global terrorism, followed closely by Asia at nearly 19 percent. The Middle East/North Africa region follows with just over 13 percent of the incidents, and Sub-Saharan Africa and North America account for the smallest proportion of terrorism events (6.10 and 1.79 percent, respectively).

The lower pie chart in Figure 6.4 shows that by percentage, the distribution of fatalities by region differs greatly from that of total incidents. While Latin America remains the leader in fatalities (31.6 percent), as well as in the proportion of total attacks, Asia has the second highest percentage of fatalities by region, accounting for more than 28 percent of all terrorism-related fatalities (28.4 percent). The chart also shows that while Europe is second in the proportion of attacks, it suffers relatively few fatalities as a result of these incidents, averaging 0.48 deaths per incident. This rate is especially low compared to that for Sub-Saharan Africa, which averages 4.9 deaths for every terrorism attack. Thus, while the Sub-Saharan African region accounts for a relatively small proportion of total terrorist attacks during this period, when there were attacks in this region, they were on average deadlier. The reasons for these differences remain to be explained, although part of

exploring these issues in much greater detail in other research. The full listing of states in this analysis is available at the *Peace and Conflict* companion Web site (*http://www.cidcm.umd.edu/pc*).

8 Mexico is counted here as part of Latin America instead of North America.

the explanation may simply be media differences in reporting and proximate access to medical care across regions.

We also classified the 162 countries with populations over 500,000 by whether they experienced at least one year of state failure at any point from 1970 to 1997, regardless of the specific year of failure or how long the failed status lasted.[9] Based on this coding criterion, there were a total of 81 failed states (termed "ever-failed" states here) and 81 nonfailed states.[10] The three regions with the most countries experiencing at least one year of state failure are Sub-Saharan Africa, Asia, and the Middle East/North Africa region, with 70, 60, and 57 percent failure rates, respectively. Latin American and European countries have far fewer failed states, with about 32 and 27 percent ever failing, respectively. Of course, neither North American country (i.e., the US and Canada) faced a state failure during the years spanned by the data.

Given these regional patterns for state failure, an examination of Figure 6.4 suggests that there may be a connection between whether a country experienced state failure and the number of terrorist attacks and fatalities it experienced—a relationship that seems to be stronger for fatalities than attacks. Thus, three of the four regions with the highest terrorism-related fatalities (Asia, Sub-Saharan Africa, and the Middle East) are also the most likely to include ever-failed states. By contrast, the two regions with the lowest fatalities (Europe, North America) also contain the smallest proportion of ever-failed states. However, the Latin American region fits this pattern less well. This region accounted for the highest proportion of terrorism-related fatalities but finished fourth among the six regions in terms of the proportion of its countries that were in the ever-failed category. And the connections between the number of terrorist attacks and state failure by region seem weaker. While Europe and Latin America top the list for terrorist attacks, both regions are in the lower half of the distribution of six regions in terms of failed states. Of course these comparisons are not very systematic and are based on a highly aggregated geographic measure.

We turn now to the distribution of terrorism activity for each region over time. Figure 6.5 shows the geographical dispersion of attacks by region from 1970 through 1997. If we examine this figure only from 1970 until 1978, it appears that terrorism is primarily a European problem. But after 1978, European attacks peak at just over 1,000 incidents in 1979 and then drop to an average of 515 incidents a year. By contrast, Latin American attacks continue to increase after 1978, peaking in 1984 with 1,758 incidents. After 1984, Latin America continues to average about 1,200 incidents a year with large fluctuations. Especially interesting for the Latin American series is the steep drop to a low point of 466 attacks in 1995. Figure 6.5 also suggests that the increases in global terrorism rates in the 1980s and

---

9 Though the loss of the 1993 GTD data is regrettable, its impact on the current analysis is negligible. No state failed exclusively in 1993. The full country listing on the *Peace and Conflict* companion Web site indicates whether any state experienced state failure at any point in the 1970–1997 period.

10 These numbers are based on the PITF country definitions, which do not correspond exactly to the GTD country definitions. Most importantly, following the original PGIS designations, GTD counts separately several territories, such as Puerto Rico and Guadeloupe, which are treated as part of other sovereign states by the state failure data.

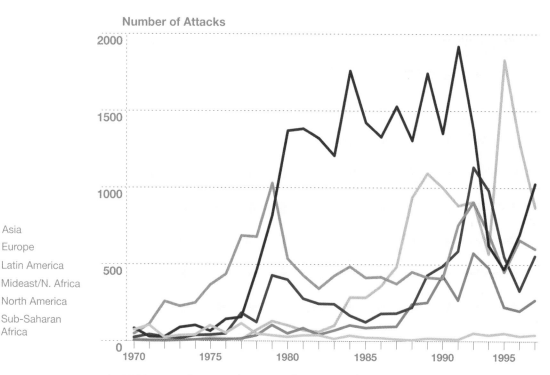

Figure 6.5: Total Regional Terrorist Activity, 1970–1997

Number of Attacks

Asia
Europe
Latin America
Mideast/N. Africa
North America
Sub-Saharan Africa

early 1990s were driven in large part by increased activity in Asia and Sub-Saharan Africa. Figure 6.5 also shows that compared to other regions, North America has experienced a relatively small proportion of terrorist attacks during this period.

Based on the substantial differences in total events by region, it is not surprising that countries vary greatly in terms of total incidents included in the GTD. In Table 6.1 we list the 25 countries that were most commonly targeted by terrorists from 1970 to 1997, along with the total number of years that each of these countries was classified as a failed state. The importance of Latin America as a regional source for terrorist incidents noted above is reinforced here: the three countries with the highest number of attacks are all Latin American—Colombia, Peru, and El Salvador. In addition, several other Latin American countries make the top 25: Chile, Guatemala, Nicaragua, and Argentina. Following Latin America, Europe contains several countries that are in the top 25 in terms of total incidents: Spain, Northern Ireland, France, Italy, Germany (East and West), Greece, and the United Kingdom (excluding Northern Ireland). Five Asian countries are in the top 25 in terms of incidents: India, Pakistan, Sri Lanka, the Philippines, and Bangaladesh. Only three Middle Eastern/North African countries are in the top 25 in terms of incidents: Turkey, Israel, and Lebanon. South Africa and Algeria are the sole countries from Sub-Saharan Africa in the top 25 most frequently targeted countries. The US finishes as 21st in terms of total attacks.

If we examine the years of state failure for the top 25 countries in terms of attacks, we see some association—although an association that is far from perfect. Only two of the top 25 terrorist attack countries (the Philippines and Guatemala) were classified as failed states for all 27 years in the series. However, 12 of the countries in the top 25 experienced at least ten years as failed states during the series and all but 8 of the top 25 countries experienced at least one year of failure during the series.

Of course the attention of policymakers and the public is drawn especially to groups that have been most active in using terrorism. Accordingly, we next examined the 25 groups with the largest number of strikes from 1970 through 1997 (Table 6.2). For each of these groups, we also classified their chief country of operation, their total number of attacks, and the number of years that the country in which each group was based was classified as a failed state. Sendero Luminoso leads the list with over 4,100 attacks from 1970 through 1997. The next highest group in terms of attacks is the Farabundo Marti National Liberation Front (FMLN). Three additional groups in the database claimed responsibility for more than 1,000 events: the IRA, ETA, and the ELN.

As with the country-level comparisons, there is clearly an imperfect relationship between whether a country is classified as a failed state and whether it has one of these top 25 terrorist groups operating within its borders. Nevertheless, there is clearly an association. Thus, three of the top 25 groups are operating in states that were classified as failed for 20 or more of the years included in the analysis; 15 of the groups were in countries classified as failed for 10 or more years; and only 8 groups were operating in countries that were never classified as failed states. We turn now to a more direct comparison between terrorist attacks and fatalities and measures of failed states over time.

Table 6.1: Top 25 Most Attacked Countries, 1970–1997

Country[1]	% of All Attacks	Num. of Years in Failure[2]
Peru*	9.15	0
Colombia	9.02	14
El Salvador	7.25	16
India†	4.57	16
Spain	4.33	0
Northern Ireland	4.32	0
Chile	3.63	4
Turkey†	3.62	18
France	3.45	0
Pakistan†	3.29	20
Sri Lanka†	3.26	14
Philippines*†	2.86	27
Guatemala†	2.76	26
Israel*	2.59	0
Italy	2.33	0
South Africa†	2.33	12
Lebanon	2.29	17
Nicaragua	1.95	11
Bangladesh	1.87	18
Algeria*	1.86	1
United States	1.73	0
Germany[3]	1.72	0
Argentina	1.21	5
Greece	1.06	0
United Kingdom*	0.81	0

[1] Countries marked with an asterisk (*) experienced protracted terrorism campaigns that were excluded from our designation of these countries as failed states, unless they also experienced other types of state failure unrelated to the terrorism campaigns.

[2] Countries marked with a dagger (†) experienced failure during 1993, a year that we excluded from the analysis because of missing GTD data. For these countries, one year of failure has been subtracted from the total number of years in failure.

[3] Prior to 1991, this figure combines attacks in both East and West Germany.

Terrorism and State Failure

In this section we examine the connections between failed states and terrorism activity by comparing the rate of terrorism, calculated from the GTD, for states that have failed to those that have not.[11] Thus, for each of the 27 years, we examine whether the state failed and the total number of terrorist attacks and fatalities during that year. In order to compare terrorism activity in failed states with that in non-

---

11 As noted above, the major exception to this strategy is that we are missing data for 1993 (see LaFree and Dugan 2007).

Table 6.2: Top 25 Terrorist Groups by Total Activity, 1970–1997			
Group	Chief Country of Operations	Total Attacks	Years as Failed State
Sendero Luminoso	Peru	4107	0
Farabundo Marti National Liberation Front (FMLN)	El Salvador	2464	16
Irish Republican Army (IRA)	Northern Ireland	2014	0
Basque Fatherland and Freedom (ETA)	Spain	1680	0
National Liberation Army of Colombia (ELN)	Colombia	1010	14
Kurdish Workers Party (PKK)	Turkey	963	18
Revolutionary Armed Forces of Colombia (FARC)	Colombia	942	14
New People's Army (NPA)	Phillipines	821	27
Manuel Rodriguez Patriotic Front (FPMR)	Chile	792	4
Liberation Tigers of Tamil Eelam (LTTE)	Sri Lanka	767	14
Tupac Amaru Revolutionary Movement	Peru	537	0
Corsican National Liberation Front (FLNC)	France	469	0
M-19 (Movement of April 19)	Colombia	457	14
People's Liberation Front (JVP)	Sri Lanka	412	14
Movement of the Revolutionary Left (MIR)	Chile	307	4
National Union for the Total Independence of Angola	Angola	284	22
Dev Sol	Turkey	246	18
Sandinista National Liberation Front (FSLN)	Nicaragua	232	11
People's Liberation Army (Colombia)	Colombia	219	14
Red Brigades	Italy	215	0
United National Party	Sri Lanka	202	14
African National Congress (ANC)	South Africa	199	12
Ulster Freedom Fighters (UFF)	Northern Ireland	189	0
Mohajir Qaumi Movement	Pakistan	185	20
Ulster Volunteer Force (UVF)	Northern Ireland	184	0

failed states, we measure failed states in two different ways.[12] First, as before, we coded any country that experienced at least one year of state failure as an "ever-failed state," regardless of when that state failed. Second, we also developed a measure that designates each country as "in failure" or "out of failure" depending on their failed-state status for each year in the analysis. Thus, using this second coding strategy, countries can move in and out of failed-state status over time, depending on how they were coded each year by the PITF. Among the 81 ever-failed states, the mean number of years that a country was in failure was 9.3.

---

12 Because of space limitations we focus here on only two variations on the state failure measure. We picked these two as illustrative because they represent strongly contrasting theoretical alternatives. The ever-failed distinction is the broadest, while the years of failure is the most specific. In ongoing research we are also exploring other coding options; notably allowing some lag period after a country moves out of the failed-state status.

In the upper graph in Figure 6.6, we compare the average number of terrorist attacks over time for ever-failed and never-failed states. As with the overall trends shown in Figure 6.1, the average number of terrorist attacks increases rapidly over time regardless of failure status. While average annual attacks for both ever-failed and never-failed states remain at or below 15 attacks per country per year until 1979, patterns for the two greatly differ. Perhaps most interesting is that terrorist attacks were initially more common against targets in never-failed states during the 1970s but then became more common against targets in ever-failed states after 1980.

Also apparent from the top graph in Figure 6.6 is that the number of attacks against targets in never-failed states varies widely between about 10 and 22 attacks per year while attacks against ever-failed states steadily increased. These two different patterns produce increasingly wide divergence in the two trends after the middle 1980s. Perhaps this shift reflects changes in the motives of terrorist groups over this period. For example, some evidence suggests that many of the terrorist groups motivated by left-wing political ideology in the 1970s struck in the never-failed states of Europe (Rapoport 2002). In contrast, terrorist groups more closely connected to religious ideologies may be more common among ever-failed states. Another possibility worth exploring in future analysis is whether the number of attacks against failed states has increased along with stronger counter terrorism measures applied in the non-failed states.

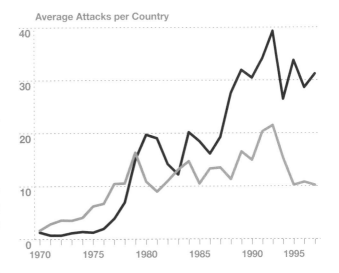

Average Attacks per Country

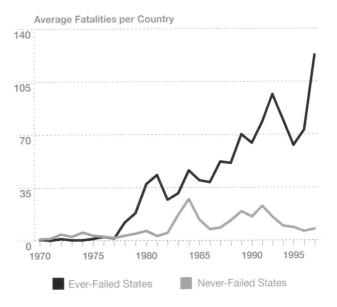

Average Fatalities per Country

■ Ever-Failed States   ■ Never-Failed States

In the bottom portion of Figure 6.6, we repeat the analysis, but instead track fatalities over time for never-failed and ever-failed states. Interestingly, compared to the results shown in the top half, the differences between ever-failed and never-failed states are much greater. Thus, for much of the 1970s, never-failed states have slightly higher fatality rates than ever-failed states. But this trend reverses in 1978, when ever-failed states have considerably higher fatalities than never-failed states. Except for 1984, never-failed states experience fewer than 25 fatalities per country per year during the entire series. A large proportion of the attacks driving the high fatalities in never-failed states in the early 1980s and 1990s were concentrated in Peru and were augmented especially by the terrorist campaign of the Maoist

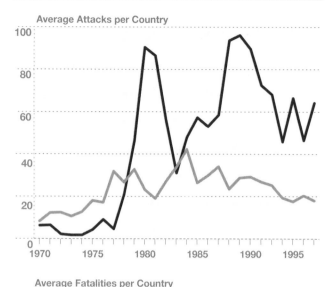

Figure 6.7: Current State Failure Status and Terrorism, 1970-1997

Average Attacks per Country

Average Fatalities per Country

■ In Failure   ■ Out of Failure

group Sendero Luminoso. In contrast, fatalities in ever-failed states continued to increase over time, rising beyond 50 per country per year by 1987, to more than 95 per country per year in 1992, and finishing the series with an average of more than 120 fatalities in 1997. Major lethal attacks among ever-failed states in 1997 included the terror campaign by Islamic militants in Algeria with more than 4,000 deaths and the terror campaign in Colombia that resulted in 1,040 fatalities in that year.

The trends in Figure 6.6 strongly suggest that terrorism has become in large part a problem for ever-failed states. Of course, it will be important to see if these patterns persist beyond 1997. Moreover, in research currently under way, we are examining whether other characteristics of ever-failed states are responsible for these observed differences in terrorism activity. Perhaps there are inherent characteristics of states that eventually experience failure that are also associated with more violence from terrorist organizations. It will also be important to determine the extent to which these differences are the result of changing strategies among terrorists and also the extent to which they reflect more effective counterterrorist methods employed by the nonfailed states over time.

Another possible explanation for these differences is that the ever-failed states only have a heightened risk of terrorist attacks during the years in which they have failed. To examine this issue more closely, we next compared the trends of terrorism activity for states "in failure" and those "out of failure" during the observation year. Thus, we only classify it as a failed state during the years of actual failure. Based on this coding strategy, in a given year there was an average of 26.6 countries in failure and 135.4 countries out of failure.

The upper portion of Figure 6.7 presents the average number of attacks per country for those states currently in failure and those out of failure. Here we see that differences between the two types of states become dramatic after 1979. Prior to 1979, stable countries had, on average, more terrorism attacks each year than states currently in failure. In the 1980s, failed states fluctuate from a high point in 1980 of 90.5 attacks per year to a decade low of 31.2 attacks per year in 1983. Then, terrorism attacks for currently failed states increase to a series high in 1989 of 96.2 average attacks per country. By contrast, stable countries show a weak positive trend from 1977 to 1992, which includes the peak of 42.3 average incidents per country in 1984. After 1984, the trend steadily declines. The large differences in magnitude between states in and out of failure for most of the series after 1979 strongly suggests that states are especially vulnerable to terrorism while experiencing state failure.

It is also worth noting that during the 1970s, countries currently experiencing state failure had virtually no recorded terrorist attacks in the GTD. In fact, total event counts for failed states during the years 1970 through 1977 were fewer than ten. A partial explanation for these striking differences might be media bias: perhaps failed states during these years had less media coverage, resulting in undercounting in open source terrorism databases such as the GTD.

The lower portion of Figure 6.7 repeats the above analysis to compare terrorism-related fatalities for countries currently in or out of failure. In general, these results are an exaggerated version of the patterns shown in the upper portion of the figure. Beginning in 1978, we observe a growing divergence in average fatalities between currently failed states and more stable countries. In 1978 the 24 countries currently in failure experienced an average of 56.4 fatalities each, compared to the 9.3 average fatalities for each of the 138 countries out of failure during that year. While this difference may seem large, the graph reveals that after 1978 the divergence between countries in and out of failed-state status becomes far greater. Terrorism-related fatalities rise to their peak at more than 219 deaths per country in 1981 for states in failure, while stable states experience an average of less than nine fatalities per country. Interestingly, both types of states end the series with a dramatic increase in fatalities in 1997. The increase in fatalities for stable states is due in large part to a rash of terrorist events in Algeria in 1997, which was coded as a stable state here but was classified as an ever failed state in the earlier analysis shown in Figure 6.6.

Conclusion

This chapter has presented a newly available terrorism open-source database that includes nearly 70,000 incidents, both domestic and international, from 1970 to 1997. Our review suggests that both total terrorist attacks and lethal attacks increased dramatically during this period. Bombings and facility attacks were the most common, followed by assassinations and kidnappings. Aerial hijackings were rare. The targets of these attacks were most often government, business, or police. The vast majority of incidents involved explosives or firearms. Latin America leads all other regions both in terms of total attacks and fatalities. While Sub-Saharan Africa and Asia are characterized by more fatalities than incidents, Europe and North America are characterized by more incidents than fatalities. By region, Sub-Saharan Africa, Asia, and the Middle East/North Africa accounted for the largest proportions of failed states during this period, suggesting a relationship between

Overall, our analysis provides strong evidence of a relationship between state failure and terrorism.

state failure and terrorism-related fatalities. The number of terrorist attacks in the Middle East/North African and Sub-Saharan African regions both increased dramatically during the 1990s.

Evidence of a relationship between state failure and terrorism activity is strengthened after examining the trends between the two. Moreover, there is strong evidence that this relationship changes over time. During the 1970s, states that never experienced failure had higher rates of attacks and fatalities; after the 1970s, states that had failed at least once had higher rates. Differences are especially great for fatalities. We are currently working on a far more detailed analysis of these issues, expecting that the relationship might depend on the type of failure that the state experiences. Further, our preliminary analysis suggests important differences when comparing states currently in failure to those not. Terrorism risk appears to be a dynamic condition that is closely related to other forms of national crisis. We intend to explore these issues in further analyses that disentangle the temporal ordering of state failure and terrorism activity. Overall, our analysis provides strong evidence of a relationship between state failure and terrorism.

7. ETHNOPOLITICAL VIOLENCE AND TERRORISM IN THE MIDDLE EAST

Victor Asal, Carter Johnson, and Jonathan Wilkenfeld[1]

Since 9/11, the academic and policy communities have accelerated efforts to explain core questions relating to the motivations of terrorists and the underlying conditions that lead to terrorist activity. The field has made great gains through a series of studies that examine particular terrorist organizations, such as al-Qaeda or the IRA, as well as through the study of particular types of terrorist groups, such as studies of Islamist organizations that engage in terrorism.[2] Despite these gains, serious obstacles have prevented us from answering the critical questions of why some organizations with political agendas engage in violence while others do not, and why some engage specifically in terrorism. One of the main obstacles to answering these questions has been a dearth of data. Until very recently, we have lacked systematically collected data on everything from incidents of domestic terrorism around the world, to characteristics of the actual organizations that perpetrate such attacks (Pynchon and Borum 1999; Silke 2004).

A new research project initiated at the National Consortium for the Study of Terrorism and Responses to Terrorism at the University of Maryland (START Center, see *http://www.start.umd.edu*) was designed to fill this void and contribute directly to our understanding of why organizations might choose terrorism. A major data collection effort was undertaken to construct a large, cross-national data set to examine both violent and nonviolent organizations for the period 1980–2004. This chapter examines the first phase of this project, which covers organizations representing minority ethnic and religious groups in the Middle East, and is structured around three themes: first, we present an overview of the findings on both ethnopolitical violence and terrorism that this new research project has generated; second, we focus specifically on terrorism, outlining four major theories that explain why organizations choose terrorism as a strategy; third, we provide a preliminary test of these theories by examining the relationships between terrorism and all organizations representing Kurds in the Middle East.

1 The authors gratefully acknowledge funding support for this work provided by the Department of Homeland Security (DHS) through the National Center for the Study of Terrorism and Responses to Terrorism (START) at the University of Maryland, grant number N00140510629. Any opinions, findings or recommendations in this document are those of the authors and do not necessarily reflect the views of DHS. We also wish to thank a dedicated group of data coders, and Amy Pate for helpful suggestions throughout the preparation of this chapter.

2 For excellent overviews of the field, see Enders and Sandler (2006), Lia and Skjolberg (2004), and Silke (2004).

Ethnopolitical Violence and Terrorism: Trends, 1980–2004

This research builds on the Minorities at Risk Project (MAR), founded by Ted Robert Gurr, which has collected data on over 300 ethnopolitical groups worldwide for the period from 1945 to 2003. Box 7.1 presents a brief overview of the project. These data have been used by academics and policy analysts to understand how ethnic conflicts begin, escalate, and end, as well as to identify broad global trends (Gurr 2000; Gurr 2005). One of the key advantages of the database is that it includes both groups that have and have not used violence. Up until now, however, MAR-based analyses have largely focused on the group as a whole (e.g., Kurds, Chechens, Tamils). While this is an important arena as far as societal preconditions for violence are concerned, it obscures the organizational nature of most violence and terrorism. Ethnic groups may describe large portions of the population, but it is particular organizations that plan, initiate, and carry out terrorist attacks. Therefore, this new database gathers information on the organizations themselves and is called Minorities at Risk Organizational Behavior (MAROB).

The MAROB database uniquely allows us to ask which organizational characteristics make it more likely that an organization will choose terrorism—defined here as the intentional targeting of civilians and civilian assets—as well as offering the potential to create risk models to help identify organizations that might adopt violence and terrorism as tactics in the future. Additionally, MAROB allows us to ask questions and develop models for organizations in particular regions of the world (e.g., the

---

Box 7.1: The Minorities at Risk (MAR) Project

The systematic collection of information on the internal affairs of states and the characteristics of societal conflict is a relatively recent endeavor, made possible by gains in information and communication technologies. One of the most accomplished of this new breed of research examining and recording information on the qualities of relations within states is the Minorities at Risk (MAR) project at the Center for International Development and Conflict Management at the University of Maryland. The MAR project was begun by Ted Robert Gurr in 1986 to examine and document the status of ethnic and religious minority groups in all countries of the world over the contemporary period, since 1945. Ethnic identity groups often compete with other political organizations, and especially the central state, for the loyalty and support of group members. On the other hand, minority identity groups can be neglected or maligned by central authorities or even excluded from equitable access to opportunities created by association with the larger state and civil society.

The MAR project focuses specifically on ethnopolitical groups, nonstate communal groups that have political significance in the contemporary world because of their status and political actions. One aspect of political significance is related to the group's size. For a group to be included in the MAR project, it must have a population of at least 100,000 or account for at least one percent of a country's total population. The group must have the membership size and, thus, the mobilization potential to influence central state politics in a meaningful way. A second aspect of political significance concerns the distinct quality of a group's relationship with state authorities. This aspect of political significance is determined by the following two criteria:

- The group collectively suffers, or benefits from, systematic discriminatory treatment vis-à-vis other groups in a society; and,
- The group is the basis for political mobilization and collective action in defense or promotion of its self-defined interests.

The MAR data collections are currently undergoing an update through 2006. For more information about the project, please visit *http://www.cidcm.umd.edu/mar*.

Middle East), about a particular transnational minority (e.g., Kurds), about a particular country (e.g., Israel and the West Bank and Gaza), or about organizations representing a particular minority inside a country (e.g., Shi'a in Iraq). Currently the MAROB database includes data on 102 organizations (112 organizations when we count different country branches as different organizations[3]) for the 29 MAR groups in the Middle East and North Africa, operating between 1980 and 2004.[4]

Diversity of Ethnopolitical Mobilization

These organizations are extremely diverse in terms of behavior and longevity. Most of the organizations exist for each of the last five years covered by the data, while 34 of them have been active since 1980 or earlier. Of the 112 organizations (counting country branches separately because different branches can behave differently in each country) that have existed from 1980 to 2004 about half have not used violence in the pursuit of political goals (e.g., Hadash in Israel), while others have used terrorism almost continuously for much of their existence (e.g., Hamas in the West Bank and Gaza Strip). Over three quarters of these organizations have pursued various forms of protest either domestically or internationally at least once (e.g., Berber Cultural Movement), and more than half have been involved in electoral politics for at least one year since 1980 (e.g., Halkin Emek Partisi in Turkey). Interestingly, some organizations have pursued protest, electoral politics, and violence, sometimes simultaneously (e.g., Hezbollah in Lebanon), while a few pursue none of these strategies at all. The United Azerbaijan Movement in Iran, for example, focused on soliciting external support and building international coalitions rather than engaging the government through violence or protest. While the majority are not using violence at all, terrorism remains a strategy for a significant number of organizations during this period, with a third of them using it at least once.

While the majority are not using violence at all, terrorism remains a strategy for a significant number of organizations during this period, with a third of them using it at least once.

An examination of organizations by ethnic group shows that the various MAR groups have significantly different levels of organizational competition. Table 7.1 displays the number of organizations by ethnopolitical group in 2004. Five ethnic groups have only one organization that claimed to represent them in 2004: Alawi in Syria, Baha'is in Iran, Copts in Egypt, Druze in Lebanon, and Saharawi in Morocco. On the other hand, the Palestinians had 28 organizations representing them across the countries where they are located (this figure includes organizations with entities in multiple countries, such as Fatah in Lebanon, Jordan, and Israel)

---

3 For example there are three Fatah/Palestinian Liberation Organizations coded, one for the West Bank, one for Lebanon, and one for Jordan. A full listing of the MAR organizations from the Middle East can be found at the *Peace and Conflict* companion Web site: *http://www.cidcm.umd.edu/pc.*

4 Identification and coding of Minority at Risk organizations for the remaining regions of the world are currently underway.

Table 7.1: Number of Organizations by Ethnopolitical Group, 2004	
Ethnopolitical Group	Number of Organizations
Alawi	1
Arabs	6
Azerbaijanis	3
Baha'is	1
Berbers	5
Copts	1
Druze	1
Kurds	16
Maronite Christians	2
Palestinians	28
Saharawi	1
Shi'a	13
Sunnis	14
Turkish Cypriots	6

the Shi'a have 13 organizations, the Kurds have 16 organizations, and the Sunnis 14 organizations representing them. If we examine the number of organizations by country in 2004 (as seen in Table 7.2) we can see a similar pattern. Egypt has only one organization—representing the Copts—while Iraq has 26, Lebanon 21, and Israel 19, representing a variety of ethnic groups. Some of this variation undoubtedly is explained by the regime type or weak state that prevailed in Lebanon and northern Iraq for much of the period covered by this study.

If we look at the development of organizations over time in the Middle East (see Figure 7.1) we can see that there have been significant changes in the practice of ethnic politics since 1980. The first and most interesting pattern is that the proportion of organizations using violence as part of their repertoire has developed in two waves, with the first peaking in 1986 when 52 percent of all organizations used violence, with a gradual decline through 1998 when only 16 percent use violence, followed by a second wave which peaked in 2000, when 26 percent of organizations used violence, followed by another decline to the lowest proportion of the entire period, 14 percent in 2004. This general decline in the proportion of organizations using violence has occurred in the context of an overall increase in the number of organizations, which stood at 69 in 1990 and 96 in 2004. We should note though that these data, which terminate in 2004, do not fully capture the developments in Iraq since the United States invasion.

Table 7.2: Number of Organizations by Country, 2004	
Country	Number of Organizations
Algeria	3
Bahrain	4
Cyprus	6
Egypt	1
Iran	6
Iraq	26
Israel	19
Jordan	4
Lebanon	21
Morocco	3
Syria	3
Turkey	2

Perhaps equally striking is the rapid rise of nonviolent forms of political activity being used by ethnopolitical organizations in the Middle East: both protest politics (which includes street protests, sit-ins, petitions, strikes) and electoral politics greatly expanded between 1980 and 2004. In the case of electoral politics, the number of organizations using this kind of political action quadrupled from

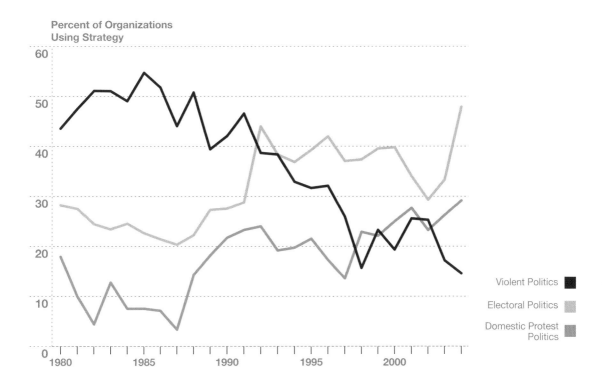

11 in 1980 to 46 in 2004, with the caveat mentioned earlier that the number of organizations also rose during this period (although at a slower pace). In other words, in 2004 half of all organizations were involved in electoral politics while in 1980 this figure stood at only 28 percent. It is important to note that many organizations used violence along with protest and electoral strategies so that the choice of nonviolent strategies does not necessarily mean a cessation of violence.

One of the key explanatory factors affecting the rise of electoral strategies is clearly at the state level: a number of countries have opened up their political systems to allow for minority participation in a number of unique ways. Turkey, for example, became a democracy once again in 1983 and, at various times, has allowed ethnic Kurdish parties to participate in elections. The Oslo process, as another example, allowed Palestinian organizations in the West Bank and the Gaza Strip to participate in elections and the political process in ways that had not been possible earlier in the occupation. With the end of the Lebanese civil war, that country also introduced a modicum of stability and renewed parliamentary activity that has allowed organizations to compete electorally. Most dramatically of course, the American invasion of Iraq profoundly changed the political system and permitted open political parties to mobilize for the elections in early 2005, which were predominantly organized along ethno-religious lines. Indeed, the number of ethno-religious organizations in Iraq committed to contesting elections doubled between 2003 and 2004, although it remains to be seen whether this expansion in ethno-religious organizations in Iraq will work positively toward a more stable

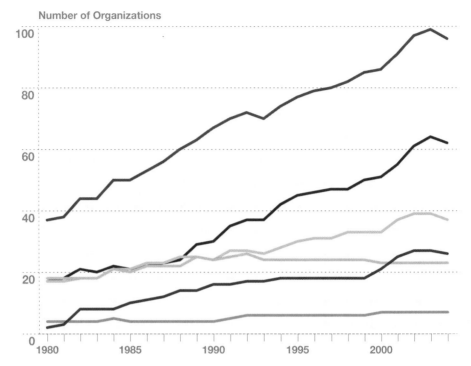

Figure 7.2: Shifts in Ideology of Ethnopolitical Organizations

Number of Organizations

Total
Democratic
Nationalist
Religious
Leftist
Rightist

political system or contribute to the further fracturing of the country into ethnic sectarianism.

A more disturbing trend within this broad opening of political contestation, however, is the evidence that political liberalization and democracy may encourage more political violence by ethnopolitical organizations.[5] According to the Polity data, only two countries were deemed democratic in the Middle East in 2004—Israel and Turkey—and both have ethnopolitical organizations using violence and terrorism to achieve their political goals.

Ideological Orientation and Violence

Political openings of governments are not the only kind of important change we see that helps explain shifts in organizational strategies. Indeed one of the biggest changes related to MAR organizations has been in their ideological motivation (see Figure 7.2). While the number of organizations on a traditional left-right economic continuum has remained fairly stable, the number of organizations motivated by religion (i.e., organizations that advocate policies expanding the role of religion in public life), nationalism (here defined as desiring either independence or autonomy), and democracy has risen dramatically. In fact many writers have made note of the global rise of religion as a political ideology in recent years. We can see this trend

---

5 There is an ongoing debate in the literature about the complicated relationship between democracy and terrorism; see Eubank and Weinberg 2001; Li 2005; Pape 2003; Reinares 1998; Stevenson 2003; Windsor 2003.

occurring in Middle Eastern organizations, as the number of organizations that want to incorporate religion into public life has risen from only two in 1980 to 23 in 2004. Some scholars propose that this shift towards more religious goals should be associated with a rise in violence and terrorism (see, for example, Juergensmeyer 2003), which has been fueled by some important examples in the region, such as Hamas and Turkish Hizbullah. In fact, our data support this hypothesis, showing a statistically significant correlation between religious ideology and use of violence by an organization, although the results are not very robust.

> *While the number of organizations on a traditional left-right economic continuum has remained fairly stable, the number of organizations motivated by religion, nationalism, and democracy has risen dramatically.*

A potentially more hopeful element has been the rapid rise in organizations that support democracy, with an increase from 17 in 1980 to 62 in 2004. Many analysts have noted the remarkable rise of democratic forms of government over the past 30 years (Huntington 1991, 1997; Jaggers and Gurr 1995), but a rise in the number of organizations that support democracy also appears to be occurring, even among organizations operating in authoritarian countries. While some organizations profess democracy as an ideology and also use violence as a strategy, they are less likely to use violence than those organizations that do not claim to be committed to democracy. From 1980 to 2004, the positive relationship between democratic aims and the rejection of violence as a strategy is statistically significant. Ironically, as we will see in the section below, while democratic ideology of organizations is associated with less violence, democratic forms of government appear to be linked to increased terrorist activity.

The Strategy of Terror

To this point, we have been discussing organizational violence and terrorism without regard to specific targets. Organizations, however, choose whether to intentionally target civilians (our definition of terrorism) or security forces, and MAROB shows clear patterns of targeting strategies during the 1980–2004 period. Some organizations have chosen primarily a strategy of insurgency, engaging with the military and police forces of the state. For example, while there were a few years before 1988 during which Polisario in the Western Sahara targeted civilians occasionally, for the most part the organization has focused on attacking the security forces of Morocco and has not launched a terror attack since 1987. On the other hand, some organizations have adopted a strategy of intentionally targeting civilians consistently throughout their existence.

Interestingly, while the number of MAR organizations that operate in the Middle East has increased dramatically since 1980, the number of organizations using terrorism has varied little (see Figure 7.3). Nevertheless, the sharp decline in the number of organizations using terrorism that appeared in the middle of the 1990s has ended, and currently the trend is rising and is sure to show an even steeper rise

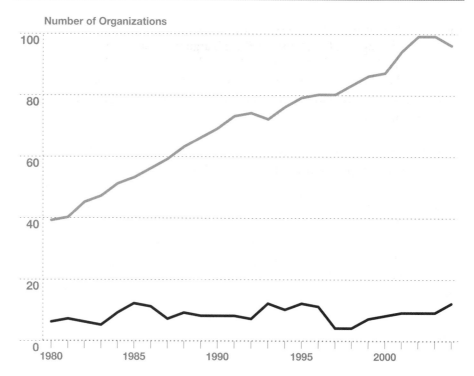

Figure 7.3: The Use of Terror by Organizations, 1980–2004

Number of Organizations

Total

Terror

once new Shi'a and Sunni organizations in Iraq are taken into account for 2005 and 2006.

Causes of Terrorism: Four Theories

A variety of causal factors have been proposed over the past three decades to explain the use of terrorism. This section will briefly outline four of those theories, while a test of these will be the focus below using data on the Kurdish minority groups of the Middle East. The first theory suggests that policies of discrimination and state repression create an incentive and motivation for oppressed group members to engage in violence against members of the dominant group (Gurr 2000). When discrimination and repression are particularly high, some analysts argue, they dehumanize the oppressors in the eyes of the organization, permitting attacks on all targets, including civilians, to destroy the "enemy" (Juergensmeyer 2003).

The second theory focuses on capabilities of organizations. Much of the literature exploring contentious politics (McCarthy and Zald 1977; McCammon et al. 2001; Alimi 2003) has focused on the impact of resource mobilization and capabilities for the rise and success of movements. Organizations that have the experience and ability to use a repertoire (Tarrow 1993) and an opening in the environment to do so (Banaszak 1996; Meyer 2004) are likely to make use of it.

The third theory focuses on political regime type, specifically identifying democracies as a core explanatory factor, but there are conflicting theoretical arguments. One group of analysts has argued that democracies have the potential to *prevent* terrorism by providing other avenues of nonviolent political action to organizations, such as legal protests or institutional access to the political system, through which grievances are addressed (Engene 2004; Gurr 2000); this argument has driven much of recent US foreign policy towards democratization in the Middle East. At the same time, however, others argue that democracy makes states uniquely susceptible to terrorist activities (Wilkinson 1986). An open political system, they argue, creates greater space for the media, which can bombard society with images of civilian deaths and destruction, putting greater pressure on governments than would be the case in authoritarian regimes that have greater control over the media (Nacos 2000). This encourages organizations to use violence because of its demonstration effects and the consequent pressure citizens apply on their governments. Recent analysis suggests that some aspects of democracy increase the likelihood of terrorism while others constrain it (Li 2005). For this reason, democracies are seen as particularly susceptible to violence and terrorism because they are more open, providing organizations with a greater ability to mobilize. Similarly, weak or failed states are expected to experience more violence and terrorism due to the lack of government control.

Finally, researchers also frequently mention ideological characteristics of organizations as an important determinant of the likelihood of terrorist activity (Drake 1998; Enders and Sandler 2000; Laqueur 1999; Sharpe 2000). Nationalist and religious ideology in particular have been identified as factors that should increase the likelihood of terrorism because they increase the ability of an organization's membership to dehumanize the enemy "other" and, particularly for religious ideology, to interpret the conflict in apocalyptic terms where any means are justifiable (Gressang IV 2001; Crenshaw 1988).

A Closer Look: The Kurds

One of the unique advantages of using the MAROB data is our ability to analyze organizations at different levels of aggregation: in addition to analyzing an entire region, as we have done to this point with the Middle East as a whole, we can also examine a single minority in a single country, all minorities in a country, or one minority found in multiple countries. For this chapter, we have chosen to take a closer look at the Kurdish organizations active in Iran, Iraq, Syria, and Turkey (see Table 7.3). Given the US invasion of Iraq in 2003, ongoing clashes in authoritarian Iran and Syria, as well as the continuing struggle in democratic Turkey, the political strategies of these Kurdish organizations have important implications for the development of policy on the problem of terrorism. In addition, there is great diversity in the situations in which we find each of the Kurdish organizations during the past 25-year period, which will better enable us to test the aforementioned theories. For example, according to MAR data, all four countries have politically discriminated against the Kurdish groups as a whole, but these levels have varied in each country over time.

Table 7.3: Kurdish Organizations—Overview		
Country	**Num.**	**Country-Level Historical Background**
Iran	2	• Varying levels of repression • Theocracy with democratic elements • No one dominant organization
Iraq	12	• Varies between highly repressed and semi-independent for large period • Dictatorship (but period of autonomy) • No one dominant organization
Syria	2	• Highly repressed for entire period • Dictatorship • No one dominant organization
Turkey	5	• Varying but mostly highly repressed for most of the period • Semi-authoritarian to new democracy • Dominant organization - Partiya Karkari Kurdistan (PKK)

Applying the Four Theories: Kurdish Organizational Behavior

Testing the first theory—that state repression of an organization leads to an increased likelihood of using terrorism—the MAROB data confirms this relationship. We find a strong, positive correlation between repression and use of terrorism that is statistically significant. In terms of capability, the second theory being tested, an astonishingly large number of the Kurdish organizations are militant in the sense that they possess violent means (explosives, armaments, etc.), regardless of whether they are used in a given year. In the Middle East as a whole, organizations have been coded militant 60 percent of the time (in itself a strikingly high number), while for the Kurds that number reaches a staggering 80 percent. In other words, most of the Kurdish organizations in the Middle East for most of the period under discussion had the capability to target civilians if they chose to do so. Yet, while Kurdish groups used violence during 54 percent of all organization years, they used terrorism (i.e., the specific targeting of civilians) only 14 percent of the time, which is roughly equivalent to the 12 percent figure for all Middle Eastern MAR organizations as a whole.

Table 7.4: Kurdish Organizations Using Terrorism		
Country	**Organization**	**Years Using Terrorism**
Iraq	Ansar al-Islam (in Iraq)	2001–2004
Iraq	Islamic Movement in Iraqi Kurdistan (in Iraq)	1993
Iraq	Kurdish Revolutionary Hezbollah of Iraq	1996
Iraq	Kurdistan Democratic Party (in Iraq)	1984, 1988, 1993, 2001, 2004
Turkey	Partiya Karkari Kurdistan (in Turkey)	1984–1999, 2004
Iraq	Patriotic Union of Kurdistan (in Iraq)	1981–1982, 1985, 1996, 2003–2004
Turkey	Turkish Hizbullah	1990–1999

Indeed of the 21 Kurdish organizations covered in the data set, only seven have used terrorism as a strategy in the past 25 years, and of these, two used this strategy during one year only and not ever again (see Table 7.4).

In terms of regime type, it is important to note that all the Kurdish organizations that resorted to terrorism were in countries that either were democratic for much of this period or in which the government was not exclusively in control of its territory, much as the theoretical literature would predict. Turkey has been a democracy since 1983, and Iraq has not been in control of all of its territory since the first Gulf war in 1991. In fact, only two Kurdish organizations used terrorism when the country in question was either not a democracy or did not have problems of territorial control (The Kurdistan Democratic Party [in Iraq] and the Patriotic Union of Kurdistan [in Iraq]), and both of these organizations were operating during the Iran-Iraq war of the 1980s.

Finally, in terms of ideology, Kurdish organizations provide some interesting findings that do not conform to the theoretical predictions outlined above. Despite larger trends related to the rise of religious organizations in the Middle East—particularly of militant religious organizations—the Kurds have not followed this pattern. More importantly, as we can see in Figure 7.4, none of the ideologies seem to track the fall and rise of terrorism particularly well, with only a democratic ideology appearing to map inversely onto the trends of terrorism, rising slightly at the same time as terrorism falls, and declining slightly as terrorism increases.

Figure 7.4: Kurdish Organizations—Ideology and Use of Terrorism (1980–2004)

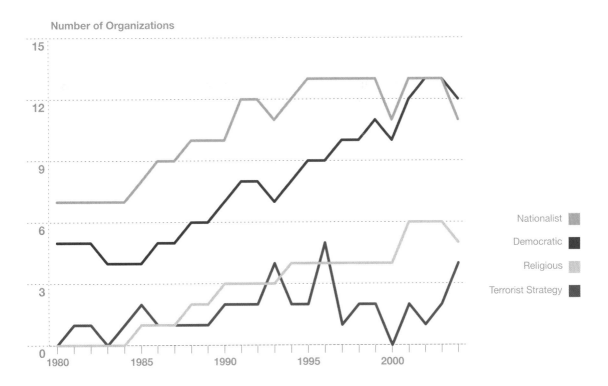

Conclusion

This chapter has provided an overview of violence and terrorism as committed by ethnopolitical organizations between 1980 and 2004. We noted a steady increase in the number of organizations using violence as a strategy until the mid-1980s, after which we noted a general but uneven decline, which is impressive given that, during this 25-year period, there has been a consistent overall growth in the number of ethnopolitical organizations in the region. We also noted a sharp increase in the number of organizations pursuing nonviolent strategies, such as electoral politics, which is probably a result of political liberalization in some countries. Overall, there was a significant rise in the number of organizations espousing democratic goals as well as religious goals, and the latter were more likely to pursue violence as a strategy to achieve their political goals.

Of the four theories explaining terrorism that we tested using the Kurdish organizations of the Middle East, we found support for two. Repression was strongly associated with terrorist activity and political openings due to liberalization or failed states appear to be associated with increased terrorism. In the case of the Kurds, only democratic ideology seemed to have a relationship with terrorism and that relationship appears to be negative. We should note though that these findings focus on the Kurdish context and generalizing across contexts may not be possible.

Taken together, this brief look at the use of political violence and terrorism as used by ethnopolitical organizations in the Middle East, both in general and by Kurdish organizations in particular, suggests a need to examine in greater detail the factors associated with both increases and decreases in the likelihood of organizations adopting terrorism as a strategy that may occur at the state level, societal level, and the organizational level. Equally important, the significant results generated by the new MAROB dataset reinforce the need for greater efforts to systematically collect data on terrorism to test the various theories in the field. These data collection efforts will enable us to both understand the causes of terrorism as well as develop forecasting models to identify, in advance, those conditions and organizational features that may be at risk for encouraging terrorist activity in the future.

Overall, there was a significant rise in the number of organizations espousing democratic goals as well as religious goals, and the latter were more likely to pursue violence as a strategy to achieve their political goals.

8. UNSTABLE STATES AND INTERNATIONAL CRISES

Jonathan Wilkenfeld[1]

The Carnegie Corporation of New York, in the most recent announcement of its International Peace and Security Program initiatives, identified "States at Risk" as a key concern:

> In the post-9/11 era, the world has become more aware that states at risk of instability and collapse threaten international peace, security and prosperity.... Linked with other major security threats, notably terrorism and the proliferation of weapons of mass destruction, as well as international crime, trafficking and humanitarian catastrophes, states at risk constitute an enduring global challenge. Effective responses will require...improved international coordination for what has become an inherently multilateral problem (Carnegie Corporation 2006).

While states at risk are not a new phenomenon, their co-occurrence in the context of the post-Cold War unipolar international structure has had the effect of unleashing tensions that had heretofore been confined generally to the domestic realm. In this chapter, we will explore the potential ramifications of state instability for the global system and regional subsystems, the implications of these possible linkages for regional and global security, and areas where a capacity for early warning may help avoid some of the more dire consequences of this linkage.

Building upon pioneering work by the Political Instability Task Force (Goldstone et al. 2005), state instability is here understood to include outbreaks of revolutionary or ethnic war, adverse regime change, and genocide (to be defined below). The occurrence of one or more of these deeply disruptive phenomena not only weakens the societies in which they flourish, but also makes the regional and global systems more insecure. Weak and unstable states might engage in diversionary tactics aimed externally in order to distract the population from deteriorating conditions at home, while external forces, be they diaspora populations, external groups with ethnic or religious ties to the homeland, or other forces seeking strategic advantage in a vulnerable locale, can come together to create a dangerous dynamic for the global system or a regional subsystem. The confluence of these conditions renders these unstable states particularly vulnerable to crisis involvement.

Our focus here will be international crises, that is, dangerous episodes that can be destabilizing not only to the actors directly involved but also to the entire international system. They can present overwhelming challenges to established institutions and belief systems and can change the basic distribution of power within the international community, regionally or globally. Indeed, Brecher and Potter (2005) liken international crises to earthquakes: the potential severity and

---

1 Michael Brecher and Ted Robert Gurr provided extensive comments on earlier drafts of this chapter.

impact of crises are parallel to that geological phenomenon, and like earthquakes, are amenable to probabilistic assessment as to vulnerability, outcome, and impact.

Seventy-seven percent of all international crises in the post-Cold War era (1990–2005) include one or more actors classified as unstable, fragile, or failed at the time of the crisis, according to the Political Instability Task Force.[2] Thus, while the yearly frequency of international crises for this period has shown a marked decline from previous eras (see Figure 3.4 in chapter 3), matching findings for other measures of sub-state and interstate conflict, those crises that do erupt show a powerful propensity to be linked to instability, fragility, and failure. The purpose of this chapter is to shed light on the phenomenon of international crisis in general, and to focus on the emerging critical relationship between state instability and involvement in international crisis.

Seventy-seven percent of all international crises in the post-Cold War era...include one or more actors classified as unstable, fragile, or failed at the time of the crisis.

A foreign policy crisis, that is, a crisis for an individual state, is a situation wherein the highest level decision-makers of the state perceive a threat to one or more basic values, an awareness of finite time for response to the value threat, and a heightened probability of involvement in military hostilities. An international crisis is characterized by a change in type and/or an increase in the intensity of disruptive (hostile verbal or physical) interactions between two or more states, with a heightened probability of military hostilities; that, in turn, destabilizes their relationship and challenges the structure of an international system--global, dominant, or subsystem (Brecher and Wilkenfeld 2000).

Reconsider Figure 3.4 from chapter 3. The figure presents a plot of the frequency of international crises for the period 1946–2004. While the Cold War era (1945–1989) was characterized by a gradual increase in the frequency of crises, there is a precipitous drop in the frequency of crises in the post-Cold War unipolar era. This recent sharp reduction in the number of international crises per year can be explained in part by the decline in power of the Soviet Union in the 1980s, culminating in its disintegration into 15 independent states, coupled with the emergence of the US as the dominant military power in the system. These events profoundly affected the nature and frequency of international crises. While the global system remains a dangerous place, the defining characteristics of international crises are less prevalent in the conflict situations that typify the post-Cold War, unipolar era. However, this should not be taken as a signal of declining crisis severity, as there were several severe crises during this era: Gulf War I 1990–1991, Serbia-Croatia-Bosnia 1992–1995, Kosovo 1998–1999, Ethiopia-Eritrea 1998–2000, Democratic Republic of the Congo 1998–2002, US/Afghanistan 2001, Iraq Regime Change/Gulf War II 2002–2003, and Israel/Lebanon (Hezbollah) 2006. Nevertheless, most of the proliferation of conflicts based on ethnicity, nationality, and religion—al Qaeda aside—do not threaten the structure of the international system. What are the key

---

2 PITF data are available at http://globalpolicy.gmu.edu/pitf.

differences between the two eras in terms of the characteristics of the crises they spawned?

Violence, either the threat of, or its actual occurrence, is a critical element of international crises. Two key indicators help us track patterns of crises in the current unipolar era: the extent to which crises are triggered by violent acts by either states or nonstate actors, and the extent to which violence is employed by the parties in the management of crises.

What makes crises particularly dangerous for the international system is the propensity for violence to escalate. Overall, 50 percent of all crises are triggered by a violent act, and 75 percent of all crises exhibit some violence. Nevertheless, it is possible to pinpoint a critical difference between crises in the Cold War and post-Cold War eras: violent triggers are followed by violent crisis management techniques in 77 percent of Cold War crises, while 96 percent of post-Cold War crises with violent triggers are followed by violent crisis management techniques. So while the frequency of crises has declined since the end of the Cold War, those that do occur are more prone than earlier crises to escalating violence. That is, a much smaller proportion are able to escape the escalation dynamic whereby violence begets violence.

International crises can be classified according to those that unfold in the context of a protracted conflict, and those that occur as more isolated eruptions. A protracted conflict is characterized by hostile interactions that extend over long periods of time with sporadic outbreaks of open warfare fluctuating in frequency and intensity. Some, like the Chad/Libya protracted conflict, are composed of recurrent crises over the same basic issue. (Between 1971 and 1986 Chad and Libya were involved in eight international crises over their mutual claims to the Aouzou Strip—45,000 square miles of northern Chad lying astride the Chad-Libya border and rich in uranium and oil deposits.) Others, like India-Pakistan (since 1947 and continuing) and Arab-Israel (since 1948 and ongoing), range across a diversity of issues. States as actors in crises arising in the context of protracted conflict are more likely to experience violent triggers and more serious threat, and to employ violent crisis management techniques.

The post-Cold War era has witnessed a modest decline in the proportion of crises that are embedded in ongoing protracted conflicts, from 61 percent of all crises in the earlier era, to 54 percent of post-Cold War crises. However, the five protracted conflicts that dominate the current era—India-Pakistan, Arab-Israel, Taiwan Strait, Korea, and Iraq Regime Change—have proven to be among the most intractable, and therefore the crises they engender constitute severe threats to the stability of the international system. All five involve at least one actor in possession of nuclear weapons, and all have the capacity for turning a minor trigger into a major conflagration, as we witnessed in the Israel-Lebanon crisis of 2006. So the downward trend in the frequency of crises spawned by protracted conflicts must be tempered with the knowledge that these crises remain the most severe with which the global system must cope.

Notwithstanding the rather precipitous decline in the frequency of crises noted in Figure 3.4, the extent to which states in crises have perceived high threat has increased from 18 percent for the earlier eras to 30 percent for the post-Cold War period, beginning in 1990. High threat includes threat to existence (e.g., threat to survival of population, genocide, existence of entity, total annexation, colonial rule, occupation) and threat of grave damage (e.g., threat of large casualties in war, mass bombings). The *Peace and Conflict* companion Web site (*http://www.cidcm.umd.edu/pc*) features a full listing of the post-Cold War international crises in which at least one of the crisis actors experienced grave threat. This is further evidence of an unfolding trend: less frequent but more severe crises, demanding the attention of the international community because of their potential for expanding beyond the immediate region in question as a threat to the stability of the entire global system. It may be that leaders of unstable states feel more threatened by international crises than do leaders of more stable states.

A key characteristic distinguishing post-Cold War crises from those of earlier eras involves the extent to which the international community has engaged in some form of mediation for purposes of crisis management or conflict resolution. As the gravity of threat in crisis has increased in the current era, so too has the frequency of mediation, from 32 percent of all crises in the Cold War era, to 46 percent in the post-Cold War system.

While all forms of mediation are evident among the crises of the post-Cold War era, the increase in the frequency of mediation has been attributable almost entirely to the increased use of formulative mediation techniques, in which the mediator conceives and proposes new solutions to the disputants but refrains from attempting to impose these solutions as would be the case in a more manipulative style of mediation. Post-Cold War mediation exhibits twice the success rate of Cold War mediation, leading to the more rapid termination of international crises, from 22 percent to 44 percent. And finally, the post-Cold War era shows a substantial increase in the number of crises mediated by single states. Several post-Cold War examples of successful mediation include the 1996 North Korea Submarine crisis (US, by President Bill Clinton), the 1996–1997 Zaire Civil War (South Africa, by Nelson Mandela), the 1998 Syria-Turkey crisis (Egypt, by Foreign Minister Amr Musa), the 1999 Kosovo crisis (US, by US Envoy Richard Holbrook, in addition to the involvement of the UN, Russia, and Finnish President Martti Ahtisaari), and the 2002 Parsley Island crisis (US, by US Secretary of State Colin Powell).

Perhaps the most significant difference between Cold War and post-Cold War international crises is the extent to which state instability impacts the dynamics of crisis. In the bipolar era following World War II (1945–1962), only 22 percent of all international crises involved at least one actor classified as unstable. This number increased to 56 percent for the polycentric period (1963–1989). By the post-Cold War era beginning in 1990, 77 percent of all international crises involved at least one unstable actor. Figure 8.1 portrays this disturbing trend. This is dramatic evidence that, not only are these states extremely prone to destabilizing events internally, but the same forces are apparently related to an inordinate propensity for these states to

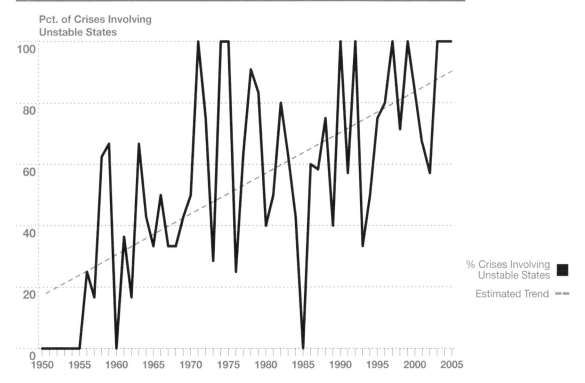

Figure 8.1: Percentage of Crises Involving Unstable States (1950–2005)

Pct. of Crises Involving
Unstable States

% Crises Involving
Unstable States ■

Estimated Trend ▬▬

become involved in external destabilizing events, i.e., international crises. The blue dashed line depicts a statistically estimated trend line (fitted with OLS regression) indicating a positively sloped trend in the data that is statistically significant. This extension of the dangers of instability from the domestic to the international realm is indeed a defining characteristic of the current international system, and one that bears close scrutiny by the members of the international community capable of intervening in such cases.

The instability-crisis nexus can also be viewed from the perspective of the state as actor. While only 11 percent of all states in the post-Cold War system exhibited significant levels of instability, 40 percent of all states involved as actors in international crises for this period were unstable. Once again, this demonstrates the disproportionate impact that unstable states have on the stability of regional subsystems and on the entire international system. It points up the importance of establishing instability watch lists, so that the international community can attempt to anticipate these escalating situations while there is still time to marshal the regional and international resources needed to defuse them.

Several of the most dangerous protracted conflicts in the international system today involve unstable states, including India-Pakistan and Arab-Israel. A number of these have erupted in recent years into crises threatening the entire international community or one of the regional subsystems—most recently wars in Afghanistan, Iraq, and Lebanon. The *Peace and Conflict* companion Web site (*http://www.cidcm.*

Unstable and
recent crisis or PC

Unstable and no
recent crisis or PC

Stable and recent
crisis or PC

umd.edu/pc) lists all international crises for the post-Cold War international system and indicates whether the crisis was part of an ongoing protracted conflict, which states were involved as actors, whether they were unstable at the time of the crisis, and the level of threat associated with the crisis.

The Crisis Vulnerability Index

A central concern of this chapter is the development of a set of indicators along which judgments can be made about states' instability and fragility and the consequences for the stability of the international system and regional subsystems. That is, we seek a way to identify those unstable and fragile situations that have serious potential to escalate to international crises. The particular metric chosen here—the *Crisis Vulnerability Index*—accounts for a state's past experience with political instability and involvement in international crisis. The index places states in one of four categories depending on whether the state experienced instability and/or crisis involvement at any point during the 2000–2005 period.

Figure 8.2 presents the global distribution of states according to degree of crisis vulnerability. Definitions of the indicators used to construct the index can be found in Box 8.1. Table 8.1 presents a regional breakdown for 54 countries that exhibit varying degrees of vulnerability. For purposes of this analysis, countries must have populations of greater than 500,000, producing a sample of 161 countries. Three categories of states are identified and color-coded for ease of reference. Unstable

Box 8.1: Crisis Vulnerabilty Index—Definitions for Key Indicators*

From the International Crisis Behavior Project

A crisis for an individual state is a situation with three necessary and sufficient conditions deriving from a change in the state's internal or external environment. All three must be perceived by the highest level decision-makers of the state actor concerned: a threat to one or more basic values, an awareness of finite time for response to the value threat, and a heightened probability of involvement in military hostilities.

A protracted conflict is defined as hostile interactions which extend over long periods of time with sporadic outbreaks of open warfare fluctuating in frequency and intensity. In the case of crises, the sporadic outbreaks can involve actual hostilities or the threat of hostilities.

From the Political Instability Task Force

Revolutionary wars are episodes of violent conflict between governments and politically organized groups (political challengers) that seek to overthrow the central government, to replace its leaders, or to seize power in one region. Conflicts must include substantial use of violence by one or both parties to qualify as "wars." "Politically organized groups" may include revolutionary and reform movements, political parties, student and labor organizations, and elements of the armed forces and the regime itself. There are two minimum thresholds for inclusion: a mobilization threshold, wherein each party must mobilize 1,000 or more people (armed agents, demonstrators, troops), and a conflict intensity threshold, whereby there must be at least 1,000 direct conflict-related deaths over the full course of the armed conflict and at least one year when the annual conflict-related death toll exceeds 100 fatalities. The fatalities may result from armed conflict, terrorism, rioting, or government repression.

Ethnic wars are episodes of violent conflict between governments and national, ethnic, religious, or other communal minorities (ethnic challengers) in which the challengers seek major changes in their status. Most ethnic wars since 1955 have been guerrilla or civil wars in which the challengers have sought independence or regional autonomy. As with revolutionary wars, there are the two minimum thresholds for inclusion: a mobilization threshold, wherein each party must mobilize 1,000 or more people (armed agents, demonstrators, troops), and a conflict intensity threshold, whereby there must be at least 1,000 direct conflict-related deaths over the full course of the armed conflict and at least one year when the annual conflict-related death toll exceeds 100 fatalities. The fatalities may result from armed conflict, terrorism, rioting, or government repression.

Adverse Regime Changes are defined as major, adverse shifts in patterns of governance, including major and abrupt shifts away from more open, electoral systems to more closed, authoritarian systems; revolutionary changes in political elites and the mode of governance; contested dissolution of federated states or secession of a substantial area of a state by extrajudicial means; and complete or near-total collapse of central state authority and the ability to govern. The main criterion used to identify adverse regime changes is the record of a six or more point drop in the value of a state's POLITY index score over a period of three years or less (see http://www.cidcm.umd.edu/polity/).

Genocide and politicide events involve the promotion, execution, and/or implied consent of sustained policies by governing elites or their agents or, in the case of civil war, either of the contending authorities that result in the deaths of a substantial portion of a communal group or politicized noncommunal group. In genocides the victimized groups are defined primarily in terms of their communal (ethnolinguistic, religious) characteristics. In politicides, by contrast, groups are defined primarily in terms of their political opposition to the regime and dominant groups. Genocide and politicide are distinguished from state repression and terror. In cases of state terror authorities arrest, persecute, or execute a few members of a group in ways designed to terrorize the majority of the group into passivity or acquiescence. In the case of genocide and politicide authorities physically exterminate enough (not necessarily all) members of a target group so that it can no longer pose any conceivable threat to their rule or interests.

* The indicators for crisis and protracted conflict are derived from the International Crisis Behavior Project data (http://www.cidcm.umd.edu/icb). The indicators of instability—adverse regime change, ethnic war, revolutionary war, and genocide/politicide, are derived from the Political Instability Task Force List of Internal Wars and Failures of Governance, 1955–2005 (http://globalpolicy.gmu.edu/pitf).

Crisis Vulnerability Index	Country	Active Protracted Conflict	Recent International Crisis	Adverse Regime Change	Ethnic War	Revolutionary War	Genocide/Politicide
North Atlantic							
●	Greece	●					
●	Spain		●				
●	United Kingdom	●	●				
●	United States	●	●				
Former Socialist Bloc							
●	Russia		●		●		
●	Azerbaijan		●				
●	Croatia	●					
●	Georgia		●				
●	Serbia	●					
●	Slovenia	●					
Latin America and the Caribbean							
●	Colombia					●	
●	Haiti			●			
Asia and the Pacific							
●	Afghanistan		●	●	●	●	
●	India	●	●		●	●	
●	Indonesia	●			●		
●	Myanmar (Burma)			●	●		
●	Pakistan	●	●		●		
●	Thailand			●	●		
●	China	●					
●	North Korea	●	●				
●	South Korea	●	●				
●	Taiwan	●					
●	Nepal			●		●	
●	Philippines				●		
●	Solomon Islands			●			
●	Sri Lanka				●		

Table 8.1: Crisis Vulnerability Index

Key
- ● Unstable and recent PC or crisis
- ● Stable and recent PC or crisis
- ● Unstable and no recent PC or crisis

states that are currently involved in a protracted conflict (PC) or a recent crisis (16 total, 10 percent) are indicated with a red bullet in Table 8.1. States currently involved in a PC or a recent crisis that are stable (21 total, 13 percent) are indicated with a blue bullet. Finally, countries that are not currently involved in a PC or a recent crisis, but are considered unstable (17 total, 11 percent) are indicated with an orange bullet. The table does not list the other 107 countries that are not designated as vulnerable. Countries are listed alphabetically within each color-coded category of the Crisis Vulnerability Index.

The 16 red-coded states representing 10 percent of the total are clearly in the most vulnerable and dangerous status for the international system, since they are already exhibiting the strong link between instability and crisis. While experts may disagree on the degree of vulnerability these red-coded states exhibit, most are on major watch lists because of their recent significant involvement in international crises, and/or significant instances of instability. Asia leads the system with six such states: Afghanistan, India, Indonesia, Myanmar (Burma), Pakistan, and Thailand. The Middle East follows with Algeria, Iran, Iraq, Israel, and Turkey. Interestingly, only six of these 16 states are among the top 25 at high risk for instability as identified in the *Peace and Conflict* Instability Ledger (see chapter 2). Crisis vulnerability adds an important dimension to the way we have traditionally conceived of instability and fragility in the international system.

By way of illustration, we will focus first on Algeria.[3] Algeria's fragility stems from the longstanding tension and political violence associated with efforts by the ruling National Liberation Front (FLN) to ensure electoral success and to prevent the Islamists—primarily the Islamic Salvation Front (FIS)—from gaining an electoral foothold. The fighting escalated into an insurgency, which saw intense fighting between 1992 and 1998 and resulted in over 100,000 deaths—many attributed to indiscriminate massacres of villagers by extremists. The government gained the upper hand by the late-1990s and FIS's armed wing, the Islamic Salvation Army, was disbanded in January 2000.

---

3 Material on Algeria and other cases discussed in this section is derived from the CIA Factbook (*https://www.cia.gov/cia/publications/factbook*); the US Department of State's Country Reports (*http://www.state.gov/r/pa/ei/bgn/*); the Political Instability Task Force List of Internal Wars and Failures of Governance, 1955–2005 (*http://globalpolicy.gmu.edu/pitf*); and the International Crisis Behavior Project (*http://www.cidcm.umd.edu/icb/dataviewer/*).

However, small numbers of armed militants persist in confronting government forces and conducting ambushes and occasional attacks on villages. On the international scene, since 1976, Algeria has supported the Polisario Front, which claims to represent the population of Western Sahara in its struggle for independence from Morocco. Algeria has provided the Sahrawi with support and sanctuary in refugee camps in southwestern Algeria. Relations between Algeria and Morocco have been frequently strained over this issue, with Mauritania drawn into the matter as well. The Western Sahara protracted conflict was responsible for ten international crises since 1975, and while dormant since 1989, has the potential to again engulf the surrounding states in conflict. Algeria's current instability, coupled with Morocco's past instability and recent crisis involvement, make this a situation fraught with potential danger for the regional and international communities.

Several ongoing protracted conflicts are characterized by instability within one or more of the adversarial actors. Perhaps most notable is the India/Pakistan protracted conflict, which has continued uninterrupted from 1947 to the present, characterized by 13 crises over that period, five during the current post-Cold War era. This protracted conflict and the crises over Junagadh, Hyderabad, Punjab, Bangladesh, and Kashmir, would appear to have a life of its own, independent of the internal situations within the two countries. Nevertheless, it would be prudent to take stock of those internal situations which, were they to become more destabilizing, might contribute at the margins to an increase in tensions between these two rival regional powers.

All five of the most recent India-Pakistan crises have been over the issue of Kashmir. During this period, India has experienced instability and fragility of a complex nature, involving both Sikh militancy in the 1990s and separatist movements with support from Pakistan in Jammu and Kashmir. Pakistan also experienced *complex* instability from 1983 to 1999, with a violent campaign by Sindhis seeking autonomy; violent attacks on Muhajirs in Karachi; and a military coup in 1999. While the India/Pakistan instability-crisis nexus has remained regional to this point, the very size and geopolitical salience of the states involved, their nuclear capabilities, and their susceptibility to international and domestic terrorism, render this situation dangerous for the entire international community.

Table 8.1: Crisis Vulnerability Index (cont.)							
Crisis Vulnerability Index	Country	Active Protracted Conflict	Recent International Crisis	Adverse Regime Change	Ethnic War	Revolutionary War	Genocide/Politicide
North Africa and the Middle East							
●	Algeria	●				●	
●	Iran		●	●			
●	Iraq	●	●	●	●		
●	Israel	●	●		●		
●	Turkey	●			●		
●	Cyprus	●					
●	Kuwait	●					
●	Lebanon	●					
●	Morocco	●	●				
●	Saudi Arabia	●					
●	Syria	●	●				
●	Yemen					●	
Africa South of the Sahara							
●	Dem. Rep. of Congo	●	●	●	●	●	
●	Ethiopia		●		●		
●	Rwanda	●	●		●		
●	Sudan	●			●		●
●	Chad		●				
●	Eritrea		●				
●	Angola				●	●	●
●	Burundi				●		
●	Central African Rep.			●			
●	Guinea Bissau			●			
●	Guinea					●	
●	Ivory Coast		●	●	●		
●	Liberia					●	
●	Sierra Leone			●		●	
●	Somalia			●	●		
●	Uganda					●	
Key							

● Unstable and recent PC or crisis
● Stable and recent PC or crisis
● Unstable and no recent PC or crisis

Two closely related protracted conflicts—Iraq/Kuwait and Iraq Regime Change—demonstrate the capacity of a single unstable state to impact the security situation of an entire region or the international system in general. Iraq's instability dates virtually to its independence in 1920, and includes ethnic tensions (Kurds, Shiites, Sunni), as well as revolutionary and genocidal elements over the years. Three significant regional wars span the Cold War and post-Cold War eras—the Iran-Iraq war (1980–1988), the Gulf War I (1991), and the Iraq Regime Change war [Gulf War II] (2003–). With both regional and international ramifications, this particular instability-crisis nexus, linked as it is to the "global war on terrorism," has proven to be perhaps the defining feature, with both regional and international ramifications, of the post-Cold War era to this point.

The 21 blue coded states representing 13 percent of the total are recent crisis participants or members of active protracted conflicts, but they are not at the moment exhibiting symptoms of instability. While these states can be found in a number of regions, they are particularly concentrated in the former Socialist bloc—Azerbaijan, Croatia, Georgia, Serbia, and Slovenia—and in the Middle East—Cyprus, Kuwait, Lebanon, Morocco, Saudi Arabia, and Syria. While these states have already become problems for the international community because of their recent crisis involvement, it is likely that were instability to emerge in any one of them, such crisis involvement would be exacerbated.

Equally important from a policy perspective is the identification of those 17 orange coded unstable states representing 11 percent of the total that have not crossed the line recently to involvement in international crises. Some are so remote or peripheral that it is unlikely that their instability will have consequences beyond the suffering that will be inflicted on their own societies. Such a group might include Haiti and Nepal.

Another group of unstable states is located in "dangerous neighborhoods" or controlling access to critical natural resources or other geopolitical considerations, but which have not been involved in recent international crises. In other words, these are states that exhibit some of the preconditions associated with the likelihood of becoming catalysts, or to being drawn into international crises. We know a good deal about the reasons for their instability, but their vulnerability for crisis involvement is less well appreciated.

While these states can be found in virtually all regions, a high concentration of such states is in Africa: Angola, Burundi, Central African Republic, Guinea Bissau, Guinea, Ivory Coast, Liberia, Sierra Leone, Somalia, and Uganda. But while the international system is aware of the widespread instability endemic to parts of the African continent, and aware of the potential spillover of many of these crises into the broader regional system, there are several similarly vulnerable states in other regions that also bear careful monitoring. These include Sri Lanka in Asia, Colombia in Latin America, and Yemen in the Middle East.

The case of Sri Lanka offers a classic pattern of this type of instability-crisis nexus. Sri Lanka's crisis vulnerability stems primarily from the longstanding ethnic Tamil grievances against the pro-Sinhalese government and their push for independence in the Tamil regions in the northern part of the country. While fighting ended with a cease-fire agreement in 2002, the recent eruption of violence in 2006 has signaled a massive deterioration of the internal situation. On the international scene, Sri Lanka's geographic proximity to India, and the existence of a large Tamil ethnic minority in India, means that India could easily be drawn into the domestic situation, as it was indeed with its intervention in June-July 1987. India has its own instability issues, stemming from the volatile situation in Kashmir and a burgeoning Maoist insurrection, as well as from local insurgencies based on ethnic divisions in other regions of the country. Further deterioration in the Sri Lanka situation, coupled with India's vulnerability, could provide the basis for a spread of instability in this region.

Colombia has experienced considerable domestic instability since 1984. A number of left-wing revolutionary groups, some in alliance with powerful drug cartels, have battled both government forces and right-wing paramilitary organizations in the rural areas of the country. The two largest insurgent groups active in Colombia are the Revolutionary Armed Forces of Colombia or FARC and the National Liberation Army or ELN. In addition, a large illegal paramilitary group, a roughly organized umbrella group of disparate paramilitary forces, is the United Self-Defense Groups of Colombia or AUC. Colombian-organized illegal narcotics, guerrilla, and paramilitary activities penetrate all of its neighbors' borders and have created a serious refugee crisis, with over 300,000 persons having fled the country, mostly into neighboring states. The US Drug Enforcement Administration estimates that more than 80 percent of the worldwide powder cocaine supply and approximately 90 percent of the powder cocaine smuggled into the United States is produced in Colombia. These conditions have the potential for igniting cross-border crises, particularly with countries with which Colombia has existing disputes—Venezuela and Nicaragua, as well as with the US to the north.

Yemen became a unified country in 1990, the Republic of Yemen, established with the merger of the Yemen Arab Republic (Yemen [Sanaa] or North Yemen) and the Marxist-dominated People's Democratic Republic of Yemen (Yemen [Aden] or South Yemen) after years of conflict between North and South Yemen that had dragged in neighboring countries including Egypt and Saudi Arabia. In recent years, Yemen has experienced revolutionary activity, attempting to suppress an uprising by dissident cleric Husain Badr al-Din al Huthi, which has resulted in serious fighting, particularly around the rebel stronghold in Saada. While Yemen has not been involved in protracted conflict and crisis activity in recent years, its unstable internal situation has the potential for spilling over into regional conflict in an extremely volatile corner of the globe. Possible conflict with both Saudi Arabia and Eritrea remain factors, with the potential for spread to other sensitive parts of the region.

Fortunately, the majority of members of the international community—107 or 66 percent of the total—are both stable domestically and not currently or recently involved in international crises. Spread across all regions of the globe, these states constitute the basis for the continued stability of the international system and its regional subsystems. They create neighborhoods of stability—much of Europe and the Western Hemisphere—where institutional and informal arrangements are in place to deal both with potential fragility and with conflict before they interact to form a lethal dynamic.

But the world will not be a secure environment until the cycle of instability and crisis, linking human security with international security, become a priority for the entire international system. As Mohamed ElBaradei, Secretary General of the International Atomic Energy Agency and 2005 Nobel Peace Laureate recently stated:

> The modern age demands that we think in terms of *human* security —a concept of security that is people-centered and without borders. A concept that acknowledges the inherent linkages between economic and social development, respect for human rights, and peace. This is the basis on which we must 're-engineer' security. While national security is just as relevant as before, the strategies to achieve it must be much more global than in the past, and our remedies must be centered on the welfare of the individual and not simply focused on the security of the state. Until we understand and act accordingly, we will not have either national or international security (ElBaradei 2006).

Fortunately, the majority of members of the international community…are both stable domestically and not currently or recently involved in international crises. Spread across all regions of the globe, these states constitute the basis for the continued stability of the international system and its regional subsystems. They create neighborhoods of stability.

9. MASS KILLING OF CIVILIANS IN TIME OF WAR, 1945–2000

Paul Huth and Benjamin Valentino[1]

The killing of civilians is a common consequence of armed conflict. We estimate that between 18 and 25 million civilians have died in civil, international, and colonial wars since 1945. In this chapter we argue that frequently civilian deaths during war are not just the result of "collateral damage" but are part of a deliberate policy of targeting noncombatant populations. Not all wars, however, result in the intentional killing of civilians on a massive scale. Why is it that some wars escalate to the massive, intentional killing of civilian populations?

Existing scholarship on genocide offers at least two possible explanations for the killing of civilians during war. First, mass killing during war may be driven by ethnic hatred and discrimination between combatant groups. Second, mass killing during war may be associated with nondemocratic regimes. These explanations have intuitive appeal, but in this chapter we argue that neither is adequate to explain variation in the intentional killing of civilians during war. We present an alternative theory, focusing on the strategic incentives for targeting civilians created by certain forms of combat. We argue that the intentional killing of civilians during war is often a calculated military strategy designed to defeat powerful guerrilla insurgencies. Unlike more conventional combatants, guerrillas often rely directly on the civilian population for logistical support. Directly defeating a large, well-organized guerrilla army can be extremely difficult because guerrilla forces themselves usually seek to avoid decisive engagements with opposing forces. As a result, counterinsurgent forces often choose to target the guerrillas' base of support in the population, which can in turn lead to the intentional killing of massive numbers of civilians.

In the remainder of the chapter we will define and discuss the term "mass killing" and present several explanations for mass killing during war derived from the literatures on genocide and guerrilla war. We will then present the results of statistical analyses to assess these explanations. A discussion of the current civil war in Darfur will follow to illustrate how our findings inform a better understanding of guerrilla warfare and its consequences for civilian populations.

Concept of Mass Killing

Mass killing is defined as *the intentional killing of a massive number of noncombatants during a war*. Victims of mass killing may be members of any kind of group

1 This chapter draws heavily upon some of our previously published work and has been reprinted with permission. See Valentino, Huth, and Balch-Lindsay (*International Organization*, volume 58, 2004). We would like to thank the National Science Foundation (SES 0241665) for its generous financial support of our research.

Table 9.1: Mass Killing in Wars (1945–2000)			
Guerrilla War	**Civil Wars**	**Start Year**	**End Year**
●	China-Communists	1946	1949
●	Colombia	1948	1962
●	China-Tibet	1956	1959
●	Vietnam, Rep. of	1960	1975
●	Iraq-Kurds	1961	1975
●	Sudan	1963	1971
	Nigeria-Biafra	1967	1969
	China-Cultural Revolution	1967	1969
●	Cambodia	1970	1975
●	Pakistan-Bangladesh	1971	1971
	Burundi	1972	1973
●	Guatemala	1974	1984
●	Ethiopia (Eritrea)	1974	1991
●	Ethiopia (Tigre-Ideology)	1974	1991
●	Angola	1975	1991
●	Indonesia-East Timor	1975	1982
●	Ethiopia (Ogaden)	1977	1982
●	Afghanistan	1978	1992
●	El Salvador	1979	1991
●	Uganda	1981	1986
●	Sudan	1983	1999
●	Iraq-Kurds	1985	1988
●	Somalia (Barre vs. SNM Isaaqs and others)	1988	1991
	Rwanda	1990	1994
●	Burundi	1991	1999
	Yugoslavia-Bosnia	1992	1995
●	Russia-Chechnya	1994	1996
Guerrilla War	**Extra-systemic Wars**	**Start Year**	**End Year**
●	Franco-Indochinese of 1945	1945	1954
●	Franco-Algerian of 1954	1954	1962
Guerrilla War	**International Wars**	**Start Year**	**End Year**
	Korean War	1950	1953

(ethnic, political, religious, etc.) as long as they are noncombatants and as long as their deaths were caused intentionally. We limit the mass killings analyzed to those carried out by national governments because states have been responsible for the great majority of mass killings since 1945. Although mass killing can occur in times of peace as well as war, we seek to explain only mass killings that occur during major armed conflicts.

A "massive number" is defined as at least 50,000 intentional deaths over the course of five years or less of warfare. Adopting this specific numerical criterion is to some extent arbitrary, but the high threshold we have selected helps establish a greater degree of confidence that massive violence has occurred despite the often poor quality of the data available on civilian fatalities. In Table 9.1 we list all 30 cases of mass killing during wars since 1945.

Two aspects of this definition require further elaboration. First, mass killing focuses on "intentional killing" in order to distinguish acts of mass killing from accidental deaths, including those caused by the spread of disease, the destruction of infrastructure, or by the interposition of civilian populations between armies during war. Deaths are considered intentional only if the affected civilian population is the *direct object* of a policy that results in widespread death. Of course, distinguishing the causes of death during war is extremely difficult in practice. In each war we have sought to identify major patterns of violence and descriptions of combatant motivations. Combined with estimates of the overall civilian fatalities during the conflict, we made the determination of whether a mass killing occurred. Second, the term "noncombatant" must be clarified. A noncombatant is defined as any unarmed person who is not a member of a professional or guerrilla military group and who does not directly participate in hostilities by attacking enemy personnel or property.[2] It should be noted that simply associating with combatants, providing food or other nonlethal military supplies to them, or participating in nonviolent political activities in support of armed forces does not convert a noncombatant to a combatant.

---

2 This definition is generally consistent with the definition of "civilian" adopted by the two 1977 additional Protocols of the Geneva Convention, see Bothe, Partsch and Solf 1982: 274–318.

Mass Killing and the Genocide Literature

The most relevant literatures to consider are those dealing with genocide. Unfortunately, adopting hypotheses from the literature on genocide to explain mass killing during war is complicated by two factors. First, scholars of genocide generally reject definitions based on absolute death tolls, focusing instead on the intent or attempt of perpetrators to destroy specific groups, in whole or in substantial part, which conforms to the UN Genocide Convention (e.g., Harff and Gurr 1996: 58). Second, genocide scholars have not developed specific theories to explain genocides that occur during war but have typically focused on theories based on common underlying motives for the violence whether it occurs during war or peace.

In light of these differences we should use caution in applying accepted arguments about the nature of genocide to explain mass killing during war. Nevertheless, there are at least three reasons for doing so. First, there is overlap between the two phenomena. For example, of the 49 episodes of genocide and politicide identified by Barbara Harff and Ted Gurr from 1945 to 2000, 31 (approximately 63 percent) meet our definition of mass killing (Harff and Gurr 1996: 49–51; Harff 2003).[3] Second, not all scholars studying genocide restrict their definitions to attempts to destroy ethnic or political groups as such. For example, the late Leo Kuper (1981: 46) believed that the intentional killing of civilians such as the strategic bombings of the Second World War should be considered genocide. Other scholars interested in this kind of violence have simply abandoned the term *genocide* to examine the broader universe of intentional killing of civilians. Thus, Rudolph Rummel has proposed the term *democide*, which he defines as the "intentional government killing of an unarmed person or people" (Rummel 1994: 36). Third, although scholars of genocide seldom limit their analyses to periods of warfare, several previous studies have suggested a strong relationship between armed conflict and some forms of genocide (Fein 1993a; Fein 1993b; Krain 1997; Markusen and Kopf 1995; Harff 2003). Indeed, 27 of the 49 (approximately 54 percent) cases of genocide and politicide identified by Harff and Gurr occurred during large-scale armed conflicts (as defined below).

From the literature on genocide we identify two factors that might plausibly account for variation in mass killing during wars.[4] First, many genocide scholars have argued that deep social cleavages, severe hatred and discrimination, or dehumanizing attitudes between ethnic groups can be important causes of genocide (Kuper 1981; Charny 1982: 206–207; Kelman 1973: 25–61; Chalk and Jonassohn 1990: 27–28; Hirsch and Smith 1988). Different scholars argue that these cleavages promote genocide by polarizing society, increasing the likelihood of intergroup conflict, facilitating the identification and collective punishment of victim groups, or by eroding norms of moral responsibility between groups. As a result, ethnic conflicts

---

3 The remaining 18 of Harff's cases were excluded as mass killing because none was estimated to have taken more than 50,000 lives in five or fewer years.

4 A broader range of factors that may contribute to genocide, although not necessarily in times of war, are described in Harff 2003.

in general are more likely to experience mass killing than conflicts waged primarily over political or economic issues.

A second factor highlighted by some scholars of genocide is the character of the regimes involved in the conflict. Several authors have suggested that the accountability of democratic political institutions and the normative orientation of democratic leaders make them less likely to engage in genocide and mass killing than other forms of government (see Fein 1993a; Fein 1993b; Poe and Tate 1994; Henderson 1991; Davenport 1999; Rummel 1995). Barbara Harff, for example, argues that democratic institutions "reduce the likelihood of armed conflict and all but eliminate the risk that it will lead to geno-/politicides" (Harff 2003: 72).

Mass Killing and Guerrilla War

We argue that understanding why states resort to mass killing during wars requires an analysis of the interaction between the specific military tactics employed by combatants. We argue that states engaged in wars with opponents employing guerrilla tactics can face significant incentives to resort to mass killing.

Guerrilla war has three central characteristics. First, guerrilla warfare relies primarily on irregular forces, organized in small, highly mobile units, and operating mostly without heavy weaponry. Second, guerrilla forces avoid decisive set-piece battles in favor of campaigns marked by limited attacks designed to increase an opponent's political, military, and economic costs, as opposed to defeating military forces directly. Third, clear lines of battle in guerrilla warfare are rare and guerrilla forces often operate in territories under the military control of their opponents.

States engaged in wars with opponents employing guerrilla tactics can face significant incentives to resort to mass killing.

It is a fourth characteristic of guerrilla warfare, however, one common to many, but not all guerrilla conflicts, that is the most critical for understanding the causal connections between guerrilla tactics and mass killing. Unlike conventional military forces, guerrilla armies often rely directly on the local population for food, shelter, supplies, and intelligence, as well as to act as a form of "human camouflage" into which the guerrillas can disappear to avoid detection.

Guerrilla warfare can be an extraordinarily powerful weapon. Skillfully applied, guerrilla tactics can provide even relatively small and weak groups with the capability to inflict significant military and political costs on an opponent, even when that opponent is capable of fielding vastly superior conventional forces. Determined guerrilla forces have proven extraordinarily difficult to defeat, even by the most advanced Western armies. Conventional military tactics are poorly suited to combating an enemy who seeks to avoid direct military confrontations, has no permanent lines of supply or communication, and whose forces are often indistinguishable from the civilian population.

The support of the local population may be one of the great strengths of guerrilla forces, but it can also be a weakness in that armies determined to defeat a guerrilla opponent may adopt a strategy designed to sever the guerrillas from their base of support in the people. Unlike guerrilla forces themselves, populated civilian centers are largely immobile and nearly impossible to conceal. As such, civilian populations offer an obvious target for counterinsurgent operations. Thus government violence against civilians during war is often designed to try to reduce civilian support for armed guerrilla forces and thereby weaken the threat posed by a guerrilla strategy. This analysis leads us to a third causal factor that may drive mass killings. The use of guerrilla tactics by an armed opposition will increase the likelihood that a state will engage in mass killing during a large-scale conflict.

Armies determined to defeat a guerrilla opponent may adopt a strategy designed to sever the guerrillas from their base of support in the people.

Our argument so far suggests that states facing guerrilla warfare should be more likely to engage in mass killing than states fighting in conventional forms of warfare. Yet most regimes facing guerrilla insurgencies have not resorted to mass killing. Of the 81 states fighting large-scale guerrilla insurgencies from 1945 to 2000, 27 used mass killing according to our research. Because we argue that mass killing during guerrilla war is a means to an end, we also argue that governments have little incentive to resort to mass killing if they believe less violent strategies will be effective. We argue therefore that two additional factors, the fourth and fifth overall, play significant roles in determining whether a regime facing a guerrilla insurgency will respond with mass killing.

States are more likely to respond to guerrilla insurgencies with massive violence when the guerrillas pose a major military threat to the regime. When guerrilla groups are small and weak, less violent tactics are more likely to keep the insurgency in check. When an insurgency, however, threatens the political stability of regimes, state leaders are more willing to accept the risks and costs associated with more violent strategies. Accordingly, the fourth overall factor that influences mass killing relates to the extent of military threat posed by the guerrillas to the regime and its political survival.

Finally, a fifth factor is the extent of the ties between the guerrillas and the local civilian population. We have argued that mass killing in counterinsurgency warfare is often a calculated government strategy intended to separate guerrilla forces from their support network in the population. Not all guerrilla forces, however, depend upon the local civilian population for support. Guerrillas may receive the majority of their support from abroad (Byman et al. 2001) rather than from the domestic civilian population, or some guerrilla groups simply may fail to win widespread support or even seek such support (e.g., Guevara 1997; Laqueur 1976: 330–338). In such cases, states face far fewer incentives to target civilians.

Box 9.1: Five Factors that Drive Mass Killing in War	
From research on genocide	Mass killing will be more likely during **ethnic or "identity conflicts"** than during political or ideological conflicts.
	Highly autocratic regimes are more likely to engage in mass killing during armed conflicts than highly democratic regimes.
From analysis of interaction between military tactics used by combatants	The use of **guerrilla tactics** by an armed opposition will increase the likelihood that a state will engage in mass killing during a large-scale conflict.
	States are more likely to respond to guerrilla insurgencies with massive violence when the **guerrillas pose a major military threat to the regime.**
	Greater civilian support for guerrillas increases the likelihood that a state will engage in mass killing during guerrilla wars.

Box 9.1 summarizes the five factors we have identified as key drivers of mass killing during wars. The first two are adapted from the literature on genocide. We have derived the latter three from an analysis of the interactions between tactics employed by combatants.

Dataset and Key Variables

Our expectations on the causes of mass killing are tested on a data set of all wars from 1945 to 2000. A war is a large-scale armed conflict between two organized armed groups.[5] These wars may take place in a civil, international, or colonial context. We limit armed conflicts to those involving at least one group that represents the national government of a state. A war is coded as starting on the first year in which direct military actions result in at least 1,000 total fatalities (including both combatants and civilians). If fewer than 200 total annual fatalities are recorded for three or more consecutive years, the war is coded as having ended on the first of those three years, even if fighting continues at very low levels in subsequent years. In addition, in order to exclude cases of completely one-sided fighting, at least 100 total military fatalities must be incurred on the part of government forces during the war.

Our analysis of wars focuses on the two primary belligerents involved in the armed conflict. The primary belligerents are defined as the forces with the primary political and military control of the combat. In the case of civil wars, only the government is considered at risk to commit mass killing. In international conflicts, on the other hand, both sides are by definition government actors and could potentially engage in mass killing. All international wars, therefore, are included as dyads in this data set, with each of the two primary belligerents in the war alternatively playing the role of the government and opposition. Utilizing these coding rules, we have

---

5 Our codings draw upon lists provided in Singer and Small (1994), Licklider (1995), Doyle and Sambanis (2000), Wallensteen and Sollenberg (2001), and Regan (2000).

identified 147 cases of war since 1945. One hundred thirteen are classified as civil wars, 20 are classified as international wars, and 14 are classified as colonial wars.[6]

To evaluate the extent to which our expectations are borne out in the data from these 147 cases of warfare, we construct a statistical model that will systematically assess the impact, if any, of each of the five factors on mass killings. Proceeding in this fashion requires us to construct quantified measurements for each of the central concepts we describe above. Due to space constraints, we offer a shortened presentation of our measurement procedures in Box 9.2. Readers interested in a full discussion can consult Valentino, Huth, and Balch-Lindsay (2004) or the *Peace and Conflict* companion Web site (*http://www.cidcm.umd.edu/pc*) for more detail.

Our descriptions of the various measurement procedures we have created are relatively straightforward, but an additional comment is warranted for one—the level of civilian support for guerrillas. One potentially serious problem with relying on the peak level of civilian support as an independent variable in our model is the possibility that mass killing itself may actually lead to increased civilian support for the guerrillas. Massive violence against civilians may cause the targeted populations to become alienated from the regime or seek protection from government attacks by giving their support to the guerrillas. In such cases, the causal arrow linking civilian support to mass killing in the model described above could be backwards. Political methodologists refer to relationships in which the possibility exists that a particular variable, in this case civilian support for guerrillas, could be both a cause and a consequence of another variable as *endogenous* relationships.

Ultimately, there is no way to exclude entirely the possibility that some of the effects of this variable on the probability of mass killing reflect endogeneity in its measurement. The results associated with this variable, therefore, should be interpreted with some degree of caution. On the other hand, there are also strong reasons to believe that this endogenous process is not the dominant cause of high civilian support for guerrilla insurgencies and, therefore, that a measure of peak civilian support may still be of considerable value in explaining mass killing during guerrilla warfare. First, approximately 47 percent of guerrilla wars with high civilian support do not experience mass killing. High civilian support for guerrillas, therefore, cannot be solely a reaction to government policies of mass killing. Second, it is important to note that even relatively widespread killings on the part of the government do not invariably generate widespread public support for guerrillas. Third, in the cases of mass killing we have identified, accounts of the military conflicts from secondary sources systematically described patterns of civilian support for guerrillas prior to large-scale government attacks on civilians. Although both support for guerrillas and the level of violence against civilians tend to escalate over the course of the conflict, government violence seems to be targeted against suspected supporters and thus causally prior to mass killing.

---

6 Our classification of civil and international conflicts differs somewhat from some other data sets. When international intervention occurs during a domestic dispute, the conflict is coded as a civil war if it met all the criteria for civil war prior to the intervention and if the subsequent combat occurred primarily within the borders of that state, even if an international power or powers subsequently assumed the primary role in the fighting.

Box 9.2: Key Concepts—Definitions and Measurement Procedures	
Dependent Variable	
Mass Killing	The intentional killing of at least 50,000 noncombatants over the course of five years or less of warfare.
Independent Variables	
Guerrilla Warfare	Defined dichotomously as either being present during the course of a war or not. Our procedure is based on the definition of guerrilla tactics presented above. The determination was based on the primary tactics utilized by the opposition (guerrilla versus conventional tactics). The primary tactics were defined as the type of tactics to which the opposition devoted the greatest amount of time during the conflict. When the opposition devoted approximately equal amounts of time and effort to both guerrilla and conventional tactics, the opposition tactics were coded as mixed. Guerrilla tactics were determined to be present whenever they were the primary tactics for opposition groups or whenever the use of tactics was mixed.
Degree of Threat Posed by Guerrillas	This measurement is based on two interrelated aspects of guerrilla opposition groups: their size and the extent of fatalities imposed on government forces engaged in the conflict. We define the degree of guerrilla threat dichotomously by setting a threshold that sets apart the cases featuring the highest and most substantial degree of threat. That threshold is satisfied when the value for either component places the case in the top quartile of all cases. For the size of the guerrilla force, a case qualifies for a high degree of threat when the size of the guerrilla force at its peak number exceeds 37,500. For government force fatalities, the threat level is determined to be high whenever the number of fatalities as a percentage of all government forces engaged in the conflict exceeds 20 percent. Whenever one or both of these conditions is satisfied, a high degree of guerrilla threat is said to be present. This measurement applies only to those cases in which opposition groups employed guerrilla or mixed tactics.
Degree of Civilian Support for Guerrillas	We define the extent of civilian support dichotomously, determining a high degree of civilian support exists whenever the number of civilians actively providing logistical support to guerrilla groups exceeds 100,000. Active logistical support is defined as providing food, shelter, information, portage, or other logistical aid to the guerrilla forces. This measurement applies only to those cases in which opposition groups employed guerrilla or mixed tactics.
Ethnic/Identity Conflict	We utilize the coding of "identity based" conflicts provided by Roy Licklider. He defines identity-based conflicts as "those driven primarily by ethnic-religious-identity issues" (Licklider 1995: 685). Since Licklider's data do not include codes for international wars, we code international wars as identity conflicts if a major issue in the conflict involved a dispute over the political control of territory populated by groups that had ethnic or religious ties to one of the primary combatants (Huth 1996; Huth and Allee 2002).
Regime Type	We utilize data on regime type collected in the Polity IV data set (Marshall and Jaggers 2000). To estimate the influence of highly democratic regimes on the probability of mass killing when compared to highly autocratic regimes, we construct two dichotomous indicators. First, regimes receiving a combined score of +7 or higher on the Polity IV scale were assigned a value of 1 and all other states received a value of 0. The second indicator, representing mid-range polities, was coded as 1 if the regime received a score between +6 to −6 inclusive.

Data Analysis and Findings

To assess the significance of each of the factors we outlined above, we estimate three statistical models. Key findings on the causes of mass killings during wars are summarized below. We will present our results without formally presenting coefficient estimation results in a series of tables. For those interested in the full equations, see Valentino, Huth, and Balch-Lindsay (2004) or the *Peace and Conflict* companion Web site. In the first model we test the general relationship between guerrilla warfare and mass killing during all wars from 1945 to 2000. In the second model we focus on our expectations regarding the specific characteristics of guerrilla wars (level of threat and extent of civilian support) to the likelihood of mass killing. In this analysis, the population of cases was limited to guerrilla wars from 1945 to 2000. In the third model we return to the population of all wars from 1945 to 2000 and test the explanatory power of these same two factors relating to guerrilla war characteristics in accounting for the incidence of mass killing.

Across all of the statistical models the results strongly support our theory of guerrilla warfare and mass killing. Guerrilla warfare proved to have highly significant and powerful effects on the likelihood of mass killing, strongly confirming our expectations. Our expectations about the characteristics of guerrilla wars were also strongly supported by the results. The guerrilla threat and civilian support variables were highly statistically significant and demonstrated major substantive effects on the probability of mass killing in all stages of the analysis. The dichotomous measure of regime type was also significant in all three equations tested and produced relatively strong substantive effects, supporting our argument about the impact of democratic government on reducing the risks of mass killing. Identity conflict was not significant in any of the three models, casting doubt on the argument that mass killings are most likely in these types of conflict settings.

> *Across all of the statistical models…guerrilla warfare proved to have highly significant and powerful effects on the likelihood of mass killing.*

Let us now turn to each of the three models to discuss the results in more detail. In the first model, which includes all wars, our expectations about the impact of guerrilla wars were strongly confirmed by the results. Guerrilla warfare was highly significant, increasing the risk of mass killing by almost five times. Democracy also proved significant. Full democracies were only 38 percent as likely as highly autocratic states to engage in mass killing during armed conflicts.

In the second model the dataset analyzed consisted of all guerrilla wars from 1945 to 2000 (75 in total). Both the level of military threat posed by the guerrillas and the level of active civilian support for the guerrillas proved to be highly significant.[7] A high guerrilla threat increased the risk of mass killing by 2.4 times, while high civilian support increased the risk of mass killing by 13.4 times.

---

7 These findings are consistent with and extend the findings of Timothy Wickham-Crowley's comparative study of several cases of guerrilla warfare in Latin America from 1956 to 1976. Wickham-Crowley found that "the deeper and more thorough the overlap between the guerrilla combatants and the civilian population, the more likely that the government would engage in terror against the civilian population" (Wickham-Crowley 1990: 226).

As we noted above, any results associated with the civilian support variable must be interpreted with a degree of caution due to the possibility of endogeneity (i.e., the possibility that the onset of mass killings causes civilian support of guerrillas to increase). On the other hand, the strong association between guerrilla war and mass killing should help to diminish these concerns to some extent. Our theoretical model suggests that guerrilla warfare is associated with mass killing because guerrilla wars tend to involve more direct civilian participation than other forms of combat. In other words, civilian support provides a single causal mechanism that explains both the general association between guerrilla warfare and mass killing, as well as the increased likelihood of mass killing in those guerrilla wars with the highest levels of civilian support. Any argument contending that civilian support simply reflects the reaction of the population to a pre-existing policy of massive violence must also explain why mass killing occurs with much less frequency in forms of combat other than guerrilla warfare.

In the second model, democracy maintains significance and produces very strong substantive effects. Highly democratic states were only 20 percent as likely as highly autocratic ones to commit mass killing during guerrilla wars. In contrast, once again we find that the identity conflict variable is not significant.

In the third model estimated, we tested the impact of variables specifically relating to guerrilla conflicts in all cases of wars from 1945 to 2000. Both the level of guerrilla threat and the level of civilian support remain highly significant, with large risk ratios. The marginal effects of these variables on the probability of mass killing during guerrilla wars are presented in Figure 9.1. In this figure we report the change in the relative risk ratios of mass killing for each of the significant variables based on the results of our third model in which a given variable is increased from low risk to high risk values while other variables in the model are held constant.

Both the level of civilian support and guerrilla threat produce extremely powerful effects on the probability of mass killing. To illustrate those effects, we use the model to examine a hypothetical baseline war in which high-level threats posed by guerrilla forces are absent. We note the estimated risk for mass killing in this setting and then modify the model to reflect the presence of a high-level guerrilla threat. In that case, the model's estimate for the risk of mass killing increases by six times. Figure 9.1 presents a graphical depiction of the estimated change in risk. The left-most vertical bar depicts the range of statistical confidence for the estimate while the red circle depicts the actual estimated change in risk resulting from the presence of a high-level guerrilla threat. Similarly, varying the level of civilian support from no support to high-level support produced very powerful effects. The risk of mass killing increased by about eight times in wars in which guerrilla insurgents received high levels of support from the civilian population. When the guerrillas both posed a major threat and received high support from the civilian population, mass killing was 18 times more likely. These variables not only produce a very strong increase in the relative probability of mass killing, they also result in very high absolute probabilities of this kind of violence. Indeed, our estimate of the probability of mass killing when both civilian support and guerrilla threat are high and other variables

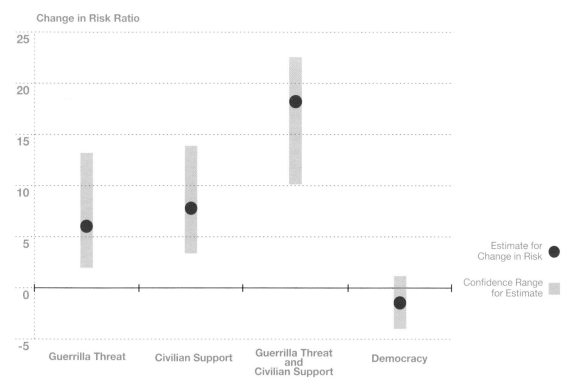

Figure 9.1: Impact of Causal Factors on Risk of Mass Killings

Change in Risk Ratio

Estimate for Change in Risk

Confidence Range for Estimate

Guerrilla Threat   Civilian Support   Guerrilla Threat and Civilian Support   Democracy

NOTE: The graph depicts the change in the relative risk of mass killings in four circumstances involving changes to key variables. The red circle represents the estimated change in the risk ratio due to changes in the value of underlying variables. The bars extending vertically from the circle represent the range of statistical confidence surrounding the estimate. The range of the bars covers a confidence interval within which we can say with 95 percent certainty that the "true" estimate lies somewhere within.

are at their moderate baseline values was about .77. Although this combination of extreme circumstances is rare, these results suggest that nondemocratic states attempting to defeat powerful and popularly backed guerrilla insurgencies face very powerful incentives to target civilian populations.

Regime type also had important effects on the probability of mass killing. The risk of mass killing decreased almost twofold when comparing highly democratic regimes to very autocratic regimes. Although this result suggests that strong democracies are substantially less likely than autocratic states to respond to powerful and popular guerrilla insurgencies with mass killing, it should be noted that even full democracies have about a .53 estimated probability of mass killing when both guerrilla threat and civilian support are set at high values while other variables are at their baseline values.[8]

---

8 Sixteen of 81 guerrilla wars involved democratic regimes, according to our definition (most of these conflicts involved democratic states engaged in extra-systemic/colonial wars). Among these wars, the guerrillas posed a major threat in four and had high levels of civilian support in eight. The guerrillas both posed a major threat and had high levels of support in four cases. Of these, three resulted in mass killings: France in Indochina, 1945–1954; France in Algeria, 1954–1962; and the US in Vietnam, 1965–1975.

Darfur as a Case Illustration

We think that much of the violence against civilians in Darfur since 2003 can be understood in terms of our general argument that state sponsored mass killing during guerrilla wars can often be an explicit counterinsurgency strategy designed to sever popular guerrilla forces from their base of civilian supporters and thereby attempt to weaken the threat posed by the guerrillas.

First, we want to establish that a policy of deliberate mass killing of civilians has been carried out by the Sudanese government and its local allies. The evidence on this question seems clear-cut in that multiple NGOs, individual researchers, the UN, and many states converge on the fact that the Sudanese armed forces in alliance with Janjaweed militia forces have engaged in a brutal and deliberate policy of targeting selected regions populated by Fur civilians. Estimates of violent civilian deaths directly caused by armed attacks range from no fewer than 80,000 to well over 200,000. In addition, approximately two million Fur civilians have been forcibly displaced from their towns and villages, resulting in 200,000 or more deaths due to conflict-related disease or hunger (e.g., de Waal 2004; Human Rights Watch 2005; Amnesty International 2006; Physicians on Human Rights 2006).

Second, this targeting of Fur civilians has taken place in the context of a guerrilla insurgency within Darfur against Sudanese regional government authorities. The recent origins of the current civil war in Darfur can be traced back to the outbreak of armed violence against the Darfur regional government since 1989 (de Waal 2004) but the insurgency escalated in early 2003. Since 2003 two armed groups have been leading the insurgency: the Sudanese Liberation Army/Movement (SLA/SLM) and the Justice and Equality Movement (JEM). Many armed groups have splintered off from these two main organizations and some have operated under an umbrella organization known as the National Redemption Front. Both the SLA and JEM have drawn considerable support from the Fur civilian populations and have operated largely in areas populated by the Fur (de Waal 2004; Human Rights Watch 2005). The SLA and JEM launched very successful attacks against Sudanese government targets in early 2003, and soon the Sudanese government realized that the insurgency posed a clear threat. As de Waal argues (2004: 12), "The rebels in Darfur had mobility, good intelligence and popular support," and he goes on to argue that the Sudanese government understood that it was "faced with a revolt that outran the capacity of the country's tired and overstretched army."

Third, the response of the Sudanese government was to terrorize the civilian Fur population through armed attacks and to forcibly displace whole towns and villages as part of what might be termed a classic counterinsurgency strategy of trying to isolate the armed rebels from their civilian base of support through a policy of "draining the sea." For example, an Amnesty International study (2006) concludes that "The Sudanese government and the Janjaweed deliberately targeted civilians of the same ethnicity as the rebel groups as a counterinsurgency strategy. Some 85,000 people have been killed, around 200,000 have died as a result of conflict-related hunger or disease, and more than two million people have been displaced." Similarly, a Human Rights Watch report argues that, "The SLA's presence and attacks prompted a massive response by the Sudanese government forces and militias that targeted civilians and civilian villages…. The government's scorched earth campaign of ground and air attacks around the Sindu Hills had removed almost all existing or potential support bases for the rebellion…" (Human Rights Watch 2005: 11). These attacks are described as systematic and coordinated over a wide geographic region and targeted specifically at towns and villages populated by Fur civilians while other nearby "Arab" towns and villages were not targeted (Human Rights Watch 2005: 11–17). As noted, the result has been that an estimated two million civilians have become refugees as a result of this policy and perhaps more than 400,000 total civilian deaths.

Conclusion: War by Other Means

In this chapter we have argued that mass killing during war can often be a calculated military strategy designed to overcome the difficult problems associated with combating major guerrilla insurgencies. Mass killing, in other words, sometimes can be war by other means. Hypotheses derived from the literature on genocide do not account for the variation in mass killing during war. We found that ethnic conflicts were not significantly more likely to escalate to mass killing than political or ideological conflicts. As some scholars expected, democracies were less likely than highly authoritarian states to resort to mass killing during war, but the impact of regime type was relatively weak. When faced with powerful and popular guerrilla insurgencies, even highly democratic states are likely to resort to mass killing.

As noted above, these findings should not be considered as conclusive evidence for or against hypotheses about the causes of genocide because of the important differences between genocide and mass killing as defined here. Because many cases commonly considered as genocide are included among the list of mass killings examined in this chapter, however, and because many of these episodes occurred in the context of guerrilla wars, the results suggest that counterinsurgency may be a motive for at least some genocides as well. Indeed, 23 of the 49 cases (approximately 47 percent) of genocide and politicide identified by Harff and Gurr during the period between 1945 and 2000 occurred during guerrilla wars.

Interestingly, although there is strong evidence that states resort to mass killing in an effort to defeat insurgencies, in practice this strategy seems to have produced decidedly mixed results for its perpetrators, especially in the long run. The Soviet Union, for example, was unable to prevail in its war in Afghanistan despite a brutal counterinsurgency campaign that left over one million people dead. As long as Soviet leaders were willing to pour troops and resources into the war, they managed to prevent the collapse of the Soviet-backed Afghani regime. Yet the Soviets were unable to defeat the Mujahideen guerrillas, and the costs of the war, including between 15,000 and 26,000 Soviet troops killed in action, ultimately proved too much to bear, prompting a withdrawal from Afghanistan in 1988.

Although we cannot examine this question in detail in this chapter, we believe that mass killing has often failed as a military strategy for the same reasons that states are hesitant to employ it in the first place. The costs and risks of mass killing, including its potential to provoke greater opposition, alienate supporters, and draw third parties into the conflict often outweigh its potential as a counterinsurgency strategy. Mass killing can keep guerrilla forces at bay, but even the most extreme levels of violence are often insufficient to decisively defeat mass-based insurgencies.

If this is so, why do states continue to employ this kind of strategy in guerrilla wars? Why, for example, did Russia revert to brutal attacks on civilians in its war in Chechnya, only a few years after its withdrawal from Afghanistan? We believe that states facing powerful and popular guerrilla opponents have continued to resort to mass killing because less violent strategies for counterinsurgency have proven at least equally costly and prone to failure. Regimes facing well-organized guerrilla opponents with strong support from the civilian population have few attractive options for meeting this threat. Counterinsurgency theorists have often touted "hearts and minds" strategies designed to win public support through the promise of material benefits and political reforms as more humane alternatives to counterinsurgency. These strategies may be effective when insurgent groups lack strong public support, but they are seldom practical for regimes facing mass-based insurgencies. Few regimes possess the resources necessary to provide meaningful, lasting improvements in the lives of hundreds of thousands or millions of disaffected citizens. For leaders determined to stave off defeat and unwilling to make major political concessions to the opposition, therefore, mass killing simply may appear as the most attractive choice among a set of highly unattractive options.

Although the results of the analyses presented in this chapter strongly suggest that guerrilla wars present a major risk of provoking mass killing, counterinsurgency clearly is not the only motivation for the intentional killing of civilians during war. The British starvation blockade of Germany during the First World War, for example, is estimated to have killed at least 250,000 civilians (Gilbert 1994: 391). In the Second World War, the United States intentionally killed between 268,000 and 900,000 Japanese civilians and, in collaboration with Great Britain, between 300,000 and 600,000 Germans (Sherry 1987: 260, 314). At least 6 of the 30 state-sponsored mass killings that occurred during armed conflict since 1945 occurred in nonguerrilla conflicts (See Table 9.1).[9] Furthermore, as noted above, sub-state groups can also perpetrate mass killing during the course of conflict. The theories developed and tested in this chapter cannot explain these events. Developing and testing theories that can help us understand these cases, therefore, represents an important area for further research.

We believe that states facing powerful and popular guerrilla opponents have continued to resort to mass killing because less violent strategies for counterinsurgency have proven at least equally costly and prone to failure. Regimes facing well-organized guerrilla opponents with strong support from the civilian population have few attractive options for meeting this threat.

---

9 Two additional mass killings occurred in mixed guerrilla/nonguerrilla cases.

10. INTERNATIONAL PEACEKEEPING: THE UN VERSUS REGIONAL ORGANIZATIONS

Peter Wallensteen and Birger Heldt

An old theme in the debate on international peacekeeping concerns whether it should be carried out by the United Nations, regional organizations (such as the OAS, OAU/AU, ECOWAS, EU, OSCE, or NATO), or ad hoc coalitions of willing states. Chapters VI and VII of the UN Charter have been used to authorize UN-led operations, whereas Chapter VIII has given additional legitimacy to non-UN operations. It may even be argued that the Charter (Article 52) expresses that the UN should be the last resort, while regional organizations and neighboring states should be given priority, when it comes to dealing with threats to international peace and security. Only when such initiatives have failed may they be referred to the UN.

Building on data compiled by Birger Heldt at the Folke Bernadotte Academy, Stockholm, Sweden, this chapter explores the empirical landscape of this old question. Covering 1948–2005, it compares peacekeeping in different organizational frameworks. Box 10.1 presents the guiding definition for a peacekeeping operation. Focusing on patterns in terms of number, location, and type of conflict, it identifies trends, similarities, as well as differences between peacekeeping operations carried out by the UN and those conducted by regional organizations or ad hoc coalitions of states. It also summarizes available evidence on success rates and offers some conclusions on the significance of the organizational framework for international action.

The Arguments

The common positive arguments favoring the use of a global organization for peacekeeping is that it has a strong standing in international law, access to global resources (finances, troops, logistics), and competence. This means it can act in an even-handed manner vis-à-vis the conflicting parties and in conflicts around the world. There are equally compelling arguments against regional organizations that consequently favor the use of the global institution. For instance, it is often claimed that regional organizations are too closely tied to the developments in their vicinity, and that strong regional powers may use the organizations to their own advantage. Thus, a global organization offers capacity and an element of protection, particularly for weaker regional or local actors. Common positive arguments for regional organizations and ad hoc coalitions contend that they may have more local knowledge and are thus more capable of dealing with local conditions, have equipment adapted to local conditions, are quicker to reach decisions on deployment, and are closer to the scene and consequently can be deployed more quickly than the UN.

| Box 10.1: Defining Peacekeeping Operations |

In this study, **a peacekeeping operation** is defined as a third-party state intervention that:

- involves the deployment of military troops and/or military observers and/or civilian police in a target state;

- is, according to the mandate (as specified in multilateral agreements, peace agreements, or resolutions of the UN or regional organizations), established for the purpose of separating conflict parties, monitoring ceasefires, maintaining buffer zones, and taking responsibility for the security situation (among other things) between formerly, potentially, or presently warring parties; and

- is neutral towards the conflict parties, but not necessarily impartial towards their behavior.

This definition has fewer implications for UN-led operations than for many peace- and capacity-building missions. Such missions, for instance by the Organization for Security and Co-operation in Europe (OSCE), the European Union (EU), and the UN, are excluded. In many of these cases, the personnel were either civilian and/or had no operational duties but focused, for instance, on training local police. The Kosovo Verification Mission and the Sri Lanka Monitoring Mission are excluded, as only civilian personnel were deployed. The definition also excludes operations such as the present, large multinational force in Iraq as well as ISAF (International Security Assistance Force) in Afghanistan. In the former case it was not a neutral force interpositioned between two or more identified warring parties, but an occupation force much like Operation Uphold Democracy in Haiti 1994–1995; in the latter case, the operation was not an interposition force, but a force initially deployed to assist in maintaining security in Kabul.

Although conflicting and possible to refute by historical examples, the various arguments are convincing. Therefore, it may not be surprising to find that during the past ten years the UN has attempted to increase the contribution of regional actors to peacekeeping, while at the same time trying to coordinate global and regional actors. This UN-led process is often said to have been initiated by the UN Secretary-General's report *An Agenda for Peace* (Boutros-Ghali 1992). Noting the dramatically increased demand on the UN for peacekeeping, the report urged a larger contribution by regional actors to peacekeeping. At the initiative of the UN, a series of high-level meetings between the UN and regional organizations were held in 1994, 1998, 2001, 2003, and 2005 (cf. Heldt and Wallensteen 2006). These meetings have touched upon how regional actors can make a larger contribution (including peacekeeping) to address threats to international peace and security, and how such efforts can be coordinated with UN efforts (Heldt and Wallensteen 2006).

However, prudence has been urged, in that the choice between UN or non-UN efforts should be made on a case-by-case basis rather than having non-UN operations as the first choice. This note of caution has been based on the observation that regions with crises and conflicts are often characterized by insufficient capacity to carry out peacekeeping. In essence, regions (such as Africa) with the greatest demand for peacekeeping are said to have the least peacekeeping capacity. This in turn implies that regions (such as Europe) with the lowest demand for peacekeeping, also have the largest capacity. This has led to concerns that a larger regional responsibility for peacekeeping will deplete the UN's pool of well-trained and well-equipped peacekeeping resources. A fear is that troop-contributing countries will use their resources for regional operations to the detriment of the most conflict-prone regions. Yet, if the regions with the lowest demand for peacekeeping also have the largest capacity, then these regions will not experience a large demand for peacekeeping in their own backyards. This suggests that, in the end, these regions' peacekeeping capacity may still be placed at the disposal of the UN.

Global Patterns

Because the arguments concerning both UN and regional organizations are compelling, it is not unexpected to find that the number of peacekeeping operations is virtually identical for the two types of organizational frameworks. There were 13 ongoing non-UN operations as of December 2005, at a time when the UN was carrying out 15 operations. This striking numerical similarity applies also when looking at all operations since 1948: from 1948 to 2005 non-UN actors initiated 67 operations, while for the UN the corresponding number is 59. The patterns are very similar also in terms of historical trends as found in Figure 10.1 (Note, Figure 10.1 and all other figures in this chapter reflect biannual observations for number of operations). During the Cold War the number of missions was small, whether within or outside the UN. Dag Hammarskjöld, the UN Secretary-General at the time, argued against activities outside the UN framework, claiming that the UN was the foremost body for international peace and security and could not be bypassed (Urquhart 1994).

Data for the period up to the end of the Cold War, around 1990, do not show dramatic shifts in absolute numbers, which are low. The number of UN operations started to increase in 1988, while the growth in operations carried out by other

Figure 10.1: Number of Peacekeeping Operations (1948–2005)

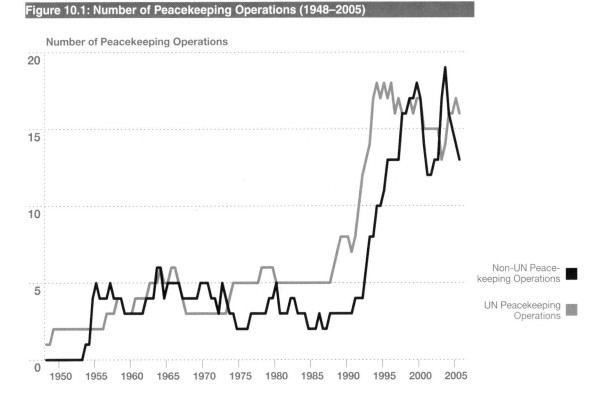

Number of Peacekeeping Operations

Non-UN Peace-keeping Operations

UN Peacekeeping Operations

actors began in 1992. This increase occurs not just as the Cold War ends, but also coincides with an increase in wars and armed conflicts in the first part of the 1990s—when more than 50 annual armed conflicts were recorded globally by the Uppsala Conflict Data Program. Another observation is that the number of both types of operations is comparable after the mid-1990s, just after the UN explicitly started to encourage more regional peacekeeping efforts. The trends appear to indicate that the UN may have inspired or induced other actors, notably regional organizations, to take on peacekeeping.

The UN may have inspired or induced…regional organizations to take on peacekeeping.

While we find more UN operations from the mid-1970s to the early 1990s, there are more ongoing non-UN operations during parts of the 1990s. That may be attributed to the developments of one particular region: Europe, and Europe's increased willingness and capacity to deal with threats to the region's peace and security. A large part of the non-UN operations in recent years consists of missions deployed by the EU, OSCE, and NATO. As such, Europe's ability and desire to deal with regional security is presently unsurpassed by any other region. Apparently, an interplay has been at work, where one body took over responsibility from another, and where many non-UN missions were either authorized, or recognized, by UN Security Council Resolutions. Thus, regional initiatives cannot be regarded as challenges to UN authority. It appears that the leading actors are in agreement on the UN's unique standing in international law. To support this, we can observe that 28 of the non-UN operations were welcomed, authorized, endorsed, commended, or approved by Security Council Resolutions. For one reason or another, the remaining operations never reached the Security Council's agenda.

While overall there have been fewer UN-led operations, there were more UN operations at almost every point in time. This pattern can best be explained by a longer average duration for UN operations and as such confirms that the UN has had a primacy in peacekeeping. There is no evidence in favor of a consistent pattern of regionalization of peacekeeping for the past ten years, as has often been claimed: only during a few brief periods have UN-led operations been in the minority. Burden-sharing may instead be a useful concept for describing this historical pattern, as it means that costs are shared regardless of their size and without concern for UN and regional peacekeeping abilities.

Whereas regional organizations can decide on their own and through their appropriate organs to welcome UN operations, UN member states are not in a legal position to decline UN action, when decisions are made under Chapter VII. However, since the end of the Cold War it has been rare for the choice of organizational framework to be stated in such a strong manner. Polemics have also given way to arguments of efficiency and capability. The discussion has moved to questions such as: Which organization is best equipped—politically, financially, militarily, culturally—to act in a particular crisis situation? Which ones are already strained by peacekeeping tasks? Where is there some free capacity?

There are differences with respect to the type of conflict in which the peacekeeping operation is placed. A significant dimension is the one of interstate and intrastate conflicts. It is worth exploring, as intrastate conflict customarily has been seen to be outside the scope of international organizations. For instance, global bodies have been regarded as more threatening to state sovereignty, partly as they appear to invite major power interests within a state's borders. Thus, interstate conflicts may get priority, particularly for a global organization.

For the whole period there were 17 UN-led operations in interstate conflicts and 18 non-UN operations. Interestingly, none of the latter was authorized or recognized by the UN Security Council. As is evident from Figure 10.2, most of the regional peacekeeping operations between states took place in 1973 or earlier. Examples are the Arab League observer mission in Yemen 1972, the cease-fire commission for the Algeria-Morocco conflict 1963–1964, and the commissions launched during different phases of the conflicts in Indochina. Since the end of the Cold War, interstate conflicts have most often seen UN missions. In other words, the Cold War period saw an element of regionalism, but that often masked action under major power tutelage. By the end of 2005, the UN led six operations in interstate conflicts, other actors only two. Given that the number of interstate wars and armed conflicts is low in comparison to intrastate conflicts, interstate peacekeeping constitutes a large proportion of all operations. The UN as well as

Figure 10.2: Peacekeeping Operations, Interstate Conflict (1948–2005)

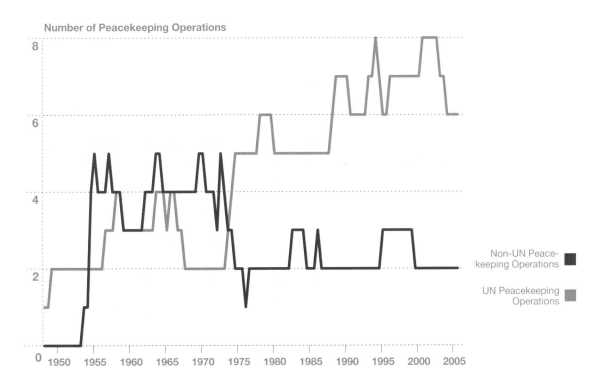

regional organizations are more likely to be used in interstate conflicts than in other conflicts.

A final observation is that there is virtually no relationship between the number of operations carried out by non-UN actors and those conducted by the UN in interstate conflicts. Whereas UN operations have a primacy, the UN does not inspire a trend in, or set a path for, the management of interstate conflicts. This observation leads us to an interesting insight: whatever factors motivate/allow the UN to intervene, they are not the same as those which motivate regional actors to intervene. From this it follows that we cannot understand why regional actors deploy peacekeepers in interstate conflicts by using the same models that can be used for understanding UN motivations.

For the whole period the UN deployed 43 operations in intrastate conflicts, while non-UN actors deployed 50 (of which, as mentioned, 28 were approved by the UN Security Council). As most conflicts are intrastate, this is the record that would be expected, or perhaps a little lower than the amount of intrastate conflict would warrant. Furthermore, the resort to non-UN led operations, with the endorsement of the UN, supports the argument that this is a matter of complementarity rather than competition. Figure 10.3 shows that for the period 1996–2005 there were more non-UN operations, but this was at a time when the UN itself was aiming at strengthening regional bodies while trying to control and coordinate their

Figure 10.3: Peacekeeping Operations, Intrastate Conflict (1948–2005)

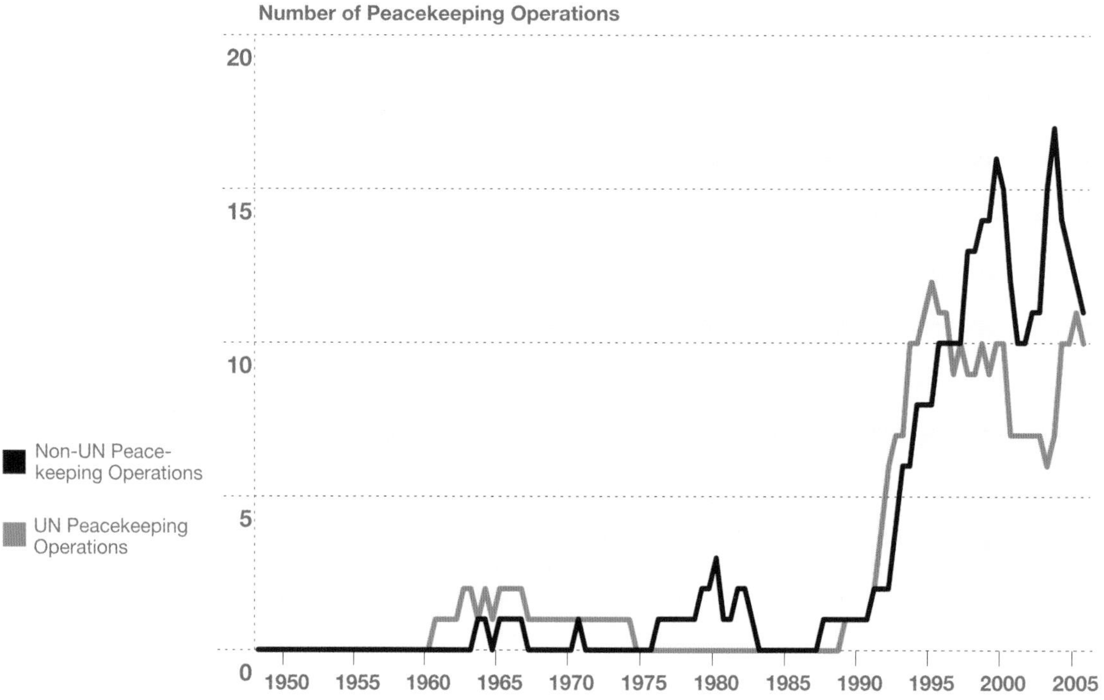

Table 10.1: Peacekeeping Operations, by Region and Conflict Type (1948–2005)				
	UN-Led Operations		Non-UN-Led Operations	
	Interstate Conflict	Intrastate Conflict	Interstate Conflict	Intrastate Conflict
Africa	3	19	3	21
Asia	3	6	6	9
Americas	0	9	5	2
Europe	2	9	0	14
Middle East	9	0	4	4

NOTE: The UN operation in Cyprus (UNFICYP) is counted twice, as it was an intrastate peacekeeping operation until 1974, after which it became an interstate operation. The UN operation in Lebanon (MNF I) is counted twice, as it was an intrastate as well as an interstate peacekeeping operation. Source: Heldt and Wallensteen (2006) for the period 1948–2004, and data collected by Heldt for 2005.

peacekeeping efforts. From the UN perspective this was not a matter of losing its preeminence but rather making it possible to concentrate on particularly urgent or demanding tasks and sharing the peacekeeping tasks.

It is important to note that for the 1989–2005 period and in particular for the period 2000–2005, Africa received a large part of UN peacekeeping resources. By December 2004, Africa had 75 percent of all UN operations and 80 percent of UN operations in intrastate conflicts in terms of all UN peacekeeping personnel. The past decade has been one of a UN focus on—not a neglect of—Africa. This observation serves to refute arguments and concerns that a larger regional responsibility for peacekeeping will deplete the UN pool of well-trained and well-equipped peacekeeping resources, to the detriment of the most conflict-prone regions. The pattern has in fact been the opposite one. It is also important to recall that by late 2004 some 45 percent of the UN peacekeepers in Africa came from African countries. In a sense, although under UN flag and with UN financing, Africa is carrying out its own peacekeeping.

Regional Patterns

Table 10.1 shows the total number of peacekeeping operations from 1948 to 2005 by region, conflict type, and organization. The most conspicuous pattern is that in the Americas the UN has been entrusted to address intrastate conflicts, and regional actors have dealt with interstate conflicts, while in the Middle East the UN has dealt only with interstate conflicts, and regional actors have addressed both types of conflict. Interestingly, the three regions of Africa, Europe, and Asia differ from the other two by displaying a similar pattern for both types of conflicts. The markedly different patterns for the Americas and the Middle East beg an explanation. A closer look at the Middle East suggests that all the non-UN intrastate operations concerned the same conflict and location. Three of the operations were deployed in Lebanon, and the fourth one in Jordan. The conflicts were also interconnected. It may therefore not be surprising that one actor, in this case the Arab League, having initiated peacekeeping, ends up handling all subsequent peace operations.

Similarly, of the nine UN operations, five were interconnected by being related to the Arab-Israeli conflict, while two were related to Iraq.

Peacekeeping is characterized by inertia.… The initial decisions…set the stage for which organization will be involved in the long run.

The same pattern applies to interstate operations in the Americas. Four out of five operations took place in Central America, often involving Honduras. Moreover, El Salvador and Nicaragua were involved in two conflicts each, and two of the conflicts were between the same parties. Again, the conflicts in Central America demonstrated a certain interconnectedness, similar to the one in the Middle East, and may offer an explanation for the pattern: having initiated peacekeeping, the same actor tends to end up handling subsequent peace operations in interconnected conflicts. Also, Europe exhibits a comparable pattern of clustering, in that eight UN operations concern conflicts of the Balkans. Such clustering of peace operations can be found in other regions. For instance, of the nine UN operations in the Americas, five dealt with Haiti. The global pattern of peacekeeping is thus characterized by inertia. It suggests that the initial decisions are important, as they set the stage for which organization will be involved in the long run.

It is important to note that 13 of the non-UN operations were carried out by actors from outside the region of conflict. Such out-of-area operations were rather common in Asia, evenly distributed in the Middle East and Africa, while rare in the Americas. Hence, two thirds of the non-UN operations in Asia, and half of the operations in the Middle East, were neither carried out by the region itself, nor by the UN. Such out-of-area operations appear to be a thing of the past: during the past 20 years only four such operations were launched.

Asia deserves some more attention, as it is unique in several aspects. First, almost half of the non-UN operations were such "out-of-area" operations. All of the operations in interstate conflicts were carried out by such actors. This includes the operation between the two Koreas—in place for more than 50 years—and the five operations established during the Vietnam War. The remaining intrastate operations consist almost entirely of those deployed in Papua New Guinea and the Solomon Islands that consisted of just a couple of small (with the exception of Australia) troop-contributing countries, and were of limited size. None of the pivotal East Asian countries contributed to these operations, while a few (Malaysia, the Philippines, Republic of Korea, and Thailand) contributed to the INTERFET operation in East Timor. This provides for a unique intervention pattern of (1) nonintervention by regional actors, and (2) ad hoc coalitions of the willing rather than regional intergovernmental organizations (IGOs).

As noted by many scholars, North East Asia is among the few regions that lack regional structures for conflict management and prevention (e.g., Swanström 2005). This means that there is no institutionalized preparedness in Asia for peacekeeping in the region. In addition, some of the conflicts are located inside pivotal member states, making peacekeeping difficult to establish. There are also a number of unresolved interstate issues that reinforce mutual distrust: the Korean peninsula is still formally in a state of war, the Taiwan issue has varied in intensity and experienced serious crises over the years, the border conflict between India and Pakistan has caused several wars, and there are many sea border disputes in North East Asia. There is also a conflict legacy from the first part of the 1900s, carrying memories of injustices that influence interstate cooperation. The absence of Asian intraregional peacekeeping, or even the absence of security-oriented IGOs, should not come as a surprise.

Impact

This brings us to the issue of the impact of peacekeeping on war and whether there is a significant difference between the different types of organizations. The issue of "success" is not easy to settle. In general, there is a detrimental confusion in the field over whether success should refer to performance (e.g., mandate fulfillment) or impact (e.g., conflict control, war avoidance, or even transitions to democracy), whether it should involve positive or negative peace, proper time frames, etc. The mandates for the operations vary, and even the time perspectives: should there be peace in terms of no war when the peacekeepers leave or should they stay for decades? What about the other goals, such as humanitarian aid, the building of democracy, state reconstruction? Many of these mandates require fairly long-term perspectives and a sharper differentiation among types of missions.

> *A series of studies…has demonstrated that peacekeeping does extend the duration of post-conflict peace, and even increases the probability of transitions to post-civil war democracy. Yet, these studies have not yet dealt with the question of the relative degree of success for UN and non-UN missions.*

Here we will settle for a minimal definition: short-term impact in terms of absence of war during deployment. That means that we ask whether the peace operation achieves what its name suggests: maintaining the peace while the operation is in place. After all, this is the fundamental responsibility and goal of peacekeeping, and is at the heart of peacekeeping operations regardless of whether the mandate is broad and borders on nation-building. Peacekeeping may contribute to peace also after its departure by leaving a legacy behind, but then a host of other factors are also likely to affect the conditions of a society or a relationship between states.

A question that carries important policy implications for the ongoing debate on whether the UN or regional actors should be entrusted with peacekeeping concerns success rates. A series of studies (e.g., Doyle and Sambanis, 2000, 2006; Fortna, 2003a, 2003b, 2004; Heldt, 2006) has demonstrated that peacekeeping does extend the duration of post-conflict peace, and even increases the probability of transitions to post-civil war democracy. Yet, these studies have not yet dealt with the question of the relative degree of success for UN and non-UN missions. Neither have they had access to the most recent data on non-UN missions. The focus on post-conflict situations also means that many operations deployed either in advance of—and during—conflicts are excluded. If we want to evaluate comparative success rates, it may be preferable to include all peacekeeping operations in the analysis.

An alternative research design could thus examine the question "under what conditions are peacekeeping operations successful?" Some operations were successful, while others were not, and this variation across cases requires an explanation. The design would thus try to account for variation in success across peacekeeping operations by examining whether type of mission makes any difference. As such it answers one important question—"Under what conditions are peacekeeping operations successful?"—but at the same time cannot answer another important question—"Is there a relationship between peacekeeping operations and the duration of peace?" With this implication in mind we will now pursue the research question with the help of the alternative research design.

Table 10.2: Operation Overlap (% of Months) with Ongoing Conflict (1948–2004)		
Conflict Type	UN	Non-UN
Intrastate Conflict	20.5%	21.4%
Interstate Conflict	1.3%	0.65%
Source: Heldt and Wallensteen (2006)		

It is often claimed that peacekeeping operations should be deployed where there is a peace to keep. This presupposes an agreement between warring parties. For the peacekeepers it would also be an "easier" task, and for the home public of the troop contributors this is reassuring: these states are not risking the lives of their citizens. In reality, and as illustrated in Table 10.2, peacekeeping operations in intrastate conflicts often find themselves deployed where there is no peace to keep, either because peace has not yet been established, or because peace has broken down during the course of the operation. There is a marked difference between the types of conflict, but not between the types of organizational frameworks: intrastate conflicts are clearly more risky, and interstate conflicts less risky, regardless of organizational framework.

In fact there is a clear pattern: peacekeeping in interstate conflicts is seldom deployed until after the parties have stopped violence; in intrastate conflicts peace operations are often launched without similar strong guarantees (Heldt 2002). Twenty percent of the time in intrastate conflicts the peace operations find themselves in situations where there is no peace to keep. One can also see this the other way around, 80 percent of the operations actually find a peace to keep, either because of their own activities or because the parties have managed to contain the violence themselves. From the point of view of the civilian population, peace only four out of five days is not likely to be satisfactory. For a war-weary world it may still sound better than continuous fighting and gives some prospect for a better future. In the medical field, treatments that are able to cure 80 percent of a very serious disease are probably hailed as very successful. Yet, over time, a 20 percent failure rate generates a large number of casualties.

The conclusion that UN and regional operations are overall and substantially equally successful during deployment appears to suggest that the two types are substitutable. However, the figures do not take into account the degree of difficulty faced by these peacekeepers. These success rates may therefore reflect either the effectiveness of different types of operations, or different degrees of difficulties. Implicit in such an argument is the plausible assumption that not all cases are equally war prone. For instance, it is sometimes claimed that the most difficult cases are referred to the UN, and if this is correct, then the equal success rates would speak in favor of the UN. Indeed, Haas (1987) reports that during the 40-year period 1945–1984, the UN was not only more likely to attempt to manage interstate disputes, but was also—with the exception of the five-year period 1971–1975—more likely to be entrusted to manage the more serious ones.

> *Peacekeeping operations in intrastate conflicts often find themselves deployed where there is no peace to keep…either because peace has not yet been established, or because peace has broken down during the course of the operation.*

A similar picture is at hand for peacekeeping, as UN-led operations are less likely to be deployed to prevent armed conflict, and consequently more likely to be deployed during and after wars. Of the 42 UN intrastate operations, only 10 were deployed where civil war had not recently taken place. The corresponding figure for the 50 non-UN-led operations is 18. Thus, UN operations were almost twice as likely to be sent to more difficult situations. For UN-led operations in interstate conflicts, the numbers are 6 out of 17, compared to 13 out of 18, suggesting a similar ratio. Regional actors are obviously more likely to deploy conflict prevention operations than the UN. One interpretation is that regional actors initially try to manage conflicts, and if they fail the conflicts are referred to the UN Security Council, just as indicated by the UN Charter. By the time a conflict reaches the UN agenda, it is more likely to have developed into war. There is a selection effect at play here: difficult cases will ultimately reach the UN agenda and end up being managed by UN peacekeepers.

Whatever interpretation, the data show that the UN tends to be entrusted with more of the difficult cases, but still is not less successful. This suggests that UN operations are in fact more likely to succeed than those carried out by other organizations. This is, however, only a rough way of treating a subject that requires more study and where more refined measurements can be developed to estimate the difficulty or severity of the challenge a peace operation faces. Moreover, as new forms of peacekeeping are developing—either involving a combination of different organizations (e.g., UN+AU); or different organizations replacing each other; or with mandates involving long-term peacebuilding—the task is increasingly complex.

The only large-scale comparative empirical study so far that has attempted to control for degree of mission difficulty finds no robust evidence of a difference in success rates (with regard to absence of war) that applies without restrictions throughout time (1948–2000) and across space (all regions of the world, cf. Heldt 2004). This means that knowing whether an operation is led by the UN or by a regional organization or ad hoc coalitions does not assist in predicting its success. While some regions, for reasons of military resources and capabilities are in a better position than others to take on peacekeeping tasks, non-UN-led operations have overall not been less successful than UN operations. Nevertheless, if peacekeeping operations are primarily confidence-building measures where physical presence rather than war fighting is essential, then issues of military resources and capabilities, or even command and control, are not of major importance.

The policy implication of these admittedly first-cut findings is that if the goal is to stop violence, then UN efforts to address international peace and security can continue to coexist with non-UN-led efforts, just as has been the case for 50 years. The UN Charter has got it right in that sense. Meanwhile, it is not possible to infer that the two types of missions are entirely substitutable. Rather, there might be a historical pattern with a selection process: the choice between UN and non-UN operations has been made on a case-by-case basis focusing on suitability and probability of success, at least in the narrow terms here defined. Meanwhile, and to complicate the picture, we have also observed a pattern where the organization that is used in the first instance, often is used also in later phases of the same conflict or in conflicts in the immediate neighborhood. This may be a choice of convenience rather than one based on close evaluation of what is most appropriate as a situation becomes more complex. Another observation is that non-UN operations are more likely than UN ones to be preventive operations. This indicates that it is not just suitability and probability of success that matters, but also inertia as well as ability to intervene at an early stage.

The policy implication of these admittedly first-cut findings is that if the goal is to stop violence, then UN efforts to address international peace and security can continue to coexist with non-UN-led efforts, just as has been the case for 50 years.…it is not possible to infer that the two types of missions are entirely substitutable.

This raises the question of how a global division of labor should be designed. There are at least three possibilities: (1) the UN takes on some missions, regional organizations (and informal coalitions) take on other missions, both basically doing the same type of peacekeeping, but in different situations; (2) UN-led and other operations coexist within one conflict and divide the tasks among themselves within that particular setting; and (3) the UN takes on some types of missions (e.g., multidimensional operations) whereas regional actors focus on others (such as traditional peacekeeping). Let us elaborate on these three possibilities.

The first form is the one that has been in existence for more than 50 years, and it appears overall to have worked, as the data presented here demonstrate. The second option has been practised only on a few occasions. However, there is no broad empirical evidence to settle the question of how this division of labor could be designed, or even whether it should be generally promoted. From experiences in development cooperation it has been observed that coordination problems are likely to arise, and local actors may play different organizations against each other. We have, however, observed a pattern of one organization being replaced by another, sometimes referred to a "re-hatting," in that regional peacekeepers are placed at the UN's disposal and change their national hat to a blue helmet, or vice versa. If different organizations develop special skills this might in fact become an effective strategy.

The third option follows from this argument and has in fact been at hand ever since the UN initiated multidimensional peacekeeping in 1989. Regional actors have almost exclusively carried out traditional short-term operations in intrastate conflicts, while the UN has more often been engaged in long-term multidimensional operations. Access to training, capacity for more complex missions, and financial resources may suffice to explain such difference. However, the desirability of this task-specific division of labor should be thoroughly assessed in future research.

Conclusion

The question asked initially in this essay was whether there is a contradiction or even competition between global and regional peacekeeping activities. The conclusion is that there has not been. Furthermore, there is a pattern of burden-sharing and a functional division of labor. Over the period, both types of missions have increased in numbers and significance, but regional initiatives and coalitions of states have almost exclusively carried out traditional peacekeeping missions even in intrastate conflicts, whereas the UN has become a provider of multidimensional operations with extensive mandates. Regional missions have often been deployed in early phases of conflict, what may amount to preventive actions. This means they may have an advantage in being able to act earlier than the UN, and at a point in time when resource demands are less restraining. UN missions, however, may more often be used at later stages of a conflict, when the difficulties are larger and the resource requirements higher. Considering the UN's larger pool of peacekeepers as well as financial resources, such a division of labor appears to be reasonable. Even so, the success rates do not differ between the organizational frameworks.

> *The question asked initially in this essay was whether there is a contradiction or even competition between global and regional peacekeeping activities. The conclusion is that there has not been.*

Regional organizations may have a stronger will, capacity, and interest in preventing conflicts in their own neighborhood from becoming serious, and this may account for the preventive nature of their peacekeeping efforts. The UN certainly can support such activities, but its decision-making may make it more likely for use in complex peacekeeping and post-conflict peacebuilding. Developing specific skills within different organizations geared to different elements in the typical conflict cycle would possibly constitute a way in which global resources for peacekeeping can be utilized in an optimal way, as far as preventing the onset, escalation, and/or diffusion of direct violence.

Developing specific skills within different organizations geared to different elements in the typical conflict cycle would possibly constitute a way in which global resources for peacekeeping can be utilized in an optimal way.

11. UNPACKING GLOBAL TRENDS IN VIOLENT CONFLICT, 1946–2005

J. Joseph Hewitt

Has global conflict been on the rise or on the decline since the end of the Cold War? Obviously, many people would be eager to get a straightforward answer to that question. Policymakers would like to know because the answer has ramifications for which policies and programs should be sustained or discontinued. If a trend in conflict could be established, academic researchers could direct their attention to possible causes. A definitive answer opens the door for increased media attention to issues related to conflict because the clarity lends itself nicely to journalistic demands for concision.

In the interest of full disclosure, this chapter will not answer the opening question with a single pronouncement. Undoubtedly, definitive answers to questions involving simple concepts would pose less of a problem. "Did Argentina's foreign debt increase or decrease last year?" is a question that can be readily answered because there is little debate about what is meant by the key terms in the question. Moreover, there is widespread agreement about how to measure the operative concept, "foreign debt." In contrast, assessing trends in global conflict is challenging because the concept of "conflict" itself is highly complex. The term covers a myriad of factors, many of which are difficult to measure.

Our answer will depend on the type of conflict we analyze, the particular attribute of conflict we measure, and whether our focus relates to global patterns or regional breakdowns. From a very large bundle of different factors that could affect overall global conflict trends, this chapter unpacks two significant items and examines them systematically. First, the chapter will explore trends in conflict diffusion, which is the extent to which armed conflict has involved countries in the global community. Second, the chapter provides an overview of trends in conflict-related fatalities. [1]

---

1 Readers familiar with past editions of *Peace and Conflict* may wonder why the index for conflict magnitude is not included in this chapter (Marshall 2001, 2003, 2005). The previous editions advanced a number of important analyses showing how the index tracked trends in conflict. The index combined into a single score the impact of the number of "…combatants and casualties, size of the affected area and dislocated populations, and extent of infrastructure damage" (Marshall 2005: 11). When applied to the set of conflicts in the Armed Conflict and Intervention Project's database (Marshall 1999), the index recorded a steady rise in conflict magnitude during the Cold War that was followed by a dramatic decline when the Cold War came to an end. One of the strengths of the index, that it accounts for multiple features of conflict, also proves problematic for pinpointing how specific factors contribute to the apparent downward trend in conflict magnitude over the past 20 years. Given this chapter's goal of deconstructing the various components of global conflict to assess their individual impact, a composite index is inappropriate for the task at hand.

Conflict Diffusion

Armed conflicts vary in terms of how many countries become involved in the fighting. While some conflicts remain relatively isolated affairs, others can involve several states. The following analyses assess the extent of the diffusion of conflict across the global community.

We begin by examining the number of countries involved in conflict in each year. As in chapter 3, these analyses will be based on data collected by the Uppsala Conflict Data Program and the International Peace Research Institute. The UCDP/PRIO Armed Conflict Dataset, which is current through the end of 2005, lists any country that becomes involved in a conflict by sending troops to actively support one of the primary actors.[2] This analysis will count the number of countries involved in conflict each year and report this figure as a percentage of the total number of independent states in that year. Reporting the total as a percentage of all countries is necessary in order to account for the increasing number of independent states that joined the international system over the post-World War II period.

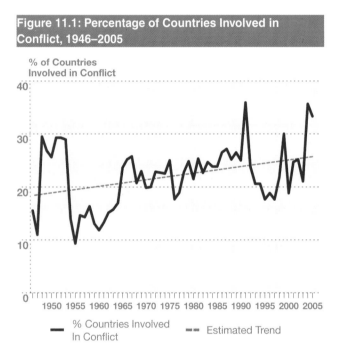

Figure 11.1: Percentage of Countries Involved in Conflict, 1946–2005

% of Countries Involved in Conflict

% Countries Involved In Conflict

Estimated Trend

Figure 11.1 presents the data on the annual number of states involved in conflict. The graph shows a modest upward trend. Again, since the figure presents the number of involved states as a percentage of total system size, the upward trend is not an artifact of a larger population of states in more recent years. The blue dashed line is an estimate of the linear trend in the data. It has been estimated with ordinary least squares regression, a statistical technique that fits a line to data by minimizing the combined distances between all data points and the line under consideration. When data are distributed randomly over time, the amount of error around the estimated trend line will be too great to conclude that the trend is statistically meaningful or significant. We will alert the reader whenever an estimated trend falls short of statistical significance.

The trend depicted in Figure 11.1 is highly significant, which means that the apparent upward trend is highly unlikely to be caused by random chance. The trend is based on data for the entire 1946–2005 period. It is important to note that while we are confident that the data on involved countries are trending upward, the magnitude of that trend is quite modest. On four separate occasions during the post-Cold War period, the percentage of countries involved in conflict exceeded any percentage reached during the Cold War. In 1991, 36 percent of the globe's countries were involved in conflict, largely because of the 1990–1991 Gulf War. After a brief decline in the diffusion of conflict in the early years of the post-Cold War period, the internationalized civil war in the Democratic Republic of Congo and the conflict in Kosovo contributed to a resurgence. In 1999, 30 percent of all countries were involved in

---

2 For a full description of the data, see Gleditsch et al. (2002).

armed conflict. In 2004 and 2005, the percentage of states involved in conflict was 36 percent and 33 percent, respectively, reflecting the large multinational forces present in both Iraq and Afghanistan. These values are greater than the highest values posted at any time during the Cold War, but not much higher. The peak value during the Korean War was 29 percent. After the Korean War, the next highest peak was recorded in 1967 at 26 percent (reflecting the impact of the Vietnam War and the multistate war involving Israel and its Arab neighbors). Given the modest differences in these values, we caution readers not to read too much into them. At the same time, one thing is patently clear. The spread of conflict over the world is not weakening. Today, as much (if not more) of the global community is involved in armed conflict as at any other time over the past six decades.[3]

The increased diffusion of conflict is partly the result of a recent string of large, multistate operations sanctioned by international bodies such as the UN or NATO. The end of the Cold War helped to bridge the fissures at the UN Security Council that once prevented authorizations of such forces. Accordingly, increased conflict diffusion can be seen as an artifact of this changed dynamic in world politics. Given this explanation for increased diffusion, there is an understandable temptation to dismiss the trend as a false indication of a worsening global condition. We caution our readers against this temptation, though. Whether authorized by the UN or not, whether symbolically deployed with no real threat for sustained fatalities, mobilization of troops to foreign territory is almost always a weighty national commitment. The substantial domestic opposition in Italy, France, Germany, and in other European governments to increased roles in the International Security Assistance Force (ISAF) in Afghanistan illustrates the point. The financial and human costs of increased involvement in conflict, not to mention the concomitant political risks for leaders who send troops abroad, are nontrivial—even when the involvement occurs in a multistate operation like ISAF. The conflict diffusion measure depicted in Figure 11.1 indirectly captures this feature of conflict by showing the annual changes in the number of governments worldwide that bear the consequences of direct involvement in armed conflict.

> *Today, as much (if not more) of the global community is involved in armed conflict as at any other time over the past six decades.*

The analysis presented in Figure 11.1 omits two important pieces of information. First, the analysis does not account for when a single country becomes involved in multiple conflicts at the same time. In 1999, for example, the UCDP/PRIO data codes India as involved in seven separate armed conflicts. The analysis in Figure 11.1 counts India as involved in conflict in 1999, but disregards the fact that the government was actually involved in seven separate affairs. Second, the previous analysis does not attempt to account for the duration of a country's involvement in conflict. We can imagine two hypothetical years in which the same number of countries were involved in conflict. In one year, the involvements might have

---

3 Note that the extent of global conflict diffusion is far more volatile during the post-Cold War period. The sudden dips and spikes in conflict diffusion mean that no statistically discernible trend exists for this period when analyzed by itself.

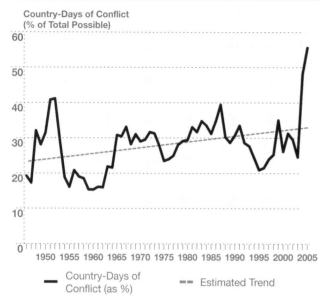

Figure 11.2: Country-Days of Conflict as % Total Possible (1946–2005)

Country-Days of Conflict
(% of Total Possible)

Country-Days of Conflict (as %)

Estimated Trend

relatively short durations, while in the other the durations might be longer. In that way, information about duration provides additional insight into which year featured "more" conflict.

The analysis in Figure 11.2 accounts for these two omissions by examining an alternative measure of conflict diffusion, country-days of conflict. Each day in which a country is involved in a single conflict is a country-day of conflict. If two countries were involved in a bilateral interstate conflict for 100 days, that conflict would produce 200 country-days of conflict. The annual totals presented in Figure 11.2 are obtained by summing the number of country-days for each country involved in a conflict during that year.[4] If a country is involved in multiple conflicts over the course of a single year, the total country-days from each are combined. The number of annual country-days of conflict is presented as a percentage of the total possible country-days of conflict that could be experienced in a given year (the total number of independent states multiplied by 365). The last step is necessary to safeguard against any trends being an artifact of the growing number of states in the system. In sum, measuring the global diffusion of conflict with country-days accounts for variation in conflict duration as well as the impact of multiple conflict involvements by a single country.

Figure 11.2 depicts an upward trend in the global diffusion of conflict measured in terms of annual country-days of conflict. The trend is based on the entire 1946–2005 period. Although the trend line is strongly statistically significant, the magnitude of the upward trend is quite modest. Notably, there is a visible decline in annual country-days of conflict in the first few years after the Cold War ends. After peaking at 39 percent in 1987, country-days of conflict plunged to a low of 21 percent in 1995. The decline in the global diffusion of conflict was short-lived, though, as it returned to Cold War levels again by 1999.

Undoubtedly, one of the most glaring features of Figure 11.2 is the sharp increase in country-days of conflict in 2004 and 2005. The UCPD/PRIO data lists three large multicountry conflicts as active in 2005. The ongoing civil war in Iraq involves troops from 30 countries, Afghanistan's internal conflict with the Taliban involves 16 countries, and the operation against al-Qaeda in the Pakistan/Afghanistan border region involves 18 countries. Also, since many of the same countries are involved in all three of these conflicts, the high number of country-days for 2005 is partly a reflection of the multiple conflict involvements.

---

4 Country-days were computed using the data available in the UCPD/PRIO "Main Conflict Table." That data set does not contain precise conflict termination dates. Another UCPD/PRIO data collection does include this information, but only for intrastate conflicts. This analysis estimates a conflict termination date as the midpoint of the last annual observation in the series of observations for a conflict.

One might question whether the values for 2004 and 2005 are the result of UCPD/PRIO's counting the two conflicts in Afghanistan as separate and distinct. Instead, a plausible argument might be made that the two should be combined. Doing so, however, would only reduce the number of country-days of conflict in 2004 and 2005 by 17 percent. That modification to the data would reduce the percentage of global country-days of conflict to about 45 percent, which would still be higher than any other year in post–World War II history.

Taken together, Figures 11.1 and 11.2 point to a sobering picture of global conflict. Global conflict touches a greater share of countries today than it ever has since the end of World War II. For many states, multiple involvements in long-lasting engagements further compound the global diffusion of conflict. The trends in the two figures should be interpreted with some caution, though, because they slope upward at a very modest rate. Having said that, we can be quite confident that the spread of conflict's reach around the world is not shrinking. At minimum, the diffusion of armed conflict has been roughly the same for a long time, and, more likely, it has become slightly more encompassing in recent years.

Conflict Lethality

Researchers and policymakers track trends in global armed conflict because they are concerned foremost with its dreadful consequences. Analysis of trends in the number of conflicts or in the diffusion of global conflict fails to capture the extent of conflict's devastation. That devastation comes in multiple forms. Armed conflicts result in dislocated populations, degradation of the natural environment, and destruction of physical property. Most of all, armed conflict leads to human suffering and death. An analysis of conflict trends that focuses only on the number of conflicts in any given year will neglect their destructive impact and lead to dubious conclusions. A comparison of the years 1950 and 2005 illustrates the point. In terms of the number of conflicts, we might be tempted to conclude that the year 1950 (with just 12 active conflicts) was a distinctively peaceful year compared to 2005 (with 25 active conflicts). But that conclusion would only invite ridicule. The active conflicts in 2005 produced about 22,000 battle-related fatalities. The 12 conflicts of 1950, one of which was the Korean War, produced about 690,000 fatalities.

The extent of conflict's devastation is an integral component of what we hope to tap into when we make claims about whether global conflict is on the rise or the decline. To make meaningful assessments, analysts must search in each conflict's scorched path for appropriate yardsticks to measure the devastation. They may choose to quantify the economic cost of lost productivity and capital, the extent of the dislocation of populations, or the harm done to the natural environment. Or, they may choose simply to count the dead bodies. One of the morbid features of the academic literature on conflict intensity is that the most painful and heart-wrenching of all of war's costs—the loss of human life—happens to be the one that is most amenable to quantification. Nonetheless, obtaining valid and reliable measurements for war-related deaths remains a challenging task with substantial complexity.

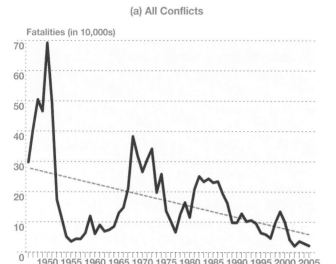

Figure 11.3: Battle Death Totals, 1946–2005

(a) All Conflicts

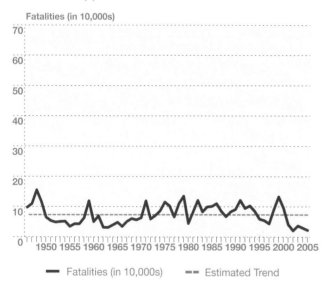

(b) 5 Deadliest Conflicts Removed

━━ Fatalities (in 10,000s)   ▬ ▬ ▬ Estimated Trend

Recognizing that there are multiple approaches for defining what qualifies as a conflict-related fatality, we use the battle death data collected by Lacina and Gleditsch (2005). Lacina and Gleditsch define a battle death as a death "resulting directly from violence inflicted through the use of armed force by a party to an armed conflict during contested combat" (2005: 162). The definition excludes some notable categories of war-related fatalities. For instance, this approach follows the UCDP/PRIO definition for armed conflict and requires that one of the parties be a sovereign state, which gives the battle death concept a state-based foundation. In addition, the definition requires that fatalities be sustained during contested combat (i.e., in situations when the parties to the conflict face a reciprocal threat of lethal force being imposed by another party to the conflict). By implication, fatalities sustained by civilians who do not threaten force against the party that carried out the violence do not qualify as battle deaths. This is the reason, at least in part, why the fatality counts for conflicts like that in Rwanda (1994) or in the current internationalized civil war in Iraq (especially in the post-invasion period) are lower in the Lacina-Gleditsch data than many observers might expect.[5]

In all, the Lacina-Gleditsch data provide a systematic accounting of fatalities for all conflicts since the end of World War II. The data have been recently updated through 2005 and are well-suited for informing assessments about trends in conflict intensity.

Figure 11.3a (the upper graph) depicts the annual total of battle deaths for the period 1946–2005. The dashed blue line shows the estimated trend line, which clearly slopes downward. The trend parallels

---

5 Ideally, future research should address how trends are affected when the analysis expands to include conflict-related fatalities beyond the battle death definition used here. Lacina and Gleditsch (2005) discuss some of the profound challenges to systematically collecting this information, which explains the relative dearth of suitable data resources. Barbara Harff's (2003) research has culminated in an excellent data collection on genocide and politicides, but the fatalities sustained in these events can often occur outside the context of an armed conflict (as defined by UCDP/PRIO or any other conflict data project). In their chapter on the determinants of mass killings, Huth and Valentino discuss this point at length (chapter 9 of this volume).

findings reported in a study by Lacina, Gleditsch, and Russett (2006) that identifies a similar trend in the ratio of battle deaths to the global population. Additionally, the trend depicted in the graph forms an important piece of the many findings reported by the Human Security Centre (2005) in its report on conflict trends. Considered by itself, this graph suggests a clear and definitive conclusion about conflict-related fatalities since World War II: they are going down. Figure 11.3a should not be considered conclusive, though.

> *Five conflicts, representing just 2 percent of the 231 conflicts since the end of World War II, account for 57 percent of all fatalities suffered across all conflicts.*

The trend in Figure 11.3a is driven by a tiny subset of highly atypical conflicts that distinguish themselves because of their exceptional lethality. Lacina and Gleditsch (2005) point out that the downward trend in battle death fatalities is driven largely by the five conflicts with the largest battle death totals. These five conflicts, representing just 2 percent of the 231 conflicts since the end of World War II, account for 57 percent of all fatalities suffered across all conflicts. This stark disproportion in the data creates the real possibility that any visible trends we find are actually driven by the exceptional impact of just a few cases. Those conflicts are (in descending order of lethality): the Vietnam War (1955–1975), the Korean War (1950–1953), the Chinese Civil War (1946–1949), the Iran–Iraq War (1980–1988), and the Afghan Civil War (1978–2002). Figure 11.3a shows four elevated peaks in fatalities that correspond to the time periods for the first four of these conflicts. The Afghan Civil War does not produce a readily distinguishable peak in the data, but does make a sizeable contribution to the overall totals in the 1978–2002 period. To illustrate the impact that these five conflicts have on any assessment of the trend in battle deaths, we replicate Lacina and Gleditsch's presentation of battle death data after removing these five conflicts. The results are displayed in Figure 11.3b.

With the five most deadly conflicts removed, there is no discernible trend in worldwide fatalities. Of the 231 armed conflicts accounted for in the battle death totals displayed in Figure 11.3a, the deadliest five create the appearance of a downward trend in the lethality of war. After setting these five aside, the destructive impact of armed conflict on human life appears to be essentially constant over the past six decades. Having said that, this analysis makes it clear that there is a downward trend in the lethality of the most severe conflicts in the last half-century. That observation is consistent with an argument that John Mueller (1989) advanced about the increasing obsolescence of major war. Mueller reasons that major wars between the most powerful members of the international system are becoming increasingly unlikely because of fundamental shifts in attitudes about warfare and the extent to which it can be used as a viable foreign policy instrument for advancing major power interests. The distinction between major power wars and other wars has potential for clarifying the interpretation of trends in armed conflict—a point we return to in the conclusion.

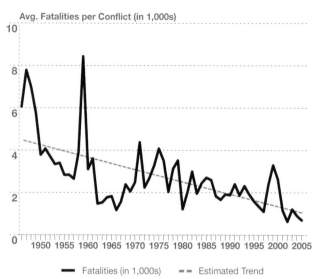

Figure 11.4: Average Fatalities per Conflict, 1946–2005

Avg. Fatalities per Conflict (in 1,000s)

Fatalities (in 1,000s) ▬▬   Estimated Trend ▬ ▬

Although Figure 11.3b suggests no clear upward or downward trend in the raw number of annual fatalities, it is conceivable that the lethality of individual conflicts is changing over time. We know from chapter 3 that the number of active conflicts in any given year grew rapidly from the mid-1960s through the end of the 1980s and then declined significantly after that. If the raw number of fatalities exhibits no trend over time, but the underlying number of conflicts changes dramatically, then that suggests that the lethality levels per conflict must have shifted. We check this line of thinking with Figure 11.4.

Figure 11.4 displays the average fatality level per conflict in each year from 1946 to 2005. As in Figure 11.3b, the five deadliest conflicts have been excluded from this analysis. The blue dashed trend line indicates a downward trend in the lethality of conflict over the period. We note that the trend line far surpasses the threshold for statistical significance despite considerable "noise" in the data, especially in the earlier years in the period.[6] The downward trend in the average lethality of conflict coincides with the rise of civil conflict.

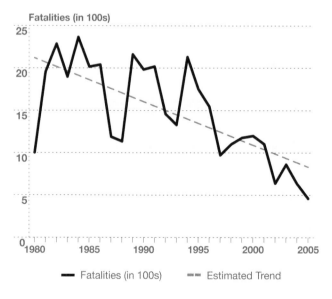

Figure 11.5: Internal Conflicts: Average Fatalities Per Conflict, 1980–2005

Fatalities (in 100s)

Fatalities (in 100s) ▬▬   Estimated Trend ▬ ▬

As chapter 3 discusses, beginning in the 1970s, civil conflicts outnumber interstate conflicts by a large margin. At the same time, civil conflicts tend to be far less lethal than interstate conflicts, a reflection of the enormous destructive capacity that multiple state governments bring to bear in interstate contests. Therefore, the recent decline in conflict lethality could be a reflection of the fact that most of the conflicts over the past two or three decades have been internal as opposed to interstate affairs.

We further explore this by assessing patterns in the average number of fatalities in internal conflicts. Figure 11.5 presents the results. Note, to ease presentation, the scale has been altered to display fatalities in hundreds. The graph shows a significant decline in the lethality of internal conflicts

6 Due to space considerations, we do not report an alternative graph showing average fatality levels per conflict in each year with the deadliest five conflicts included. As one might expect, the downward trend is even more apparent when we include these atypical conflicts.

over the 1980–2005 period. Here then is a clear piece of encouraging news. Not only have the last 20 years witnessed a significant decline in the number of internal conflicts, but the average lethality of those conflicts has declined as well. We also examined the per conflict averages for interstate and internationalized internal conflicts, although space limitations prevent a presentation of the corresponding graphs. Not surprisingly, the findings are sensitive to whether the most deadly conflicts are included (the Iran-Iraq war in the case of interstate conflicts; the Afghan Civil War in the case of internationalized internal conflicts). No trend is apparent when these conflicts are excluded from the analysis. When they are included, it appears as if conflict lethality has trended downward over the past two decades.

Figure 11.6 presents disaggregated fatality totals for each of the three conflict types to further explore additional insights into trends in conflict lethality. We continue to be attentive to the impact of the deadliest of conflicts on our results. Figure 11.6a displays the trend in battle deaths for interstate wars during the 1980–2005 period. The solid red line shows annual fatality totals excluding the impact of the Iran-Iraq War. The dashed blue line shows that the estimated trend for these data is essentially flat. When the impact of the Iran-Iraq War is included, depicted with a dashed red line, a significant downward trend becomes visible in the data. Figure 11.6b shows a clear downward trend in battle deaths in all internal conflicts, an expected finding given the pattern presented in Figure 11.5. Since none of the five deadliest conflicts qualify as an internal conflict, the finding does not depend on the exceptional lethality of any one of these affairs. The trend is especially pronounced in the post-Cold War period. Figure 11.6c presents data on battle deaths in internationalized internal conflicts. These are internal conflicts in which the government of another state intervenes on behalf of one of the sides (the government or an opposition group). When battle deaths from the Afghan Civil War are excluded (depicted with the dashed red line), no statistically significant trend exists in the data. A

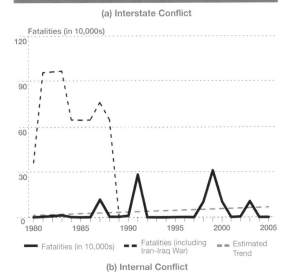

Figure 11.6: Battle Deaths by Conflict Type, 1980–2005

(a) Interstate Conflict

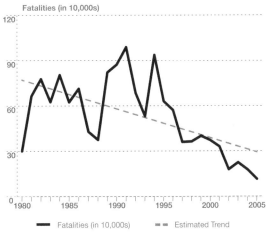

(b) Internal Conflict

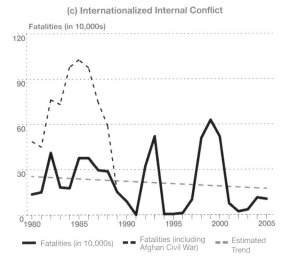

(c) Internationalized Internal Conflict

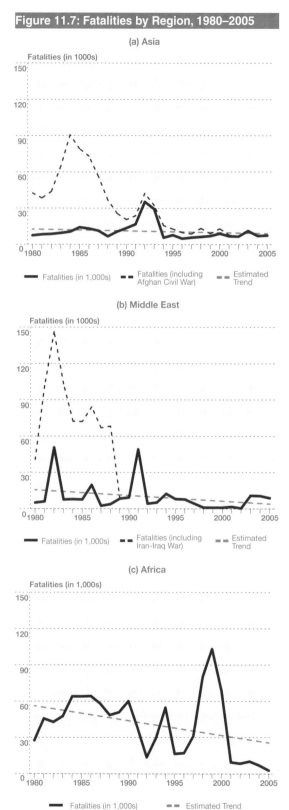

Figure 11.7: Fatalities by Region, 1980–2005

(a) Asia

Fatalities (in 1000s)

— Fatalities (in 1,000s)　■ ■ Fatalities (including Afghan Civil War)　= = Estimated Trend

(b) Middle East

Fatalities (in 1000s)

— Fatalities (in 1,000s)　■ ■ Fatalities (including Iran-Iraq War)　= = Estimated Trend

(c) Africa

Fatalities (in 1,000s)

— Fatalities (in 1,000s)　= = Estimated Trend

statistically discernible trend exists only when the singular impact of the Afghan war is included.

We also examine battle death trends by region to determine the extent to which patterns in a particular part of the globe diverge noticeably from others. Figure 11.7 presents five graphs that depict regional trends.

For all five regions of the globe, we find very little evidence suggesting any change in fatality levels over the past 25 years. The clearest evidence of a downward trend appears in Asia and the Middle East (Figures 11.7a and 11.7b, respectively). But the existence of a downward trend depends on including the Afghan Civil War and the Iran-Iraq War, in their respective analyses. The trend lines in both regions are flat when these exceptionally lethal conflicts have been removed. A slightly downward trend is visible in the African data (Figure 11.7c), but the trend line is not statistically significant. That is, a wide margin of error on the estimated trend line includes the possibility of a perfectly flat trend.

The only global region in which conflict-related fatalities are clearly trending downward is the Americas. Figure 11.7d displays fatality data for the region. Note, we have changed the scale in this graph. Maintaining the same scale for this region would make it impossible to see the trend on the graph because conflict in this region has produced dramatically fewer fatalities. Even on the smaller scale, it can be seen in Figure 11.7d that fatalities in the Americas have declined markedly. For most of the 1980–2005 period, combined fatalities for the entire region decline steadily. The noticeable increase in fatalities in 2001 is due to the fatalities sustained in the September 11 attacks and also to the subsequent use of force in Afghanistan by the US-led coalition.

Finally, Figure 11.7e displays fatality data for Europe. As with the data for the Americas, we use a smaller scale for the European data to ease review. Due to the series of conflicts in the Balkans during the 1990s, there is a visible upward trend in the data. However, the estimated trend line is not statistically significant over the 1980–2005 period owing to the extreme volatility in the recorded values.

In all, the many analyses we have presented about conflict-related fatalities do not allow us to tell a single, coherent story that confidently asserts that worldwide conflict is getting more benign or more lethal. Instead, our conclusions are somewhat more tentative and conditional.

Conclusion

Overall, the trends presented in this chapter do not provide sufficient evidence to definitively answer the question about whether armed conflict is either on the rise or the decline. This chapter has demonstrated that any answer about trends in conflict depends on the way one asks the question. True, the raw number of conflicts around the world has been declining more or less steadily since the end of the Cold War (as reported in chapter 3). That fact would surely be a source of encouragement if a number of other features of armed conflict were unmistakably trending downward as well. That, however, is not the case.

The share of countries with direct involvement in armed conflicts has risen slowly since the end of World War II. The three years featuring the highest percentage of states involved in conflict were all recorded after the Cold War ended. When we measure the diffusion of conflict worldwide in terms of country-days, the picture is similar. The trend in the annual total of country-days of conflict has been creeping upward, with a significant spike in the last two years. It is notable that the diffusion of worldwide conflict declined considerably in the early years of the post-Cold War period. While that trend prompted some to speculate that the end of the Cold War had fundamentally altered the nature of global conflict, the downward trend appears to have been short-lived. The diffusion of global conflict returned to Cold War levels and subsequently surpassed them a few short years later.

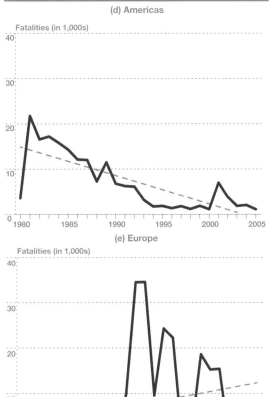

Figure 11.7 (cont.): Fatalities by Region (1980–2005)

Although there is little positive news to be drawn from this chapter's analysis on conflict diffusion, there are small glints of encouragement to be gleaned from the analyses on fatalities. These findings are far from definitive, though. Annual totals for battle deaths have been declining more or less steadily since the end of World War II. However, the downward trend in annual battle death totals is driven by the impact of five particularly lethal conflicts representing just 2 percent of all the conflicts that have occurred since 1946. In the other 98 percent of the conflicts, there is no discernible upward or downward trend. Over the same period, there is a statistically discernible downward trend, albeit a weak one, in the average lethality of individual conflicts. This trend does not depend on whether the five deadliest conflicts are included in the analysis.

Fatality levels in internal conflicts that remain isolated (i.e., do not become internationalized) are trending downward. Of course, part of this is related to the decline in the number of internal conflicts. But internal conflicts are becoming less deadly over time, too. The average number of fatalities per internal conflict has been dropping steadily since 1980.

The same optimism cannot be extended to interstate and internationalized internal conflicts. For these types of conflict, the appearance of downward trends in fatalities depends on including the idiosyncratic impact of a single conflict. Excluding the impact of the Iran-Iraq War, for example, we find no trend in fatality data for interstate conflicts. The same is true when the experience of the Afghan Civil War is removed from the set of internationalized internal conflicts.

Our analyses of the five global regions revealed little evidence of any significant upward or downward trends in fatalities when we removed the impact of the most deadly conflicts. A very slight downward trend exists for Africa, but the margin of error is too large to accept the trend as statistically significant. As before, a downward trend becomes apparent in the Middle East and Asia when we add the impact of the Iran-Iraq War and the Afghan Civil War, respectively. The only global region in which conflict-related fatalities declined significantly was the Americas.

Whether we examine all fatalities for the entire 1946–2005 period or break the data down by conflict type or by region, nearly all of the downward trends in conflict that we find disappear when any of the five deadliest wars are removed from the analysis. What does it mean when downward trends in various slices of conflict fatality data are essentially artifacts of the exceptional impact made by the deadliest of all conflicts? For starters, we think these findings point to the need for caution before making general claims about the alleged decline in global conflict. The causes for any downward trend may be idiosyncratic to the peculiarities of the five deadly conflicts upon which the appearance of the trend depends. As discussed earlier, Mueller (1989) has catalyzed a lively academic exchange about the possibility that major wars may be on the wane because of unique characteristics of the major powers. This certainly helps to delineate our understanding of why a downward trend in lethality is evident among major wars, but no such trend is discernible among all the others. A general explanation that credits the spread of democratic governments worldwide or greater effectiveness in conflict management and resolution by international institutions cannot speak to the remaining 98 percent of the cases that exhibit no downward or upward trend. The qualitative difference between the five deadliest wars and the rest of the global conflicts should be accounted for when making any claims about trends in armed conflict around the world.

APPENDIX

This appendix identifies all major armed conflicts as of December 31, 2005, and tracks their origins as well as changes in the status of these conflicts since the previous volume of *Peace and Conflict*. It also updates these conflict descriptions through 2006 where developments warranted. To compile this appendix, we have relied almost exclusively on information in the Conflict Database maintained by the Uppsala Conflict Data Program (UCDP) at Uppsala University, Sweden (*http://www.pcr.uu.se/research/UCDP/*). The brief updates for further developments in 2006 rely primarily on material posted by the International Crisis Group (*http://www.crisisgroup.org*).[1] Readers familiar with previous publications of *Peace and Conflict* will note that this is a significant change from its earlier reliance on data from the Armed Conflict and Intervention (ACI) project maintained by the Center for Systemic Peace (http://members.aol.com/cspmgm). This change reflects an editorial policy decision to base all present and future *Peace and Conflict* analyses exclusively on open-source and publicly available data.

The appendix provides descriptions for the 25 major armed conflicts that were ongoing in 21 countries as of December 31, 2005. These cases have two key characteristics: (a) they were reported as active in 2005 (i.e., at least 25 battle-related deaths were reported for that year), and (b) the accumulated battle deaths in the conflict exceeded 1,000.[2] Three major armed conflicts have terminated since the publication of *Peace and Conflict 2005*: Sudan-SPLM/A at the end of 2004; Indonesia-Aceh at the beginning of 2005; and Nepal-CPN-M/UPS in 2006. One additional conflict—Uganda-LRA—appeared to

be moving toward resolution in late 2006. A drastic escalation in the armed conflict between Israel and Hezbollah occurred in mid-2006 (covered in the Israel section below). In addition, a new armed conflict involving Ethiopian intervention in Somalia was developing as the 2008 issue was going to press.

The Uppsala Conflict Data Program defines an *armed conflict* as a contested incompatibility which concerns government and/or territory where the use of armed force between two parties, of which at least one is the government of a state, results in at least 25 battle-related deaths. A *major armed conflict* is one in which at least 1,000 battle-related deaths have occurred during the course of the conflict. An *incompatibility* can pertain to government (type of political system, the replacement of the central government or a change in its composition) or territory (the status of a specified territory, e.g., a change of the state in control of a certain territory (interstate conflict), secession, or autonomy (intrastate conflict)).

Conflict Type and Intensity Scores: Conflicts are classified as *interstate* (between two or more governments), *intrastate* (between a government and a non-government party), or *intrastate with foreign involvement* (the government or opposition party or both receive troop support from other governments). UCDP classifies conflicts into three intensity levels: *minor* (at least 25 battle-related deaths per year and fewer than 1,000 battle-related deaths during the course of the conflict), *intermediate* (at least 25 battle-related deaths per year and an accumulated total of at least 1,000 deaths but fewer than 1,000 in any given year), and *war* (at least 1,000 battle-related deaths per year). For purposes of the current study, only conflicts classified as intermediate or war are considered as armed conflicts.

Current Status: The current status of the armed conflicts as of December 2005 can fall into two categories—*terminated* or *ongoing*. A terminated conflict is categorized according to any of the following types: 1) peace agreement; 2) victory; 3) ceasefire

---

1 Readers should note that the conflict updates through 2006 reported below have not yet been incorporated into the datasets used in the analytic chapters of *Peace and Conflict 2008*; those analyses are based on empirical data current through 2005.

2 These 25 conflicts are identified through data provided by UCDP-PRIO for 1946–2005 (http://www.pcr.uu.se/database). In 2005, UCDP reported a total of 31 active armed conflicts, of which six had not exceeded a total of 1,000 battle-related deaths since 1946 (see Harbom, Hogbladh and Wallensteen 2006).

agreement; 4) low activity; or 5) no activity (the latter three are sometimes grouped as other outcome); or 6) other.

Afghanistan

Ongoing, Intrastate with the Taliban, with foreign involvement

Afghanistan has been at war since 1978. Several factors have converged to make the country a fertile ground for protracted guerrilla war and transregional insurgencies: the existence of distinct tribal identities, a salient religious element, Afghanistan's geopolitical location as a meeting place of three regions, and the country's landlocked and mountainous geography. The two prominent groups at the onset of the insurgency were Jamiat-i-Islami and Hezb-i-Islami, which have remained among the central warring parties to the present. Both groups aimed at overthrowing the "atheist, communist and pro-Soviet" government of Afghanistan, and declared a Jihad (holy war) against the state-power in March 1979. The Soviet invasion in December 1979 added the dimension of a national freedom struggle to the religious war. The Soviet troop withdrawal in February 1989 ended the first phase of the Afghan civil war, after approximately 1 million deaths. As the Soviet troops withdrew, heavy fighting erupted between the Afghan army and Mujahideen forces. The strategic situation on the ground changed in 1992, when parts of the factionalized opposition movement joined forces. It was against this background that the Taliban movement first emerged on the military scene in August 1994. Led by Mullah Mohammad Omar, its stated goal was liberating Afghanistan from the corrupt leadership of warlords and establishing a pure Islamic society. On September 28, 1996, the Taliban forces took control of Kabul and proclaimed the Islamic State of Afghanistan and the enforcement of Sharia (Islamic rule). The anti-Taliban opposition formed a political and military alliance in June 1996 that came to be known as the Northern Alliance (UIFSA). The balance of forces changed drastically with the entrance of the US-led multinational coalition into the conflict in response to the 9/11/2001 bombings. The Northern Alliance, backed by US and UK military force, took control of Kabul, and on December 7 the last Taliban stronghold of Kandahar fell. Following intense diplomatic pressure, the parties agreed

to the creation of a 29-member interim government headed by Hamid Karzai to lead the country for six months, until a broad-based administration could take over. The security situation in Afghanistan deteriorated in 2004, with stepped-up attacks against local and international NGOs, as well as against military and peacekeeping personnel, and Afghan citizens believed to be cooperating with the government or Western forces. In 2005 the armed conflict between remnants of the ousted Taliban regime and the Afghan government escalated further, with violence reaching an unprecedented level. The Afghan government remains dependent on the US-led multinational coalition and the NATO-led peacekeeping force to provide security.

[2006 update: The insurgency continues in the southern and eastern regions bordering Pakistan.]

Algeria

Ongoing, Intrastate with GSPC

Algeria gained independence from France in 1962 after a bloody war. Severe economic problems persisted during the following 27 years of socialist one-party rule under the Front de libération nationale (FLN). During the late 1980s, these economic problems led to violent strikes and riots, leading to the introduction of a multiparty system. The Front islamique du salut (FIS) became the most potent opposition force in the country, as its anti-regime stance and Islamic values appealed to the urban poor. After the FIS won the first round of parliamentary elections in 1991, the army canceled the second round. Amidst increasing political violence, FIS was outlawed in 1992. Groups that fought the regime with arms came to dominate the struggle and the FIS lost the initiative. In response, the party endorsed MIA's (Mouvement islamique armée) armed struggle in 1993, and its armed wing, Armée islamique du salut (AIS). In 1992, a number of small extremist groups set up the Groupe islamique armé (GIA). The most prominent splinter group was the Groupe salafite pour la prédication et la combat (GSPC), appearing in 1998. In 1999 Bouteflika won the presidential election after all other candidates withdrew. In the wake of 9/11, the Algerian government has received significant international support, much of it from the US, for its fight against Muslim extremism. The character of the violence in Algeria has changed dramatically over the years and has expanded to include government officials, representatives of the opposition, foreigners, and journalists. In the mid-1990s the conflict turned into carnage. GIA, issuing a fatwa that charged the whole Algerian society with apostasy, launched a new strategy, specifically targeting the civilian population. The army's countermeasures became increasingly brutal, resulting in accusations of gross human rights abuses. In 2000, the AIS agreed to disband. As of late 2005, the conflict was still ongoing. However, only one of the insurgency groups was active. In a September 2005 referendum, 97.43 percent of Algerians voted in favor of the government's proposal on partial amnesty for former rebels.

[2006 update: Despite a government-declared amnesty beginning in March, GSPC continued to perpetrate violence at a relatively low level throughout the year.]

Azerbaijan
Ongoing, Intrastate with Republic of Nagorno-Karabakh

Nagorno Karabakh is a region in Azerbaijan populated mainly by Armenians. At the beginning of the 20th century Nagorno Karabakh was a part of Armenia, but in the 1920s it was decided that the area was to belong to Azerbaijan. During the Soviet era the underlying conflict in the area was suppressed, but re-emerged with perestroika at the end of the 1980s. In February 1988 the regional council in Nagorno Karabakh voted to integrate the region into Armenia. Following this Moscow imposed direct rule over the territory, but as soon as this was ended in November 1989 Armenia declared the enclave to be part of a unified Armenian republic. Armenia fought with the USSR over Nagorno Karabakh for two years. The collapse of the Soviet Union in 1991 did not end the conflict. Rather, the dispute continued within the newly independent Azerbaijan as Nagorno Karabakh proclaimed itself a republic. The Azerbaijani leadership responded to Nagorno Karabakh's proclamation by imposing direct presidential rule over the region. The conflict resulted in tens of thousands of deaths between 1992 and 1994. The President of Armenia announced in March 1992

that the status of Nagorno Karabakh was an internal matter of Azerbaijan, and the problem was thus to be solved by Azerbaijan only. However, Armenia remained involved in the conflict over Nagorno Karabakh also after 1992. After negotiations in Moscow in May 1994 with CIS delegates, the chair of the National Assembly in Azerbaijan signed a protocol calling for a ceasefire in the war and the deployment of international peacekeeping forces. The agreement was given legal status and was extended indefinitely on July 27 by the Defense Ministers of Armenia and Azerbaijan and the military leader of Nagorno Karabakh. Low-level fighting resumed in 2005.

Burundi
Ongoing, Intrastate with Palipehutu-FNL

Burundi's population is roughly 85 percent Hutu and 15 percent Tutsi. Since independence in 1962, the Tutsi minority has controlled the government and society. In 1972, the armed repression was on the verge of genocide, and many Hutu survivors sought refuge in Rwanda and in Tanzania. In 1987, President Buyoya, a Tutsi, came to power and in 1988 anti-Hutu pogroms took place once again. The Hutus have been radicalized by their experiences and extremism has flourished in the refugee camps. Thus, in the early 1990s, Hutu rebels launched an armed struggle consisting mainly of attacks from Tanzania. From 1998 on some Hutus were included in the government. Since 2000, this side in the conflict has been represented by a transitional government, with cabinet posts split between Hutus and Tutsis. The other side in the conflict consists of a number of Hutu rebel groups including Ubumwé, PALIPEHUTU, PALIPEHUTU-FNL, CNDD, FROLINA, and CNDD-FDD. In the mid-1990s the country was drawn into the conflict in neighboring Zaire/DRC. Since then, it is difficult to separate the Burundian conflict from this regional context. The government has since 1996 cooperated militarily with the Rwandan armed forces, both in DRC and along the common border. Together these two armies have fought both Burundian and Rwandan rebel forces. During recent years, Rwandan troops have also been active within Burundi in pursuing Rwandan rebels. CNDD-FDD and to some extent also PALIPEHUTU-FNL have been fighting alongside the

DRC government army, inside DRC, against the Burundian armed forces. As the conflict in the DRC subsided in 2001, thousands of rebel fighters previously based in eastern DRC filtered back into Burundi, along with numerous Rwandan rebels. In 1996, multiparty talks were initiated, mediated first by former Tanzanian President Julius Nyerere and later by Nelson Mandela. In 2003 agreements were signed endorsing power-sharing. In January 2004 the first face-to-face negotiations between the government and Palipehutu-FNL Rwasa took place in The Netherlands, but talks soon broke down. The government and their new allies, CNDD-FDD, continued to clash with Palipehutu-FNL.

[2006 update: In April, South Africa agreed to mediate between the government and FNL rebels. The security situation improved in parts of Burundi. FNL rebels signed a surprise ceasefire agreement with the government in September in Dar es Salaam, but full implementation had not taken place at year's end.]

Chad
Ongoing, Intrastate with MDJT, RDL

Since gaining independence from France in 1960, Chad has been almost continually enveloped in civil war including immense ethnic diversity, a tradition of factionalism, as well as animosity between the mainly Muslim north and the Christian and animist south. After independence, southerners controlled the central government. The politically marginalized north launched a Libya-backed rebellion, and in 1973 Libya became directly involved by annexing the Aozou Strip on the Chad-Libya border. Forces armées du nord (FAN), a northern anti-Libyan rebel movement led by Hissèn Habré seized power in N'djamena in 1982. During the 1980s Libyan troops supported the rebels and France supported the Habré government. Idriss Deby and his former guerrilla group MPS came to power in 1990. The latest rebel group to appear was Mouvement pour la démocratie et la justice au Tchad (MDJT), which launched its armed struggle in 1998, seeking to topple the government, accusing it of being authoritarian and corrupt. The US provided extensive support to the earlier Habré regime as a part of its strategy to contain Libya and, if possible, remove Colonel Gha-

dafi from power. Traditionally, Chad has had close relations with France, the former colonial power, and in the early 1980s, France sent troops in aid of the Habré regime. Like the US, France too was aiming to stop Libya from gaining an upper hand in the region. Sudan also supported the rebels, allowing both the Islamic Front and MPS to have rear bases on its territory. Indeed, Sudan continued to function as a safe haven for at least one rebel group, FNT, even after Habré was overthrown. However, it is unclear if the Sudanese government actively allowed the rebels to use its territory. Niger, Nigeria, Algeria, Cameroon and Central African Republic have all harbored rebel groups on their soil. The locus of the violence in the 1990s and 2000s has changing as regionally based rebel groups have formed and disappeared. The situation in Chad during 2005 was volatile, with spill-over effects from the Western Region of Sudan-Darfur to the adjacent eastern part of Chad. On December 18, 2005, a newly formed rebel group called RDL (Rally for Democracy and Liberty) claimed responsibility for a large-scale attack. The origin of RDL is unclear; the Government of Chad says that RDL is a Sudanese militia and holds Sudan entirely responsible for the attack.

[2006 update: Relations with Sudan improved with a February agreement to end support to each other's rebel groups. Cross-border raids continued despite the accord, and high-level defections from Chad's army to Darfur-based Chadian rebels have increased the likelihood of continued escalation. Many refugees fled to Darfur to escape the fighting. Sudanese and Chadian militias from Darfur, with apparent Sudanese government backing, reportedly were behind the attacks. Despite rebel threats of violence, peaceful presidential elections were held in May. President Déby was reelected with 65 percent of the vote. Janjaweed continued attacks on border towns, and Sudanese SLA rebels continued to infiltrate refugee camps to forcibly recruit civilians, causing 10,000 to flee to Darfur. In October and November, Darfur-based Chadian rebels launched a major new offensive in eastern Chad. At year's end, Nour's FUCD faction signed a peace accord with Chad's president, but other rebel groups vowed to continue fighting the Déby regime.]

Colombia

Ongoing, Intrastate with FARC, EPL, ELN

The Colombian government is involved in a long-term armed conflict with several guerrilla organizations. The conflict, which is active throughout the country, causes the death of thousands of people every year, 40,000 in the past decade alone. The weakness of the Colombian state in the 1970s resulted in the formation of self-defense groups as private armies for rich landowners and drug lords. Subsequently lucrative drug trafficking and kidnappings made these paramilitary forces increasingly independent. In 1995 the United Self-defense Forces of Colombia (AUC) was formed as an umbrella organization for several local paramilitary groups. In 2002, President Uribe was determined to fight "outlaws" both on the political left and right. AUC declared a cease-fire in December 2002, and Uribe's hope was that the two main left guerrilla groups FARC-EP (Revolutionary Armed Forces of Colombia—the People's Army—most often referred to as FARC) and ELN, National Liberation Army) would follow AUC's example. In June 2003 the government, AUC, and Catholic Church representatives signed an accord stipulating complete AUC demobilization by 31 December 2005. As of the end of 2005, half of AUC's 20,000 fighters had handed in their arms. Although there were several groups which fought the government at the beginning of the 1990s, today only two groups remain active: FARC and ELN (EPL, People's Liberation Army) has also been active as late as in 2004). FARC is the only peasant-based guerrilla movement. ELN was created by a group of students whose objective was to bring down the government and to declare itself the military wing of the PCML (Communist Party of Colombia Marxist Leninist). The US has supported Colombia mainly by providing financial support for the government's anti-narcotics policies, expanded to counter-terrorism in 2001. FARC, ELN, and AUC are listed on the US Department of State's Current List of Designated Foreign Terrorist Organizations.

[2006 update: Demobilization of the AUC was completed in 2006. Paramilitary control over local socio-economic structures was left virtually untouched by the Justice and Peace Law (JPL). The uncovering of links between secret police DAS and paramilitaries in late 2005 and the killing of 10 elite counternarcotics policemen by an army unit in May 2006 raised fears of drug mafia's and paramilitaries' infiltration of key state institutions. Attacks conducted by illegally armed groups decreased considerably from 2002 to 2005, but FARC attacks resumed in January 2006. In December 2005 ELN began a new round of talks with the Colombian government in Cuba, and they met again February and May 2006.]

Ethiopia

Ongoing, Intrastate in ONLF

In 1984 the ONLF (Ogaden National Liberation Front) was established to struggle for self-determination. In January 1996 armed conflict broke out when ONLF declared a holy war against Ethiopia and launched an attack on Ethiopian government troops with the stated aim of liberating Ogaden from the Ethiopian colonial power. ONLF offered the government a negotiated dialogue, but these proposals were turned down. The same year in June ONLF signed a military agreement on an alliance with the Oromo Liberation Front (OLF), although the parties still acted separately. In 1997, however, the conflict was inactive but erupted again the following year. On August 15, 1997, ONLF and one faction of Afar Revolutionary Democratic Unity Front (ARDUF) signed a document in which the two organizations agreed to cooperate and coordinate their political, diplomatic, and military efforts. Moreover, the ONLF was split into two factions: one that wanted to continue armed operations against the regime in Addis Ababa, and one that saw its fight as within the framework of the Somali regional state (which was now led by one of its officials, Mohamed Maalim). This led to a definite split of ONLF in June 1998 when one of its factions merged with the Ethiopian-Somali Democratic League (ESDL) and formed a new party called the Somali Democratic Party, with the intention of establishing a new regional government. Remaining ONLF continued the armed struggle. The conflict in Ethiopia continued, although accurate information is difficult to locate.

[2006 update: In August, the security situation remained tense in the Ogaden region as the military said it killed 13 ONLF ethnic Somali separatists crossing into Ethiopia, days after ONLF said it was "ready for talks." Eritrean-backed Oromo Liberation Front (OLF) rebels called for mediation by African nations. Oromo media reported OLF killed 35 soldiers in the south in November.]

India
Ongoing, Intrastate with CPI-M

In the late 1960s several elements of the Indian Communist movement revolted against the prevailing communist party of India (CPI-M), accusing it of being counterrevolutionary. This so-called Naxalite movement became a revolutionary party with the establishment of the Communist Party of India (Marxist-Leninist) in 1969. Other groups that formed during this period and later with differing views on the best strategy for agrarian revolutionary struggle included the Maoist Communist Centre (MCC) and the Communist Party of India (M-L) People's War Group (PWG). The MCC and PWG led the Maoist insurgency against the Indian state in the 1990s. The revolutionary aim included the abolition of the feudal order in rural India through protracted armed struggle. The Naxalite organizations have primarily mobilized among the peasantry, particularly among the tribals and landless poor in the jungle districts of Andhra Pradesh, Maharahstra, Madhya Pradesh, and Orissa. The warring strategy of the insurgents has been directed at undermining government authority. The low-intensity conflict between the Indian government and the rebel opposition was only one dimension of the deteriorating security situation in the Naxalite strongholds of Bihar and Andhra Pradesh during the 1990s. Both warring parties have taken initiatives to find a political solution to the conflict during the last three years, most of which proved fruitless. During 2004 the MCC and PWG were extending and consolidating their influence in their communist strongholds—the states of Jharkand, Bihar, and Andrah Pradesh—while also further strengthening cross-border links with Nepalese Maoist cadres. The state government in Andrah Pradesh declared a unilateral ceasefire with the PWG in June 2004. Peace talks were initiated in October, but ended without any substantial progress. On October 14, 2004, the MCC announced its merger with the PWG to form the Communist Party of India. Negotiations between CPI (Maoist) and the Andhra

Pradesh state government broke down in mid-January 2005 after the rebels accused the authorities of not addressing their demands for a written truce, release of prisoners, and redistribution of land. CPI (Maoist) continued to consolidate its hold on large rural areas in several Indian states (Andhra Pradesh, Bihar, Jharkand, Chattisgarh, etc.). The conflict remained active throughout 2005.

India
Ongoing, Intrastate with NSCN-K, with foreign involvement

Among the ethnic groups and tribes in the northeast, in 1947 the Nagas were the first to seek a separate state. In seeking a political settlement of the conflict, Nagaland was established as a separate state under the Indian constitution in 1963. The NNC continued the insurgency but was eventually forced to sign the Shillong agreement in 1975, whereby NNC accepted the Indian constitution and agreed to surrender. In 1978 a new underground movement was formed, called the National Socialist Council of Nagaland (NSCN), demanding the establishment of a "greater Nagaland." The Konyak tribe, which formed the rank and file of the NSCN, formed a breakaway faction. In 1988, the Tangkhuls continued to dominate the command structure of the NSCN. As part of a deliberate strategy to enforce the vision of a "greater Nagaland," the insurgents have targeted other ethnic groups and forced their violent expulsion from the territory. It has been estimated that the conflict has claimed 20,000 lives during the last four decades. Strong regional linkages have remained between territorial insurgencies in the neighboring Indian states. NSCN has allegedly also received secondary support from regions within Bangladesh, Thailand, Burma, and Myanmar, and training from the Pakistani intelligence service. Improved relations between India and Myanmar led to increased cooperation in fighting against the NSCN-K. In early 1997, several factors coincided to put pressure on the NSCN-IM and facilitate negotiations for a political solution: the success of the government's counteroperations; the arrest of several prominent NSCN-IM leaders; Myanmar's hostile attitude towards NSCN activity on its territory; Indo-Bangladesh cooperation on preventing rebel activity along their border; and the strengthening of the hostile Khalang-faction of the

NSCN. The government signed a ceasefire with the NSCN-K in 2000 to limit the occasional cross-border attacks. Both the ceasefire with NSCN-K and the ceasefire with NSCN-IM have been extended on several occasions and remain in effect as of December 2005. Almost no armed activity was reported for NSCN-IM in 2005. The 2005 offensives by Indian-Myanmar forces against NSCN-K bases have been criticized by both factions as a major setback in the peace process. The conflict was active in December 2005 but all fighting was taking place between NSCN-K and the Myanmar army across the border from Indian Nagaland.

[2006 update: In February, deadly clashes were reported between the military and NSCN-K separatist groups based in Myanmar.]

India
Ongoing, Intrastate with Kashmir Insurgents

The most protracted and serious regional problem confronting India is the territorial insurgency in Kashmir resulting from the state's disputed accession to India following partition in 1947. The dispute escalated into full-fledged war with Pakistan in 1948. The UN-mediated ceasefire line agreed to in 1949 divided Kashmir between Indian and Pakistani controlled sections. Sympathy for the militant groups advocating violent secession from India increased dramatically by the end of the 1980s. Anti-government demonstrations, strikes, and violent attacks on government targets launched in 1988 marked the onset of the Kashmir insurgency. In 1989, the Jammu and Kashmir Liberation Front (JKLF) was the single dominant rebel group. By January 1990, as many as 40 different militant groups existed. The main division is between the pro-Pakistani elements favoring accession to Pakistan and the pro-Azadi elements favoring Kashmir's complete independence. The intrastate conflict has become closely entangled with the interstate relations between Pakistan and India. India has repeatedly accused Pakistan of supporting the Kashmir separatists, while Pakistan has denied these allegations and stated that its support to the insurgents is limited to political, cultural, and diplomatic areas. In meeting the mounting Kashmir insurgency, the army and paramilitary forces have remained the preferred strategy of India through-

out the conflict. Positive moves by both parties in mid-2000 and early 2001 raised hope for a political dialogue, but no progress was made. Discussions have been deadlocked by irreconcilable preconditions: the Indian government insists that all talks must take place within the framework of the Indian constitution, while the insurgents demand that any talks must address the Kashmiri's demand for independence. The rebel opposition has demanded that Pakistan participate in the negotiations, but India insists that Kashmir is a purely internal matter. The conflict continued at the level of war in 2005. While cross-border infiltration has dipped thanks to the building of a new fence along the Line of Control and the secession of military hostilities between India and Pakistan, Kashmir insurgents continued to engage the Indian army. The earthquake in October 2005 appeared to affect insurgent forces, who initially declared the suspension of military operations. They quickly regrouped, however, and violence continued throughout the year.

[2006 update: In early 2006, and again late in the year, India and Pakistan met and agreed on continued dialogue on normalization. Cross-border travel links increased. In May and June, there was an upsurge in attacks by separatists. Violence continued in Indian-controlled Kashmir in apparent reaction to positive talks between Indian PM Singh and the main moderate faction of APHC that set up an unprecedented framework for future talks. Foreign secretary-level talks between India and Pakistan in mid-November yielded little progress on Kashmir sticking points.]

Indonesia
Ongoing (termination August 15, 2005), Intrastate with Aceh

The Aceh region of northern Sumatra is rich in natural resources such as oil and natural gas; the uneven distribution of the wealth has been central to the conflict. With Indonesian independence in 1949, the province of Aceh was granted local autonomy. This autonomy was withdrawn in 1950 as Aceh was incorporated into the province of North Sumatra. In 1959, President Sukarno restored Aceh as an autonomous province, but this status was removed by President Suharto in the mid-1960s. Religious and economic grievances led to the second Acehnese rebellion beginning in 1976 and the founding of GAM (Free Aceh Movement). Swift Indonesian response soon ended the rebellion. The increasing influx of migrant workers and their non-Islamic behavior led to widespread dissatisfaction among the Acehnese population throughout the 1980s, leading to a reinvented GAM in 1989.

After an increasing number of violent incidents, the government launched a large-scale campaign in 1990 against GAM and Acehnese civilians. In the late 1990s GAM established alternative local administrations in parts of Aceh. Swiss mediation resulted in a "Humanitarian Pause" in the fighting on May 12, 2000, later extended to January 2001. Negotiations continued until April 2001 when President Wahid initiated a renewed government offensive, reversed by President Megawati Sukarnoputri signing of a law in August 2001 that proclaimed special autonomy to Aceh. A Cessation of Hostilities Agreement was signed on December 9, 2002. However, when the peace negotiations failed on May 19, 2003, the conflict intensified. Aceh was hit hard by the December 26, 2004, Indian Ocean tsunami, with a death toll of 160,000. GAM and the Indonesian Government declared unilateral ceasefires. Pressure from international donors led to a memorandum of understanding on August 15, 2005, stipulating the demobilization and disbanding of GAM's rebel troops and restricting of the presence of government troops. The province is to govern itself in all sectors of public affairs except foreign affairs, external defense, national security, monetary and fiscal matters, justice, and freedom of religion. An Aceh Monitoring Mission is to monitor and verify the implementation of the peace agreement, with EU and ASEAN observers. Finally a general amnesty was proclaimed. In fall 2005 governmental forces withdrew from Aceh and GAM carried out decommissioning of its weapons; violence decreased substantially.

Iran

Ongoing, Intrastate with PJAK

Mujahideen e Khalq (MEK) roots are in the early 1960s in a nationalistic, liberal, lay-religious party, called the Liberation Movement. After a failed uprising against the Shah in 1963, many of the movement's leaders were imprisoned and the younger generation advocated armed struggle. It was the younger members of the Liberation Movement who formed MEK, which became the more religiously oriented, anti-American offspring to the Liberation Movement. The group's potential for violence was developed as members were sent to train in PLO camps in Lebanon and Jordan. In 1971 the group attempted to attack the state, but the operations were foiled, leading to the execution of the founders and the arrest of many members of the group. This led to an influx of new leaders and members with a more Marxist-centered ideology, causing the group to eventually splinter. In the period leading up to the 1979 Islamic Revolution, MEK leaders were released from prison and they managed to become Iran's largest political movement. The Marxist-Leninist splinter group became known as the Paykar Organization during the revolution. MEK ended up opposing the regime through violent means. After a major violent incident in June 1981, leaders of the group fled to Paris. In 1987 most of the group moved to Iraq, where they remain today. Their support of the Iraqi side in the Iran-Iraq war had a negative effect on their popular support in Iran. There was not much activity in the conflict immediately after the Iran-Iraq war, but in 1991 the conflict started again. The capture of the Kurdish leader Abdullah Ocalan by Turkish security forces in 1999 led to protests and demonstrations in the Kurdish parts of Iran. As a result of these protests Iranian PKK members created a new movement with the name Democratic Union Movement. On April 25, 2004, this movement held its first congress and formed a more structured organization with the name PJAK—The Free Life Party of Kurdistan (Partî Jiyanî Azadî Kurdistan). At this congress PJAK also presented its political motives and goals. As of early 2006, the conflict is considered active.

Iraq

Ongoing, Intrastate with TQJBR, Al-Mahdi Army, Jaish Ansar Al-Sunna, IAI

After Iraq was defeated in the interstate conflict against the US, UK, and Australia in 2003, forces from a US-led coalition of countries remained in Iraq to support the new government in providing security, policing, and reconstruction in the years that followed. The situation remains complex, with the Shi'i dominated government unable to control the spreading violence among insurgent groups. It appears that the violence is associated with three primary groups during the period since the US-led invasion, but many other groups have been involved. One of the groups that wanted to overthrow the Iraqi government in the fall of 2003 was Jaish Ansar Al-Sunna (Army of Ansar Al-Sunna) in northern Iraq. As the number of casualties increased in the early months of 2004, the Iraqi government accused a Jordanian named Abu Mus'ab al-Zarqawi as heading the insurgency. There were no official statements from al-Zarqawi that could be confirmed. On April 24, 2004, the "Military Department" of the Zarqawi group stated their intention to overthrow the government, expel the US forces, and establish a Sunni Islamic state with Sharia law. The group started its activity in 2004 and named itself TQJBR (Tanzim Qa'idat al-Jihad fi Bilad al-Rafidayn; The Organization of Jihad's Base in the Country of the Two Rivers). In early 2004, political discontent grew among the Shi'i population, especially targeting the foreign presence in the country. One of the more outspoken critics was Muqtada al-Sadr who previously had formed a militia, the Al-Mahdi Army. The Al-Mahdi Army launched coordinated attacks on government positions in southern Iraq as well as in Baghdad in April 2004. The Al-Mahdi Army fought the government intensively during that year. In late August, the prime Shi'ite cleric in Iraq, Ayatollah Ali al-Sistani, intervened and negotiated a ceasefire between the two forces. Some clashes continued in September in the Al-Sadr suburb of Baghdad, but Muqtada al-Sadr focused more on preparing for the elections in January 2005. In the elections, Al-Sadr and his supporters won 30 seats in the new parliament. In 2005, activity by TQJBR and the Jaish Ansar al-Sunna escalated. There has been an increase in deliberate attacks on civilians and intercommunal violence. At the same time, there remains a great deal of uncertainty about the perpetrators of much of the violence.

[2006 update: The December 2005 elections resulted in a victory for the Islamist Shiite-led United Iraqi Alliance. There was continued and escalating sectarian violence throughout the year. After five months of negotiations, parliament approved a 37-member "unity government" on May 20th. The brutal insurgency and sectarian violence continued throughout the country. Al-Qaeda in Iraq (TQJBR) leader al-Zarqawi was killed in a US-Iraqi operation in June. PM Maliki presented a national reconciliation plan in an attempt to reduce sectarian violence: offered amnesty to some insurgents, militia disarmament and improvement of security forces. By November, sectarian violence rose to the worst levels since the US-led 2003 invasion. On December 30, former Iraqi president Saddam Hussein was hanged by the government after his conviction for having ordered the murders of 148 Shi'ites in a failed assassination attempt in 1982.]

Israel

Ongoing, Intrastate with Fatah, Palestinian Islamic Jihad, Hamas, (Hezbollah 2006)

There have been nine different Palestinian groups active in clashes with the government of Israel; Fatah, the Popular Front for the Liberation of Palestine (PFLP), the Popular Front for the Liberation of Palestine-General Command (PFLP-GC), Hezbollah, Amal, Hamas, Palestinian Islamic Jihad (PIJ), Palestinian National Authority (PNA) and Al-Aqsa Martyr's Brigades (AMB). The roots of the conflict lie in ancient and competing claims for the territory known as Palestine. The UN-mandated partition of Palestine in 1947 led to the establishment of the State of Israel in 1948 and was followed by five interstate wars with Arab countries between 1948 and the present. Two key factors that resulted from the wars and that fed the Israeli-Palestinian part of the Israeli-Arab conflict were; Palestinian refugees growing out of the 1948–49 war, and the occupation of the West Bank and Gaza from Jordan and Egypt in 1967. In 1959 Yasser Arafat founded Fatah and became an important player in the umbrella organization PLO (Palestinian Liberation Organization). Other Palestinian organizations took up arms soon after Fatah. Hezbollah has its origins in the Israeli occupation of southern Lebanon, after its intervention in the Lebanese civil war in 1982. In the West Bank and Gaza, Islamic groups such as the PIJ (Palestinian Islamic Jihad) and Hamas conducted their first attacks during the latter half of the 1980s. Local Palestinian leaders in December 1987 initiated violent demonstrations against the Israeli occupation, the so-called Intifada (Uprising). The Oslo Accord, signed on September 13, 1993, called for the establishment of a Palestinian Interim Self-Government Authority and a preparatory transfer of power and responsibilities from Israel to authorized Palestinians, with a final settlement to be reached within five years. The second Intifada began in 2000 and all but ended any chance that the Olso Accord would be implemented. In early 2005 Israel proceeded with the construction of a security wall roughly along the Green Line separating Israel from the West Bank, and began preparations for the withdrawal of forces from parts of the West Bank and Gaza. On the Palestinian side, the efforts of new President and Fatah leader Mahmud Abbas to establish control over all militant factions seemed to be successful. A ceasefire came into effect and elections in the Palestinian Authority were extended to January 2006. The Israeli pullout from Gaza during June–September 2005 and the official ceasefire led to a decrease in conflict activity in 2005 relative to the previous three years.

[2006 update: 2006 began with an overwhelming Hamas victory in legislative elections in the West Bank and Gaza, and Israeli Prime Minister Sharon's incapacitation due to a stroke, followed by Olmert's Kadima Party victory in March elections. The Hamas cabinet won a parliamentary confidence vote. Violence escalated between Israelis and Palestinians while tensions rose between Hamas and Fatah. Mounting violence in Gaza was fuelled by a power struggle between Fatah and Hamas loyalists. Rivalries focused on respective control of Palestinian President Abbas and Islamist Palestinian Authority government over security forces. In June, tensions rose dramatically as the Israeli military launched an operation in the Gaza Strip following the kidnapping by Palestinian militants of an Israeli soldier and an increase in shelling of Israeli towns from Gaza. Full-scale conflict between Israel and Hezbollah erupted following the abduction of two Israeli soldiers in July along the Lebanese border. Israel responded to the abductions with a sea, land, and air blockade, attacks on Hezbollah positions in south Lebanon, and countrywide bombing of infrastructure. Hezbollah replied with indiscriminate rocket attacks into northern Israel. A fragile UN-brokered ceasefire commenced on August 14: approximately 1,000 Lebanese and 159 Israelis were killed. UNSC Resolution 1701, which led to the ceasefire, called for Hezbollah to move north of the Litani River to allow the Lebanese army and strengthened UN force (UNIFIL) of 15,000 to deploy to southern Lebanon. In Gaza, a fragile ceasefire took hold in November.]

Myanmar (Burma)
Ongoing, Intrastate with KNU

The Union of Myanmar (Burma until 1989) consists of several ethnic groups. The Karen's traditional homeland is along the border with Thailand. The KNU (Karen National Union) was formed in 1947. Shortly after independence in 1948, the KNU demanded the formation of an independent Karen state. Tensions continued to grow and in January 1949 fierce fighting erupted between KNU forces and a combination of government troops and affiliated paramilitary forces. KNU has formed alliances with other insurgent groups, especially those in close areas such as the Karenni, Mon, and Pao. Myanmar has accused Thailand of backing the KNU, as the group has been able to retreat to bases on Thai territory. The KNU had great military success until an internal split, and ensuing government offensive in 1994–95. In late 1994, disenchantment with the Christian leadership of KNU among a group of Buddhist Karen led to a split in the organization and the formation of the Democratic Kayin Buddhist Army (DKBA). The DKBA quickly signed a ceasefire with the Myanmar government and began an armed struggle against the KNU. The KNU has relied mostly on the tactic of armed attacks on government troops, while the government offensives have been large-scale operations lasting for months. After the fall of the KNU headquarters in 1995 and a tougher stance towards border-crossings from the Thai authorities, KNU has adopted more of a guerrilla strategy. After decreasing clashes in 2003, the KNU and the government announced a "gentleman's agreement" ceasefire in December 2003, although occasional breaches of the ceasefire were reported. As of December 2005, the conflict between the government and KNU over the Karen territory is active.

[2006 update: In March 2006, a counterinsurgency action by the military in western Karen state reportedly forced villagers to flee homes, bringing the total number of internally displaced to 5,000 since January. In April, the army intensified its offensive against Karen communities near the new capital Pyinmana and along the Thai border. A KNU delegation was due to hold peace talks with the junta in September.]

Myanmar (Burma)
Ongoing, Intrastate with SSA/S

The 1947 constitution of the Union of Burma stipulated that the Shan State had the right to leave the union ten years after the country became independent in 1948. Two years later, the Karen rebellion (see above) spread into Shan State as the Karen insurgents were supported by fleeing Chinese Kuomintang (KMT) troops; as a result the Burmese government sent additional troops to the area. With the alleged assistance of the American CIA, the KMT maintained bases in Burma during the next decade in their struggle against the Chinese communist government. They also developed into the largest opium-dealing army in the world. The Shan nationalist movement started gaining strength in the mid-1950s. They managed to take over most of the drug business after the KMT left in 1961. Following the Burmese military coup in 1962, the elected Shan administration came under virtual military occupation by the government. The three largest Shan rebel organizations merged in 1964 as the SSA (Shan State Army). In the late 1980s and early 1990s, most of the Shan insurgent organizations either signed ceasefire agreements with the government or became affiliated (or incorporated) with the MTA (Mong Tai Army). In 1989, several ethnic groups emerged from the disintegration of the Burmese communist party (CPB). The strongest militarily was the UWSA (Wa), which signed a ceasefire with the government with the promise to help the government against MTA. Throughout 1995, the members of the MTA split into several different factions. Several of these were involved in fighting against the government but finally three main groups united as the Shan State Army – South Command (SSA-S.) The SSA-S continued fighting in the Shan conflict, as well as fighting UWSA, which allegedly took over the drug business left by MTA. The SSA-S relied on cross-border attacks from Thailand. The fighting had slowly intensified between the government and SSA-S after a year of almost no conflict activity in 2003. Small clashes were reported in 2004 as the government reportedly increased its military presence in Shan state. In April 2005, there was intensive fighting between SSA-S and government forces supported by the UWSA. As the year continued, several other incidents of fighting were reported. As of December 2005, the conflict between the government and Shan State Army-South Command over the territory of Shan State was active.

Nepal
Ongoing (terminated 2006), Intrastate with CPN-M/UPF

The roots of the Nepalese insurgency originate in the turbulent transition from an absolutist system of monarchy to a constitutional monarchy under multiparty democracy. The present system was introduced in 1990, but the system has been flawed by a lack of stability and unrealized expectations. The Communist Party of Nepal-Maoist (CPN-M) publicly launched its armed struggle in 1996, calling for the installation of a communist government. There followed a series of attacks on political, military, and commercial targets all over the country. The violence marked the onset of an insurgency that by 1999 affected half of Nepal's 75 districts. Popular sympathy for the insurgents was strengthened by the crude force used in police reprisals. In mid-2001 the deteriorating security situation in the country was further aggravated by the killing of the royal family. The Maoists used the general sense of disorder as an opportunity to further destabilize the government. The Nepalese government declared a nationwide state of emergency and deployed the army to counter the insurgents. Following several failed attempts at negotiation, on February 1, 2005, the king seized power in what was widely seen as a royal coup. The rule of law was suspended as hundreds of political leaders, activists, journalists, and rights workers were arrested. The king's actions met with widespread international condemnation, even by traditional allies, such as India, the UK, and the US. The coup led to an escalation in violence that continued until September 3, 2005, when the Maoists declared a unilateral three-month ceasefire as they held talks with political parties. Nepal's mainstream political parties and the Maoists engaged in talks throughout the ceasefire and eventually came to an agreement in November on mutual goals and cooperation.

[2006 update: Political turmoil continued ahead of the planned February 8, 2006, municipal elections, and a major escalation of violence occurred. In April, after 19 days of mass anti-monarchy protests, King Gyanendra agreed to restore parliament for the first time since its dissolution in 2002. In May, the new government and Maoists met for the first peace talks since 2003. The sides agreed to a ceasefire and code of conduct which committed both to a multiparty system, elections for a constituent assembly, and an end to provocations. Previously, the government had dropped terrorism charges against the Maoists and released hundreds from prison. In May, Parliament voted unanimously to restrict royal powers, putting the Nepal Army under the control of parliament. The Maoists and the interim government signed an historic peace deal on November 21, 2006, ending the 10-year war.]

Philippines

Ongoing, Intrastate with MILF and Abu Sayyef Group

The government of the Philippines has long been involved in fighting communist and Muslim (Moro) insurgencies on Mindanao Island. The term "Moro" is more specific than the universal "Muslim" since it denotes the political identity of the local Muslims. During the 1970s, the Moro National Liberation Front (MNLF) and its military wing engaged in armed struggle against the central government, leading to as many as 120,000 deaths. Under pressure from the Organization of the Islamic Conference, in 1976 the MNLF dropped its demands for independence and settled for autonomy. The agreement provided for the granting of autonomy to 13 of the 23 provinces in Mindanao, Sulu, and Palewan islands. When the MNLF dropped its demand for independence, breakaway factions emerged including the Moro Islamic Liberation Front (MILF). Hostilities resumed and continued into the early 1980s. In the early 1990s, increased international attention was directed towards Mindanao, resulting from several high-profile kidnappings by criminal gangs and conflict parties. Most notorious was the Abu Sayyaf

Group (ASG), which was also responsible for several attacks on civilians. In 1996 the Final Peace Agreement was signed; even though the MILF did not participate in the 1996 agreement, the group had committed not to block peace, and fighting decreased in the following years. After formal negotiations had resumed, the government launched an "all-out war" policy against the Moro groups in 2000, leading to an escalation in conflict and the breakdown of peace talks. In 2003 the conflict between the government and MILF escalated again. During the second half of 2003 several attempts to start peace talks were made. The ceasefire lasted for much of 2004 as well. However, sporadic clashes continued in 2004 and 2005 amidst fresh peace talks. With both MILF and Abu Sayyaf involved in fighting, the conflict over Mindanao is ongoing as of December 2005.

[Update 2006: The military and the MNLF, based on Jolo, agreed to a truce in January. Clashes continued between the military and suspected Abu Sayyaf members on Basilan. In June 2006, despite initial optimism, informal MILF-Manila talks stalled over territorial delimitation and jurisdiction of an ancestral homeland on Mindanao. Deadly clashes continued on the southern island of Jolo between the military—backed by US technical support—and the Abu Sayyaf terrorist group.]

Philippines

Ongoing, Intrastate with the CPP

Increasing criticism of US involvement in Filipino affairs led to the formation of several protest groups in the early 1960s. Inspired by the successful revolutions in China, Cuba, and Vietnam, younger members of the Partido Komunista ng Pilipinas (PKP) were eager for the party to resume the type of armed activity that had characterized the party immediately after World War II. In 1968 the Huk established the CPP (Communist Party of the Philippines). The CPP looked to the Maoist idea of an agrarian revolution and developed plans for a military struggle. CPP's military wing, the NPA (New People's Army) was established in 1969. In the following years, the NPA kept expanding and in 1972 President Marcos declared countrywide martial law to suppress the "state of rebellion" caused by the Communists as well as the increasing communal conflicts between Moros and Christians in Mindanao (see above). Several factors led to a decrease in fighting between the CPP and the government in the early 1990s. The military was preoccupied with internal struggles. Changes also occurred within the CPP, namely, there was diminishing international political support as well as internal divisions on what tactics to pursue. As a consequence, several factions left the CPP to pursue urban guerrilla warfare. Conflict activity decreased as more formal peace negotiations were held in the mid-1990s. Under President Estrada in 1998 peace negotiations stalled. The economic crisis of 1998–99 also led to widespread criticism of the government, and the different factions of CPP seemed to unite. As a consequence, both the ranks of the CPP and the conflict itself escalated in 1999–2002. Since the CPP tactics were to connect with rural support and establish strongholds in the two largest islands, Luzon and Mindanao, it has been able at times to control substantial territory. The violence during 2005 continued at about the same level as in previous years.

[2006 update: Clashes continued between the military and NPA south of the capital and on Mindanao throughout 2006.]

Russia
Ongoing, Intrastate with Republic of Chechnya

During the Soviet era, the Autonomous Republic of Chechen-Ingush was under the authority of the Russian Republic. After the Soviet Union was dissolved in 1991 and the Russian Federation was formed, the new Russian government considered Chechen-Inguish to be one of the federated states. The Chechens aspired to political as well as cultural independence; Chechnya declared independence in 1991. In 1994 the conflict escalated radically when the Russian army launched a large-scale military intervention into Chechnya. During the first war, from 1994 to 1996, the Yeltsin government's intervention in Chechnya was unpopular in Russia. The second war broke out in 1999 and is still ongoing; President Putin has consistently referred to the Russian action in Chechnya as a "campaign against terrorism." This approach has enjoyed both strong popular and political support in Russia. During both conflict phases, "the Republic of Chechnya" has been obstructed by an internal power struggle. From the outset of the conflict, the fighting took the form of violence against civilians and indiscriminate killings. In 2004, the conflict escalated as the rebels instigated attacks in neighboring republics such as Dagestan, Ingushetia, and Northern Ossetia, with terrorist acts reaching as far as Moscow. During the course of the conflict, few serious efforts have been made to negotiate a solution. In the second phase, the Russian government's approach was a refusal to recognize "President" Maskhadov's authority. As of the end of 2005, Russia maintained a certain degree of control over the Chechnya territory. The Russian leadership also dictated Chechnya's political future through Alu Alkhanov and his puppet government. Nevertheless, the rebels continue to be an active threat both for Chechnya and for the neighboring areas.

[2006 update: In July 2006, rebel commander and deputy leader Shamil Basayev was killed with three other militants in Ingushetia. In August, Russian President Putin asked defense and interior ministries to formulate a plan for withdrawal of all nonpermanent troops from Chechnya by 2008. Pro-Kremlin Chechen PM Kadyrov welcomed the proposal.]

Sri Lanka
Ongoing, Intrastate with LTTE

Tamil militancy in Sri Lanka arose when the Tamils expressed fear that the unitary constitutional arrangements of the new state in 1948 would not give minorities adequate protection against the possible discriminatory consequences of majoritarian Sinhalese rule, including the constitutional stipulation of the primacy of Sinhala and Buddhism—the language and religion of the Sinhalese majority. The constitutional status of the predominantly Tamil area in the northeast of the island has remained the core of the conflict. The Liberation Tigers of Tamil Eelam (LTTE) was established in 1976 as a purely military organization, pursuing separatist demands. The LTTE initiated regular fighting by 1983, with an estimated 65,000 killed and 1.8 million displaced (as of 2003). The LTTE is one of the world's most sophisticated armed rebel groups, organized along conventional army lines and with suicide-cadres called the Black Tigers. The Indian-Sri Lankan accord of 1987 provided for the establishment of a regional provincial council in the Tamil areas and the disarming of Tamil militants. The Indian Peace Keeping Force (IPKF) was subsequently deployed on the island to guarantee the implementation of the political solution and the cessation of hostilities. When IPKF troops withdrew from Sri Lanka in 1990 full-fledged fighting resumed. Intense interfactional fighting exhausted the previously Indian-backed more moderate Tamil alliance and left the LTTE unchallenged to progressively take over the area abandoned by the IPKF, including nearly the whole Jaffna peninsula in the north. The most violent phase of the conflict began in 1995, aimed at eliminating the military capacity of the LTTE. The "Third Eelam war" brought military victories to the government, which recaptured the LTTE stronghold, Jaffna, in 1996. By late 2000 war fatigue led the Tamil Tigers to declare a unilateral ceasefire. The LTTE and the government signed a memorandum of Cessation of Hostilities in 2002. Hopes were raised in early 2005 that the tsunami disaster would result in increased cooperation and lasting peace. Instead, the situation deteriorated. By the end of the year, the situation deteriorated even further. As of late 2005, the conflict was still active.

[2006 update: After four years of relative peace, military conflict has again broken out between the government and LTTE. More than 2,500 people, many of them civilians, have been killed since January 2006. Human rights abuses and political killings were carried out with impunity by both sides. Talks in February and October 2006 failed to restart discussion of a political settlement.]

Sudan
Ongoing, Intrastate with SLM/A, JEM

In early 2003, while the government and SPLM/A were negotiating a settlement of the conflict in southern Sudan, another conflict broke out in Darfur, western Sudan. The SLM/A (Sudan Liberation Movement/Army) declared that it would fight the government to change the political system in Sudan. It demanded a united democratic Sudan based on equality, the separation of religion and the state, complete restructuring and devolution of power, more even development, and cultural and political pluralism. Subsequently another opposition group, JEM

(Justice and Equality Movement), also launched an armed struggle against the government, fighting for a federal system with autonomy for all states, a rotating presidency, and an equal distribution of natural resources. The two groups have cooperated both militarily and politically, but there has also been internal disagreement and fighting between them. Negotiations between the government of Sudan and SLM/A and JEM (jointly and separately) were held throughout the 2003–2005 period, mediated first by Chad, and later by the African Union (AU), but stalled on power-sharing and security arrangements. The situation in Darfur has been disastrous for the population. Besides the fighting between the two rebel groups and the army, there is a government-aligned militia called Janjaweed, which has been burning villages, looting, and killing. The government took some positive steps to investigate and address human rights violations in 2005, although implementation has been slow. Armed conflict continued in Darfur during 2005, albeit at a significantly lower level. The lower level of conflict is due to a number of factors, including the presence of AMIS (African Union Mission in Sudan) forces, the flight of most of the population to Internally Displaced Persons (IDP) and refugee camps, pressure by the international community, and consolidation of areas of control by the warring parties. Eritrea, Chad, and Libya have supported SLA and JEM. An estimated 180,000 to 300,000 people have died in Darfur since the civil conflict erupted in 2003, with some 2.6 million civilians left homeless. Currently, a complicating factor is the fractionalization among the rebels with internal fighting within SLA, with two rival groups struggling for power, fighting between JEM and SLA/M and splinter groups emerging from JEM.

[2006 update: In February, the UN Security Council authorized planning for the expected re-hatting of the AU mission in Darfur, despite strong objections from Khartoum. Severe insecurity in Darfur continued, spilling over into Chad, with Janjaweed militias raiding refugee camps inside Chadian border. In May, under intense international pressure, the government and the largest SLA rebel faction signed the Darfur Peace Agreement. The plan called for creation of temporary regional authority with rebel participation, Janjaweed disarmament, incorporation of rebels into the army, and Sudanese government funds for reconstruction and compensation. But other rebel group refused to sign. The UN Security Council voted in August to approve a force for Darfur with some Chapter VII powers, "inviting" consent from Khartoum. In November, major fighting erupted in the south between Sudan People's Liberation Army (SPLA) and Sudanese Armed Forces (SAF) in the first major violation of the 2005 north-south peace agreement.]

Turkey
Ongoing, Intrastate with PKK

Abdullah Öcalan founded the PKK (Kurdistan Workers' Party) in 1974 as a Marxist-Leninist group with the goal of establishing an independent and democratic Kurdish state. In August 1984 PKK forces began ambushing Turkish troops on Kurdish territory. Unlike many other Kurdish organizations, such as KDPI in Iran and KDP and PUK in Iraq, the PKK originally demanded an independent Kurdish state instead of Kurdish autonomy. After Öcalan was arrested and tried in 1999 he gave up the idea of a Kurdish state and convinced the PKK's Presidential Council to drop the word "Kurdistan" from the names of PKK's military and political wings (ARGK and ERNK). The PKK retained its sizeable "Public-defense Force." Syria, Greece, and Iran have provided the PKK with shelter, training grounds, and/or financial support. Northern Iraq has been a safe-haven for PKK fighters. In April 2002 the PKK changed its name, announcing that it had fulfilled its historical mission and that it was now dissolved. At the same time the Congress for Freedom and Democracy in Kurdistan (KADEK) announced its establishment to continue PKK's struggle for the liberation of the Kurds through dialogue and democracy rather than violence. KADEK was dissolved after the summer of 2003 and a new Kurdish group intended to attract broader support, KONGRA-GEL (People's Congress of Kurdistan), was formed. In 2005 a sharp increase in clashes was reported. On August 19, 2005, the PKK unilaterally declared a ceasefire after Prime Minister Erdogan announced that his government wanted more reforms for the Kurds. The PKK stated that it might permanently extend the ceasefire if the Turkish government met its conditions. Attacks decreased but nevertheless continued, indicating the ceasefire was not recognized or adhered to by either side. The PKK's ceasefire appeared to be an effort to get their case onto the political agenda during sensitive negotiations leading up to Turkey's October 3rd date for the start of entry talks with the EU.

[2006 update: The PKK continued its attacks during most of the year, particularly in Istanbul and the southeast. Turkey called on both Iran and Iraq to curb PKK activities in northern Iraq. The government called on the US and Iraq to crack down on the PKK in Northern Iraq, signaling it would mount cross-border operations to halt PKK incursions otherwise. The PKK announced a unilateral ceasefire September 30th, following a call from imprisoned leader Ocalan, but Prime Minister Erdogan said the PKK must surrender weapons unconditionally. Violence in the southeast and east continued.]

Uganda
Ongoing, Intrastate with LRA

Uganda's history since independence in 1962 has been characterized by violence, much of it based on regional interests. The current conflict with the Lord's Resistance Army (LRA) has its roots in 1986, when Museveni seized power and NRA forces began to commit human rights abuses throughout the Acholi region. Acholi soldiers from Obote's defunct national army and youths fleeing from NRA operations either hid or crossed the border into Sudan to take up arms. In August 1986, these fighters, under the name Uganda People's Democratic Army (UPDA), launched the first attack against NRA troops. UPDA signed a peace agreement with the government in 1988. Meanwhile, in 1985, an Acholi woman named Alice Auma claimed to have been possessed by an alien Christian spirit and in 1986 began raising an army. In November 1986 Uganda Democratic Christian Army (UPCA) began attacking NRA units stationed in Acholi. The UDCA has its roots in both of these movements, and is led by Joseph Kony. When Alice's forces were defeated in late 1987, Kony declared that he would keep fighting the regime, and in 1992 formed the Lord's Resistance Army (LRA). The Khartoum regime until the early 2000s supported LRA, providing bases, weapons, and military training. In return,

LRA fought alongside Sudanese government forces against SPLA/M. Zaire/DRC has also actively supported rebels opposing Museveni's government. However, in 1998 this situation changed and DRC switched sides in the conflict. In 1994 LRA became increasingly brutal, often specifically targeting the civilian Acholi population, including the mass abductions of children. The UPDF subsequently received permission from Sudan to carry out operations against LRA in southern Sudan, and to some extent the conflict was moved eastwards to the Teso region in mid-2003. The rebels came under even further military pressure when Sudan struck a deal with Uganda allowing UPDF to go even further into Sudan. During the last two months of 2004, a ceasefire was respected and peace talks were initiated. The peace agreement between the Sudanese government and SPLM/A meant that LRA came under increasing pressure in southern Sudan.

[2006 update: In August 2006, the government and the LRA reached a ceasefire agreement, in peace talks that began in Sudan in July. A revised cessation of hostilities agreement had been signed November 1 to specify assembly points, provide for security and humanitarian assistance, and removal of UPDF from near assembly points. The negotiations were plagued by dissatisfaction within the LRA delegation and lack of monitoring mechanisms of LRA and UPDF. These talks were suspended by LRA in late November.]

United States
Ongoing, Intrastate with al-Qaeda, with foreign involvement

The conflict between the US and al-Qaeda constitutes an untraditional case of internal conflict with most of the activity taking place outside of the US and including armed forces from over 20 different countries. Following the Iraq-Kuwait conflict 1990–91, the US maintained airbases in Saudi Arabia, a cause for much criticism of the US and its regional allies. Al-Qaeda had been formed in 1988 by volunteer forces that were fighting alongside the rebels in the Afghanistan conflict (see Afghanistan above). Encouraged by the 1989 withdrawal of Soviet troops

that had supported the Afghan government in that conflict, al-Qaeda declared its intent to continue the jihad in defense of Islamic movements. Al-Qaeda's founder Osama bin Laden from Saudi Arabia became increasingly critical of the US and its presence in the Islamic world. On September 11, 2001, al-Qaeda launched attacks on the Pentagon in Washington DC and civilian targets in New York City. The goal was to force the US to abandon its involvement overseas, and specifically in the Middle East. Following these attacks, US President Bush declared "war on terror" and al-Qaeda. Several other countries quickly supported the US. In October–November 2001, troops were deployed from the United Kingdom, Canada, Australia, Germany, France, Poland, Italy, and Turkey, while other countries offered other types of support. By March 2002, more than 17,000 military personnel from 17 countries had been deployed together with US forces as the so-called "coalition of the willing." US demands that the Taliban government of Afghanistan extradite the al-Qaeda leaders based in that country were rejected. The US-led "Operation Enduring Freedom" that started in October 2001 then targeted suspected al-Qaeda bases in Afghanistan, but also the Taliban regime itself for its support of al-Qaeda. With the defeat of the Taliban government, the US attacks on al-Qaeda intensified. Most surviving al-Qaeda operatives fled across the border into Pakistan in 2002–03, while others regrouped in Saudi Arabia. When the conflict resumed in 2004, almost all the activity took place in the Pakistani tribal areas of South Waziristan and in Saudi Arabia. During 2005, most of the activity in the conflict was in the border region between Afghanistan and Pakistan.

[2006 update: In September, President Musharraf of Pakistan made a controversial deal with North Waziristan tribal militants allied with the Taliban: it ended military operations against border militants in exchange for an end to attacks on the army and across the border in Afghanistan. But heightened tensions between Islamabad and Kabul may also have strained Pakistan's relations with NATO, while the local governor admitted the presence of hundreds of al-Qaeda-linked militants in North Waziristan.]

REFERENCES

Alimi, Eitan. 2003. "The Effects of Opportunities on Insurgencies." *Terrorism and Political Violence* 15 (3):111-138.

Amnesty International. 2006. "Background Information." http://web.amnesty.org/library/Index/ENGAFR540732006?open&of=ENG-SDN. (Accessed Nov. 14, 2006).

Banaszak, Lee Ann. 1996. *Why Movements Succeed or Fail*. Princeton: Princeton University Press.

Bates, Robert H., David L. Epstein, Jack A. Goldstone, Ted Robert Gurr, Barbara Harff, Colin H. Kahl, Marc A. Levy, Michael Lustik, Monty G. Marshall, Thomas M. Parris, Jay Ulfelder, and Mark R. Woodward. 2006. *Political Instability Task Force Report: Phase IV Findings*.

Bothe, Michael, Karl Josef Partsch, and Waldemar A. Solf. 1982. *New Rules for Victims of Armed Conflicts: Commentary on the two 1977 Protocols Additional to the Geneva Conventions of 1949*. The Hague: Martinus Nijhoff.

Boutros-Ghali, Boutros. 1992. *An Agenda for Peace: Report of the Secretary-General to the Security Council*. New York: United Nations Publications.

Brecher, Michael, and Philip B.K. Potter. 2005. "The Severity and Impact of International Crises: Models and Findings" Meeting of the International Studies Association, Honolulu, March 2005.

Brecher, Michael, and Jonathan Wilkenfeld. 2000. *A Study of Crisis*. Ann Arbor, Michigan: University of Michigan Press.

Byman, Daniel, Peter Chalk, Bruce Hoffman, William Rosenau, and David Brannan. 2001. *Trends in Outside Support for Insurgent Movements*. Santa Monica: RAND.

Carnegie Corporation of New York. 2006. "States at Risk." International Peace and Security Program. http://www.carnegie.org/sub/program/intl_peace.html (Accessed Dec. 9, 2006).

Chalk, Frank, and Kurt Jonassohn. 1990. *The History and Sociology of Genocide*. New Haven: Yale University Press.

Charny, Israel W. 1982. *How Can We Commit the Unthinkable? Genocide: The Human Cancer*. Boulder: Westview.

Collier, Paul, and Anke Hoeffler. 2004. "Greed and Grievance in Civil War," *Oxford Economic Papers* 56:563-95.

Crenshaw, Martha. 1988. "The Subjective Reality of the Terrorist: Ideological and Psychological Factors in Terrorism." In *Current Perspectives in International Terrorism*, eds. R.O. Slater and M. Stohl.

Davenport, Christian. 1999. "Human Rights and the Democratic Proposition." *Journal of Conflict Resolution* 43 (1):92-116.

de Waal, Alex. 2004. "Counter-Insurgency on the Cheap." *London Review of Books* 26 (15):1-15.

Doyle, Michael, and Nicholas Sambanis. 2000. "International Peacebuilding: A Theoretical and Quantitative Analysis," *American Political Science Review* 92:779-801.

Doyle, Michael W., and Nicholas Sambanis. 2006. *Making War and Building Peace: The United Nations since the 1990s*. Princeton: Princeton University Press.

Drake, C.J.M. 1998. "The Role of Ideology in Terrorists' Target Selection." *Terrorism & Political Violence* 10 (2):53.

Easterbrook, Gregg. 2005. "The End of War? Explaining 15 Years of Diminishing Violence," *The New Republic*, May 30, 2005.

ElBaradei, Mohamed. 2006. "Human Security and the Quest for Peace in the Middle East." Sadat Lecture for Peace. University of Maryland, October 24, 2006.

Enders, Walter, and Todd Sandler. 2000. "Is Transnational Terrorism Becoming More Threatening? A Time-Series Investigation." *Journal of Conflict Resolution* 44 (3):307-332.

Enders, W., and T. Sandler. 2006. *The Political Economy of Terrorism*. Cambridge: Cambridge University Press.

Engene, Jan Oskar. 2004. *Terrorism in Western Europe: Explaining the Trends since 1950*. Cheltenham: Edward Elgar Publishing.

Esty, Daniel C., Jack Goldstone, Ted Robert Gurr, Pamela T. Surko, and Alan N. Unger. 1995. *Working Papers: State Failure Task Force Report*. McLean, Virginia: Science Applications International Corporation.

Esty, Daniel C., Jack Goldstone, Ted Robert Gurr, Barbara Harff, Marc Levy, Geoffrey D. Dabelko, Pamela T. Surko, and Alan N. Unger. 1999. *The State Failure Report: Phase II Findings*.

Eubank, William, and Leonard B. Weinberg. 2001. "Terrorism and Democracy: Perpetrators and Victims." *Terrorism & Political Violence* 13 (1):155.

Fearon, James D., and David D. Laitin. 2003. "Ethnicity, Insurgency, and Civil War." *American Political Science Review* 97:75-90.

Fein, Helen. 1993a. "Accounting for Genocide after 1945: Theories and Some Findings." *International Journal on Group Rights* 1:79-106.

Fein, Helen. 1993b. *Genocide: A Sociological Perspective*. London: Sage.

Fortna, Page V. 2003a. "Inside and Out: Peacekeeping and the Duration of Peace after Civil and Interstate Wars." *International Studies Review* 5:97-114.

Fortna, Page V. 2003b. "Scraps of Paper? Agreements and the Durability of Peace." *International Organization* 57:337-372.

Fortna, Page V. 2004. "Does Peacekeeping Keep Peace? International Intervention and the Duration of Peace after Civil War." *International Studies Quarterly* 48: 269-292.

Galvin, Dennis. 2001. "Political Turnover and Social Change in Senegal." *Journal of Democracy.* 12 (3):51-62.

Gates, Scott, Håvard Hegre, Mark P. Jones, and Håvard Strand. 2006. "Institutional Inconsistency and Political Instability: Polity Duration, 1800-2000." *American Journal of Political Science* 50 (4):893-908.

Gilbert, Martin. 1994. *The First World War: A Complete History.* New York: Henry Holt.

Gleditsch, Nils Petter, Peter Wallensteen, Mikael Eriksson, Margareta Sollenberg, and Håvard Strand. 2002. "Armed Conflict 1946-2001: A New Dataset." *Journal of Peace Research* 39 (5):615-637.

Goldstone, Jack A., Ted Robert Gurr, Barbara Harff, Marc A. Levy, Monty G. Marshall, Robert H. Bates, David L. Epstein, Colin H. Kahl, Pamela T. Surko, John Ulfelder, and Alan N. Unger. 2000. *State Failure Task Force Report: Phase III Findings.* McLean, VA: Science Applications International Corporation (SAIC).

Goldstone, Jack A. Robert H. Bates, Ted Robert Gurr, Michael Lustik, Monty G. Marshall, Jay Ulfelder, and Mark Woodward. 2005. "A Global Forecasting Model of Political Instability." Presented at the Annual Meeting of the American Political Science Association, Washington, DC. September 1-4.

Gressang IV, Daniel S. 2001. "Audience and Message: Assessing Terrorist WMD Potential." *Terrorism & Political Violence* 13 (3):83.

Guevara, Che. [1961] 1997. *Guerrilla Warfare*, ed. Brian Loveman and Thomas M. Davies Jr. Wilmington: Scholarly Resources.

Gurr, Ted Robert. 1974. "Persistence and Change in Political Systems, 1800-1971." *American Political Science Review* 68 (4):1482-1504.

Gurr, Ted Robert. 2000. *People vs. States*. Washington D.C: United States Institute of Peace.

Gurr, Ted Robert. 2004. The Minorities at Risk (MAR) Project July 8, 2004 (Accessed Aug. 1, 2006). Available from http://www.cidcm. umd.edu/inscr/mar/.

Gurr, Ted Robert, Monty G. Marshall, and Deepa Khosla. 2001. *Peace and Conflict, 2001.* The Center for International Development and Conflict Management, University of Maryland, College Park, Maryland.

Haas, Ernst B., 1987. "The Collective Management of International Conflict, 1945-1984," pp. 7-70 in *The United Nations and Maintenance of International Peace and Security.* Dordrecht: Martinus Nijhoff Publishers.

Harbom, Lotta, ed. 2005. *States in Armed Conflict 2004.* Uppsala: Department of Peace and Conflict Research, Uppsala University.

Harbom, Lotta, and Peter Wallensteen. 2005. "Armed Conflict and Its International Dimensions, 1946-2004." *Journal of Peace Research* 42 (5):623-635.

Harff, Barbara. 2003. "No Lessons Learned from the Holocaust? Assessing the Risks of Genocide and Political Mass Murder since 1955." *American Political Science Review* 97 (1):57-73.

Harff, Barbara, and Ted Robert Gurr. 1996. "Victims of the State: Genocides, Politicides and Group Repression from 1945-1995." In *Contemporary Genocide: Causes, Cases, Consequences*, ed. Albert Jongman. Leiden: Den Haag: 33-58.

Hegre, Håvard, Tanja Ellingsen, Scott Gates, and Nils Petter Gleditsch. 2001. "Toward a Democratci Civil Peace? Democracy, Political Change, and Civil War, 1816-1992." *American Political Science Review* 95 (1):33-48.

Hegre, Håvard, Ranveig Gissinger, and Nils Petter Gleditsch. 2003. "Globalization and Internal Conflict," in *Globalization and Armed Conflict* by Gerald Schneider, Katherine Barbieri, and Nils Petter Gleditsch. Lanham, Maryland: Rowman & Littlefield Publishers.

Hegre, Håvard, and Nicholas Sambanis. 2006. "Sensitivity Analysis of Empirical Results on Civil War Onset." *Journal of Conflict Resolution* 50:508-35.

Henderson, Conway W. March 1991. "Conditions Affecting the Use of Political Repression." Hirsch, Herbert, and Roger Smith. 1988. "The Language of Extermination in Genocide." In Genocide: A Critical Bibliographical Review. Vol. 2. ed. Israel Charny. New York: Facts on File, 386-403.

Hoffman, Bruce. 1998. "Recent Trends and Future Prospects of Terrorism in the United States." Santa Monica: Rand.

Human Rights Watch. 2005. "Targeting the Fur: Mass Killing in Darfur." Washington, DC.

Human Security Centre. 2005. *Human Security Report 2005: War and Peace in the 21st Century.* New York: Oxford University Press.

Huntington, Samuel P. 1997. "After Twenty Years: The Future of the Third Wave." *Journal of Democracy* 8 (4):3-12.

Huntington, Samuel P. 1991. *The Third Wave: Democratization in the Late Twentieth Century.* Norman: University of Oklahoma Press.

Huth, Paul. 1996. *Standing Your Ground.* Ann Arbor: University of Michigan Press.

Huth, Paul, and Todd Allee. 2002. *The Democratic Peace and Territorial Conflict in the Twentieth Century.* New York: Cambridge University Press.

International Crisis Group. 2003. "Côte d'Ivoire: 'The War is Not Over Yet.'" http://www.crisisgroup.org/library/documents/africa/072_ _cote_d_ivoire_war_not_yet_over.pdf. (Accessed Jan. 2, 2007).

Jaggers, K., and T. R. Gurr. 1995. "Tracking Democracy's Third Wave with the Polity III Data." *Journal of Peace Research* 32 (4):469.

Juergensmeyer, Mark. 2003. *Terror in the Mind of God: The Global Rise of Religious Violence.* third edition. Berkeley: University of California Press.

Kelman, Herbert C. 1973. "Violence Without Moral Restraint: Reflections on the Dehumanization of Victims and Victimizers." *Journal of the Social Issues* 29 (4):25-61.

King, Gary, and Langche Zeng. 2001. "Improving Forecasts of State Failure." *World Politics* 53:623-58.

Krain, Matthew. 1997. "State Sponsored Mass Murder: The Onset and Severity of Genocides and Politicides." *Journal of Conflict Resolution* 41 (3):331-360.

Kuper, Leo. 1981. *Genocide.* New Haven: Yale University Press.

Lacina, Bethany, and Nils Petter Gleditsch. 2005. "Monitoring Trends in Global Combat: A New Dataset of Battle Deaths," *European Journal of Population* 21:145-166.

Lacina, Bethany, Nils Petter Gleditsch, and Bruce Russett. 2006. "The Declining Risk of Death in Battle." *International Studies Quarterly* 50 (3):673-680.

LaFree, Gary, and Laura Dugan. 2007. "Introducing the Global Terrorism Data Base," *Terrorism and Political Violence.* forthcoming.

Laqueur, Walter. 1976. *Guerrilla: A Historical and Critical Study.* Boston: Little Brown.

Laqueur, Walter. 1999. *The New Terrorism: Fanaticism and the Arms of Mass Destruction.* New York: Oxford University Press.

Li, Quan. 2005. "Does Democracy Promote or Reduce Transnational Terrorist Incidents?" *Journal of Conflict Resolution* 49 (2):278-297.

Lia, Brynjar, and Katja Skjolberg. 2004. *CAUSES OF TERRORISM: An Expanded and Updated Review of the Literature.* Kjeller, Norway: Norwegian Defence Research Establishment.

Licklider, Roy. 1995. "The Consequences of Negotiated Settlements in Civil Wars, 1945-1993." *American Political Science Review* 89 (3):681-690.

Markusen, Eric, and David Kopf. 1995. *The Holocaust and Strategic Bombing: Genocide and Total War in the Twentieth Century.* Boulder: Westview.

Marshall, Monty G. 1999. *Third World War: System, Process, and Conflict Dynamics.* Lanham, Maryland: Rowman & Littlefield.

Marshall, Monty G. 2001. "Global Trends in Violent Conflict," in *Peace and Conflict, 2001: A Global Survey of Armed Conflicts, Self-Determination Movements, and Democracy,* by Ted Robert Gurr, Monty G. Marshall, and Deepa Khosla, The Center for International Development and Conflict Management, University of Maryland, College Park, Maryland.

Marshall, Monty G. 2003. "Global Trends in Violent Conflict" in *Peace and Conflict, 2003,* by Monty G. Marshall and Ted Robert Gurr, The Center for International Development and Conflict Management, University of Maryland, College Park, Maryland.

Marshall, Monty G. 2005. "Global Trends in Violent Conflict" in *Peace and Conflict, 2005,* by Monty G. Marshall and Ted Robert Gurr, The Center for International Development and Conflict Management, University of Maryland, College Park, Maryland.

Marshall, Monty G. 2005. "The Peace and Conflict Ledger: Country Ratings of Peace-Building Capacity in 2005" in *Peace and Conflict, 2005,* by Monty G. Marshall and Ted Robert Gurr, The Center for International Development and Conflict Management, University of Maryland, College Park, Maryland.

Marshall, Monty G., and Keith Jaggers. 2000. *POLITY IV Data Set Users Manual.* College Park: Center for International Development and Conflict Management, University of Maryland.

Marshall, Monty G., and Ted Robert Gurr. (2005) *Peace and Conflict, 2005.* The Center for International Development and Conflict Management, University of Maryland, College Park.

McCammon, Holly J., Ellen M. Granberg, Karen E. Campbell, and Christine Mowery. 2001. "How Movements Win: Gendered Opportunity Structures and U.S. Women's Suffrage Movements, 1866 to 1919." *American Sociological Review* 66 (1):49.

McCarthy, John D., and Mayer N. Zald. 1977. "Resource Mobilization and Social Movements: A Partial Theory." *American Journal of Sociology* 82 (6):1212-1241.

Meyer, David S. 2004. "Protests and Political Opportunities." *Annual Review of Sociology* 30 (1):125-145.

Mueller, John. 1989. *Retreat from Doomsday: The Obsolescence of Major War.* New York: Basic Books.

Muller, Edward N., and Erich Weede. 1990. "Cross-National Variation in Political Violence: A Rational Action Approach." *The Journal of Conflict Resolution* 34 (4):624-651.

Nacos, Brigitte L. 2000. "Accomplice or Witness? The Media's Role in Terrorism." In *Current History*: Current History Inc.

Pape, Robert A. 2003. "The Strategic Logic of Suicide Terrorism." *American Political Science Review* 97 (3):343-361.

Poe, Steven C., and C. Neal Tate. 1994. "Repression of Human Rights to Personal Integrity in the 1980s: A Global Analysis." *American Political Science Review* 88 (4):853-872.

Physicians on Human Rights. 2006. "New Report on Genocide in Darfur, Sudan, Documents Systematic Destruction of Livelihoods of Three Villages in Unprecedented Detail." http://www.phrusa.org/research/sudan/news_2006-01-11.html (Accessed: Nov. 14, 2006).

Pynchon, Marisa Reddy, and Randy Borum. 1999. "Assessing Threats of Targeted Group Violence: Contributions from Social Psychology." *Behavioral Sciences & the Law* 17 (3):339.

Rapoport, David C. 2002. "The Four Waves of Rebel Terror and September 11." *Anthropoetics* 8:1-18.

Regan, Patrick. 2000. *Civil Wars and Foreign Powers*. Ann Arbor: University of Michigan Press.

Reinares, Fernando. 1998. "Democratic Regimes, Internal Security Policy and the Threat of Terrorism." *Australian Journal of Politics & History*: Blackwell Publishing Limited.

Rummel, Rudolph J. 1994. *Death by Government*. New Brunswick: Transaction Publishers.

Rummel, Rudolph J. 1995. "Democracy, Power, Genocide and Mass Murder," *Journal of Conflict Resolution* 39 (1):3-26.

Sambanis, Nicholas. 2001. "Do Ethnic and Non-Ethnic Civil Wars Have the Same Causes? A Theoretical and Empirical Inquiry (Part 1)" *Journal of Conflict Resolution* 45:259-82.

Sambanis, Nicholas. 2002. "A Review of Recent Advances and Future Directions in the Quantitative Literature on Civil Wars." *Defense and Peace Economics* 13:215-43.

Sambanis, Nicholas. 2004. "What Is a Civil War? Conceptual and Empirical Complexities of an Operational Definition." *Journal of Conflict Resolution* 48:814-58.

Schmid, Alex P., and A.J. Jongman. 1988. *Political Terrorism: A New Guide to Actors, Authors, Concepts, Databases, Theories and Literature*. Amsterdam: North-Holland Publishing Company.

Sharpe, Tanya Telfair. 2000. "The Identity Christian Movement: Ideology of Domestic Terrorism." *Journal of Black Studies* 30 (4):604-623.

Sherry, Michael. 1987. *The Rise of American Air Power*. New Haven: Yale University Press.

Silke, Andrew, ed. 2004. *Research on Terrorism*. London: Frank Cass.

Singer, J. David, and Melvin Small. 1994. *Correlates of War Project: International and Civil War Data, 1816-1992* [computer file] (Study #9905). Ann Arbor: Inter-University Consortium for Political and Social Research.

Stevenson, Jonathan. 2003. "Exploiting Democracy: The IRA's Tactical Cease-Fire." *Review of International Affairs* 2 (3):159-170.

Swanström, Niklas. ed. 2005. *Conflict Management and Conflict Prevention in Northeast Asia*. Uppsala: Uppsala University, Silk Road Studies Program.

Tarrow, Sidney. 1993. *Power in Movements*. Cambridge: Cambridge University Press.

Tierney, John. 2005. "Give Peace a Chance," *The New York Times*. May 28, 2005.

Toungara, Jeanne Maddox. 2001. "Ethnicity and Political Crisis in Côte d'Ivoire." *Journal of Democracy* 12 (3):63-72.

UN Secretary-General, 2005. "In Larger Freedom: Toward Security, Development, and Human Freedom for All." Report of the UN Secretary General. http://www.un.org/largerfreedom/ (Accessed Nov. 23, 2006).

United States Agency for International Development (2005) *Measuring Fragility: Indicators and Methods for Rating State Performance*. Washington DC.

Urquhart, Brian. 1994. *Hammarskjold*. London, New York: Norton.

Valentino, Benjamin, Paul Huth, and Dylan Balch-Lindsay. 2004 "Draining the Sea": Mass Killing and Guerrilla Warfare." *International Organization* 58 (2):375-407.

Wallensteen, Peter. 2007. *Understanding Conflict Resolution. War, Peace and the Global System*. London: Sage, second edition.

Wallensteen, Peter, and Margareta Sollenberg, 2001. "Armed Conflict, 1989-2000." *Journal of Peace Research* 38 (5):629-644.

Wickham-Crowley, Timothy P. 1990. "Terror and Guerrilla Warfare in Latin America, 1956-1970." *Comparative Studies in Society and History* 32 (2): 201-237.

Wilkinson, Paul. 1986. *Terrorism and the Liberal State*. New York: NYU Press.

Windsor, Jennifer L. 2003. "Promoting Democratization Can Combat Terrorism." *The Washington Quarterly* 26 (3):43-58.

Peace and Conflict Editorial Advisory Board

Ted Robert Gurr, Chair
Distinguished University Professor Emeritus
University of Maryland

Mary Caprioli
Assistant Professor
Department of Political Science
University of Minnesota at Duluth

Nils Petter Gleditsch
Editor, Journal of Peace Research
International Peace Research Institute (PRIO)
Oslo, Norway

Krishna Kumar
Senior Social Scientist
U.S. Agency for International Development

Mark Irving Lichbach
Professor and Chair
Department of Government and Politics
University of Maryland

Will H. Moore
Professor and Director of Graduate Studies
Department of Political Science
Florida State University

Alex Peter Schmid
Director, Center for the Study of Terrorism and
Political Violence
St. Andrews University, Scotland

Monica Duffy Toft
Associate Professor of Government
Kennedy School of Government
Harvard University

Acknowledgments

A large team of devoted people invested great energy and enthusiasm into producing *Peace and Conflict, 2008*. We benefitted from many discussions with our colleagues at CIDCM. In particular, Andrew Blum and Kelvin Wong offered consistently helpful guidance about several aspects of the volume. Courtney Blachly provided crucial administrative support to the project. We also thank Dan McCormack for his assistance in data preparation and for creating some of the book's graphics. The layout and design of *Peace and Conflict, 2008* is based on the original design created by Alexandra Weil in previous volumes. We thank Alexandra for her assistance in adapting the design for this book.

We are also indebted to the Uppsala Conflict Data Program at the International Peace Research Institute not only for making their data available, but for their helpful comments about the Appendix. Additionally, we wish to acknowledge Monty Marshall's past contributions to the *Peace and Conflict* publications, upon which we hope to continue to build.

We owe a special word of thanks to Jennifer Knerr at Paradigm Publishers for her guidance in seeing this project through. We are also most appreciative of her enthusiasm for the project, which was always a source of renewed motivation for us.

Finally, and most of all, we are grateful to Elizabeth Kielman, the Deputy Director of CIDCM. She tirelessly pushed us to strengthen and clarify the overall presentation, including the narrative, graphical elements, and analyses. Betsy was involved in every aspect of this project—from original conception to the final copy editing. Wherever she focused her energies, improvements were the result.

About the Authors

J. Joseph Hewitt (University of Maryland) is Assistant Director and Director of Government Relations at CIDCM. His particular responsibilities for the center include projects funded by government contracts and grants. His research focuses on the causes of armed interstate conflict, conflict early-warning, international crisis bargaining, and the connections between government attributes and conflict behavior.

Jonathan Wilkenfeld (University of Maryland) is Professor in the Department of Government and Politics and Director of the Center for International Development and Conflict Management. He is also Co-Principal Investigator for the Center for the Study of Terrorism and Responses to Terrorism. His research focuses on international conflict and crisis, foreign policy decision making, experimental and simulation techniques in political science and, most recently, the role of third-party mediation in international disputes.

Ted Robert Gurr (University of Maryland) is Distinguished University Professor at the University of Maryland. He is the founder of the Polity project and the Minorities at Risk project. His most recent book is Peoples versus States: Minorities at Risk in the New Century (United States Institute of Peace Press 2000). Professor Gurr has been a core member of the Political Instability Task Force since its inception in 1994 and has written or edited twenty other books and monographs including the award-winning Why Men Rebel (Princeton 1970) and Ethnic Conflict in World Politics (Westview 1994, 2003 with Barbara Harff).

About the Contributors

Victor Asal (University at Albany, State University of New York) is an Assistant Professor of Political Science and a researcher for the START (Study of Terrorism and Responses to Terrorism) center and for CIDCM. His research interests focus on political violence, particularly terrorism, and ethnic conflict, as well as the process of political inclusion.

Laura Dugan (University of Maryland) is an Associate Professor in the Department of Criminology and Criminal Justice. She is an active member of the National Center for the Study of Terrorism and Responses to Terrorism, the National Consortium on Violence Research, and the Maryland Population Research Center. Her research examines the causes of and policy responses to terrorism. She also designs methodological strategies to overcome data limitations inherent in the social sciences.

Susan Fahey (University of Maryland) is a doctoral student in the Department of Criminology and Criminal Justice. Her research interests include the environmental context of terrorism, including the context of failed states, the situational characteristics of airline hijackings, and the functioning and desistance of terrorist organizations.

Birger Heldt (Folke Bernadotte Academy, Sweden) is research adviser and Associate Professor of Peace and Conflict Research. His research focuses on conflict management (conditions for success, exit strategies, and trends in peacekeeping operations) and conflict prevention with regard to third-party intervention in intrastate conflicts.

Carter Johnson (University of Maryland) is a doctoral student and former Project Coordinator for the Minorities at Risk Project. His research interests include identity and conflict, minority politics, civil war, and the former Soviet Union.

Gary LaFree (University of Maryland) is Director of the National Consortium for the Study of Terrorism and Responses to Terrorism (START) and Professor of Criminology and Criminal Justice. His recent research deals with national and international macro-level trends in violent crimes and terrorism. LaFree is the author of *The Changing Nature of Crime in America* (National Institute of Justice 2000) and *Losing Legitimacy: Street Crime and the Decline of Social Institutions in America* (Westview 1998).

Paul Huth (University of Maryland) is Professor of Government and Politics and Research Director of CIDCM. He has published widely on subjects related to the study of international conflict and war, including deterrence behavior, crisis decision making, territorial disputes, and the democratic peace. In addition, he has more recently published on the topic of the civilian consequences of war. Professor Huth is the recipient of numerous grants from the National Science Foundation and the Karl Deutsch Award from the International Studies Association. He is the author of *Standing Your Ground* (Michigan 1996) and *The Democratic Peace and Territorial Conflict in the Twentieth Century* (Cambridge 2002).

Amy Pate (University of Maryland) is a Doctoral Candidate in the Department of Government and Politics. She is the Project Coordinator for the Minorities at Risk Project. Her dissertation is on ethnic rebellion in democratizing states.

David Quinn (University of Maryland) is a Doctoral Candidate in the Department of Government and Politics. He works with the Minorities at Risk project examining various aspects of self-determination and autonomy movements. He is co-author of *Mediating International Crises* (Routledge, 2005).

Benjamin Valentino (Dartmouth College) is Assistant Professor of Government. His research focuses on international security and human rights, especially the use of violence against civilian populations. His most recent book is *Final Solutions: Mass Killing and Genocide in the 20th Century* (2004).

Peter Wallensteen (Uppsala University) is Dag Hammarskjöld Professor of Peace Research at Uppsala University, Uppsala, Sweden, and Richard G. Starmann Sr. Research Professor at the Joan B. Kroc Institute of International Peace Studies, University of Notre Dame, USA. He directs the Uppsala Conflict Data Program, which publishes annual updates on global conflicts (www.pcr.uu.se/database) in SIPRI Yearbooks, the *Journal of Peace Research*, and *States in Armed Conflict* (Uppsala, Sweden). He also leads the Special Program on the Implementation of Targeted Sanctions, focusing on the effectiveness of modern UN and EU sanctions (www.smartsanctions.se). His most recent book is *Understanding Conflict Resolution* (Sage, 2007, 2nd, rev. ed.).

CIDCM Center for International Development and Conflict Management

The Center for International Development and Conflict Management (CIDCM) is an interdisciplinary research center at the University of Maryland. CIDCM seeks to prevent and transform conflict, to understand the interplay between conflict and development, and to help societies create sustainable futures for themselves. Using the insights of researchers, practitioners, and policymakers, CIDCM devises effective tools and pathways to constructive change.

For more than 20 years, scholars and practitioners at CIDCM have sought ways to understand and address conflicts over security, identity, and distributive justice. CIDCM programs are based on the belief that "peace building and development-with-justice are two sides of the same coin." (CIDCM Founding Director, Edward Azar, 1987).

CIDCM's accomplished scholars, its expertise in data collection and analysis, and its direct involvement in regional conflict management efforts make the Center a unique resource for discovering enduring solutions to the world's most intractable conflicts.

Please visit the Center's Web site at **http://www.cidcm.umd.edu.**